The RAF Staff College by Ben Irish.

SERVICE WITH A SMILE

by

Wing Commander
Norman Conquer, OBE

Neil

With all good wishes

Norman

Feb '08

Privately published 2006

© 2006 Norman Conquer

All rights reserved. No part of this publication can be reproduced, stored in a retrieval system, or transmitted in any form or by any means without the prior consent, in writing, of the author, nor be otherwise circulated in any form of binding or cover other than that in which it is published.

ISBN 0-9552277-0-4
978-0-9552277-0-7 (January 2007)

Every effort has been made to obtain the necessary permissions for photographs used in this book, should there be any omissions in this respect we apologise and shall be pleased to make the appropriate acknowledgements in future editions.

Printed in Great Britain by
Short Run Press Ltd, Exeter

For Joan, my loving wife of 60 years, with my gratitude for her patience and support, especially during those early years.

Also for my many colleagues and friends, of all ranks, who contributed so much to the fun and the 'smiles', and in memory of those who were less fortunate than we lucky survivors.

CONTENTS

Preface 1
Personal Introduction 3

PART ONE

Chapter One 7
    Uxbridge   *Dec 1939*   7
    Blackpool   *Feb–Mar 1940*   7
    White Waltham   *Mar–Aug 1940*   8
    Dumfries   *Sep–Dec 1940*   9

Chapter Two 11
    10 ITW, Scarborough   *Dec 1940–Mar 1941*   11
    10 B & GS, Dumfries   *Mar–May 1941*   12
    3 AONS, Bobbington   *May–Aug 1941*   14

Chapter Three 17
    13 OTU, Bicester   *Sep–Nov 1941*   17

Chapter Four 22
    Radcliffe Inf., Oxford   *Nov 1941–Mar 1942*   22
    RAF Hospital, Halton   *April/May 1942*   22
    Palace Hotel, Torquay   *June/July 1942*   22

Chapter Five 27
    13 OTU, Bicester (again)   *July 1942–March 1943*   27

Chapter Six 34
    13 OTU, Bicester   *March–June 1943*   34
    60 OTU, High Ercall   *June–Sep 1943*   36
    Lyneham & Portreath   *Oct 1943*   40

Chapter Seven 42
    Gibraltar & Malta, 23 Sqn   *Oct 1943*   42

Chapter Eight			48
	23 Squadron, Pomigliano	*Nov 1943–Jan 1944*	48
Chapter Nine			55
	23 Squadron, Alghero	*Jan–May 1944*	55
Chapter Ten			70
	Return from the Med	*May//June 1944*	70
Chapter Eleven			74
	23 Squadron, Little Snoring	*Jun–Sep 1944*	74
Chapter Twelve			80
	51 OTU, Cranfield	*Sep 1944–May 1945*	80
	54 OTU, Charter Hall	*June–Sep 1945*	82

Half Way Note	84
Foreword to Part Two	85

PART TWO

Chapter Thirteen			89
	EANS, Shawbury	*Sep 1945–July 1947*	89
Chapter Fourteen			98
	228 OCU, Leeming	*July 1947–Oct 1949*	98
Chapter Fifteen			106
	115 Squadron, Mildenhall	*Oct 1949–Mar 1950*	106
	RAF Lakenheath	*Mar 1950–April 1951*	107
Chapter Sixteen			114
	Air Ministry, Adastral	*April 1951–Feb 1954*	114
Chapter Seventeen			123
	Interval – Swinderby	*Mar 1954*	123
	527 Squadron, Watton	*Mar 1954–Jan 1956*	125
Chapter Eighteen			136
	46 Course, RAF Staff College, Bracknell	*Jan 1956–April 1957*	136
Chapter Nineteen			145
	83 Group, Wahn	*April 1957–May 1958*	145
	2 TOC, Sundern	*May 1958–Feb 1960*	152
Chapter Twenty			162
	DS at RAF Staff College, Bracknell	*April 1960–Mar 1963*	162
Chapter Twenty-one			174
	RAF Bruggen	*April 1963–Sep 1965*	174
Chapter Twenty-two			189
	OASC, Biggin Hill	*Oct 1965–Feb 1968*	189

PREFACE

When I started to write this book, my intention was merely to set down experiences in 'my war' ('39–'45). But, in the telling, I came to realise that those six years were by no means what I now regard as the most serious, the most enjoyable, the most important years of my life. Those adjectives are probably more applicable to the following twenty years or so of my peacetime service in the Royal Air Force. Hence the two Parts which are included herein.

Much has been written and filmed about World War II – the heroisms, the disasters, the horrors and the successes. Nothing can, or should, be said to detract from the seriousness and the sacrifices of those years. Yet, for many there was a lighter side, fun and games which were a safety valve, a release of tensions, a 'letting off of steam', so necessary to the successful prosecution of the painful duties of the war.

And sometimes there were bizarre, occasionally hilarious, aspects to the most serious of occasions – such as the mess party that followed two apparent air combat successes: the RAF fighter crew's claim of a German bomber damaged and a USAAF bomber crew's claim of a German fighter beaten off and damaged; over many glasses they discovered they had been shooting at each other!

Such 'comic cuts' events were not restricted to wartime either. The writer recalls many hilarious moments during the years of peacetime service which followed, some directly concerning flying and operational matters, many others relating to personal and family experiences in a wide variety of postings. One's memories of the serious side gradually fade, excluding the worst and highlighting the amusing aspects. Personal diaries show how lighter moments served to soften the hairy events, so many of which have been chronicled elsewhere.

PERSONAL INTRODUCTION

I joined the Royal Air Force to fly in December 1939 but did not reach an operational squadron until October 1943. The many delays in my progress began right there in the initial selection process: given the choice of 'immediate service' or 'go home to await the call for training' I naively asked which would get me into training the sooner (keen type!). "Enter now and you'll soon be called" the recruiting sergeant said; result – almost a year as a gunner on Ground Defence (forerunner of the RAF Regiment). Yet that was an experience I wouldn't have missed for the worlds.

Eventually I went through the full training machine as an Observer, Initial Training Wing (ITW) to Operational Training Unit (OTU), via Bombing and Gunnery School (B&GS) and Air Observer Navigation School (AONS), between December 1940 and November 1941, only to land up in hospital for eight months as the sole survivor of a Blenheim prang on the final OTU training flight. Recuperation in a ground job for six months was followed by a second Blenheim course, conversion to Mosquitos, then finally, after a few exasperating weeks of equipping at Lyneham (including a week's course of lectures and practice flights on how to navigate to Gibraltar!), we left Portreath, Cornwall, to spend a wonderful 24 hours in Gib., arriving at Luqa, Malta, in October 1943.

There followed an unsettled period for the Squadron during the earliest stages of the Italy invasion, engaged in ground support of the Army and intruder operations over southern Italy, then on detachment to Sicily (an airstrip on the lower slopes of Mount Etna!), a further detachment to Naples (Pomigliano airstrip on the north side of Mount Vesuvious!) and finally a full squadron move to Alghero, Sardinia (a mini-mountain rose to 1500 feet right beside the runway!), from where we operated from December 1943 to June 1944 – intruding over enemy airfields in northern Italy and southern France, train and transport busting and occasional sea patrols against German reconnaissance aircraft trailing our convoys. (We never did discover who ordained that we must always fly from a mountainside!). Thereafter, the Squadron returned to UK in support of the Second Front.

Part 1 of my book is concerned not so much with the actual business of flying in wartime but with the pleasures and fun we enjoyed in the process. I must not detract from the seriousness of the task, the tragedies along the way, the loss of comrades who did not survive, the inevitable killing of the enemy, military and civilian – but that side of the story is told in countless historical records and serious books by writers far better qualified than I. Perhaps the light-hearted touch herein can be forgiven.

PART ONE

CHAPTER ONE

Uxbridge, December 1939

"Please Sir, I'd like to join the R.A.F." "To fly?" "Of course." "Very well, fill in this form, sit this test, breath in/out, read that card left eye/right eye, jump up and down, blow in this bag and pee in that one, I see you've got two of everything and the one most important – you're in!"

Then came what seemed to be two innocent questions, I gave the wrong answer both times and learned my first two lessons in the Service: don't be too keen and never volunteer for anything!

"I see you claim Maths to be your strongest subject – over 90% in Matric, eh? We desperately need good mathematicians to be navigator/observers – would you be willing to change your application for pilot and volunteer as a navigator?" "Yes Sir, if you think that's best" (sucker!). "Do you wish to opt for immediate service or would you prefer to go home to await call for aircrew training?" "Which would get me into training quicker, Sir?" "Why immediate service, of course". Of course!

Entry January 1940, Aircrew Receiving Centre Blackpool, followed by 10 months as a gunner on Ground Defence. Not until December 1940 was I to reach I.T.W. to start aircrew training.

Blackpool, February/March 1940

Apart from the horrifying effects of the initial vaccination/ inoculations, our three weeks at A.C.R.C. was not only bearable, it was almost holiday fun. Our squad was "controlled", if that's not too strong a word, by a delightful corporal with the welfare of his men always at heart. Our drill parades were short and snappy on the parade ground and always followed by an hour on the beach. During our second and third weeks we were detailed for several route marches: some of the other squads did 8–10 miles; we marched along the promenade and at a suitable ramp to the beach were given "right wheel" followed by "Halt, Sit. Off boots and socks. Paddle". How unlike so many other N.C.O.s it was not my pleasure to meet!

Our landlady at the "digs" was certainly not the harridan so often depicted in Blackpool stories; in fact she was a sweetie, a real "Mum" to us all and made our stay home from home. Some may say that this sojourn at the seaside failed in the essential "hardening" process. For some, maybe, but my real "toughening up" was still to come.

White Waltham, March–August 1940

March the month, march the exercise to get us fit – all over Berkshire. Guard duties day and night; most prized duty, when considered capable, manning the gun defences around the airfield. One night, imagine the scene if you can, it's the midnight to 2 a.m. shift (2359 to 0200 to the initiated), in the middle of a cornfield, in a sand-bagged emplacement with a multiple Lewis gun mounting (all loaded), when an air-raid on London is at its height. Orders: fire only when ordered and with an N.CO. present. I'm alone, when there, plain as a pikestaff, is a Ju88 approaching my field at about 1000 feet – what would you do? Too right, both barrels! Hopeless miss, of course but, though I didn't expect a medal, I thought 7 days c.c. was a bit harsh!

All my mates on the ground defence flight were Welsh, all destined to serve out the war as R.A.F. soldiers. They all laughed when they heard I was awaiting aircrew training – fat chance, they said, now you're one of us. Most of them were from the mining valleys with very little education, several could neither read nor write; one of my more enjoyable tasks was writing letters home for them. For this, and presumably because of the outside chance of my becoming officer/aircrew, they dubbed me "the Duke". What a grand bunch they were – solid in friendship, loyal and dependable. In August came a move and we were posted en bloc.

Dumfries, September–December 1940

Similar duties awaited us in Scotland but with some notable differences – mainly brought about by a pompous ass recently commissioned and appointed Station Defence Officer. Our flight organisation was unchanged, except that I was now appointed one of the junior guard commanders.

One of our guard posts was a road bridge over a stream on the approach to aircraft dispersals on the outskirts of the airfield. One night at around 0100 hrs., said officer approached the bridge under cover of a hedge, jumped out and surprised the airman on guard – then ordered him to hand over his rifle "for inspection". The lad complied and was promptly put under close arrest to be charged with giving up possession of his weapon. I stood as "accused's friend; circumstances explained – case dismissed". Now said officer disliked me – I thought he might try something similar on me. A few days later as i/c guard on that bridge, with the normal guard in place, I took up support watch on the wrong side of the bridge. Sure enough, his car drew up on the main road half a mile away, lights doused, and some minutes later I detected his approach behind the hedge. His head appeared above the bridge parapet, looking for the guard on the camp side of the bridge – "HaltwhogoesthereHaltwhogoesthereHaltorIfire" in one breath – bang! Right over his head. He could have taken a Gold at the Olympics that night! Repercussions? I immediately reported to our Flight Commander a surreptitious approach to our aircraft by a suspicious character who fled when challenged. He never did own up!

One night whilst guarding "the bridge" came the storm. Guards could not stand up in 100 mph gusts, so the whole point of a guard seemed lost. One Handley Page Harrow, that ancient high-winged monster which frightened me on my first flight, got airborne when its tethers snapped and was projected (flew?) full tilt into a hangar wall. What a mess!

It was inexplicable, and seemed pathetic, to be warned that Hitler was preparing to invade England and that we must therefore be brought to full alert – on the west coast of Scotland?! But said officer went further: we dug ditches, built sandbag walls à la W.W.I front line, then manned them continuously for 7 days and nights, in snow, the first four days at full strength without a break, subsisting on tea and sandwiches. We had our rifles and several Lewis machine guns – but all the ammunition was locked in the Station Armoury a mile away! Years later, we heard that our Station Defence Officer was sacked not long after that episode.

Now it is mid-December; we are well on with plans for our forthcoming Christmas and are holding a discussion in our billets over the arrangements for a flight party. Having spent the afternoon on the practice firing range, "Taff" is sitting on his bed cleaning his rifle. "I hope that bloody thing isn't loaded", says his mate; "Of course not", says "Taff" and pulls the trigger to demonstrate. Fortunately, the gun points heavenward; but the roofs of seco huts are not really made of the stuff to withstand 303 bullets and a sizable chunk of debris descends on "Taff's" head. It was funny at the time – until the flight sergeant crashed through the hut door in rather a panic. Poor "Taff" – I often wonder what happened to him.

Next day startling news: I'm posted to No. 10 Initial Training Wing forthwith to start my aircrew training. The squaddies can't believe it – they really never thought it could happen; someone up above must actually have read the Uxbridge papers.

CHAPTER TWO

No. 10 I.T.W., Scarborough, December 1940–March 1941

After some eight months as a ground gunner I had thought myself fairly fit – not by the standards of the P.T. sergeant at I.T.W. On the day after arrival, and every day for several weeks after, 0630 on the beach in shorts and gym shoes, 20 minutes minimum. Cold? I think it was the first time I believed the brass monkey story.

Two seafront hotels had been taken over by the Wing, I was billeted in the Grand – rather different to the seco huts, but four to a room was crowded. Initially, bags of "bull", but though that was rough on some of the others straight from home, I was well used to it; lodging with "the gunners" had been worthwhile grounding after all. Lectures formed the main working part of the course: maths, geography, meteorology, basic astronomy, Air Force Law, R.A.F. organisation, theory of flight, etc. Several lasting friendships were formed here, the first leg on the road to active participation in the war. Of the four I was closest to, one failed to survive training, two were lost on operations, the last was the sole survivor of an entire squadron destroyed on one raid in the Mediterranean: we met again, 35 years later, in a pub in East Grinstead!

But the run of things changed dramatically for me after the first few weeks; though I was compelled to complete all the essential theory training, I was soon to be excused all outside labour and subsidiary duties (marches, guards, clerical, P.T!) by the arrival of eight very special bods – all from (if I remember correctly) Carol

Gibbons' Savoy Hotel Orpheans. I think they had volunteered en bloc to join the Service as a band, figuring their speciality would be a great boost to the Service throughout the war. How right they were, though to my everlasting regret I was to be associated with them for only three months.

For the previous six years all my spare time, evenings and weekends had been devoted to music, starting on drums with the local philharmonic orchestra and the town silver prize band, graduating to tympanist with the London Civil Service Orchestra and, just before joining the R.A.F., auditioning for the B.B.C. Symphony (they would have offered me the appointment had I been free!). Throughout those years I had also played with local dance bands and formed a small band of my own – strictly semi-pro. The eight gentlemen mentioned above contributed two alto and one tenor sax, two doubling clarinet and one baritone, two on trumpet and one trombone, piano and bass; they were only short of guitar and drums – enter yours truly and one of the Wing clerks. With our very popular signature tune – The World is Waiting for the Sunrise – we were soon known all over the North and Midlands, travelling frequently at weekends to other stations and giving concerts in various towns. I could willingly have foregone all else to spend not only the war years but the rest of my life with that outfit. Dream on!

Came March and the eagerly awaited (for some!) postings to flying training. Where to? Why, back to Dumfries, of course.

No. 10 Bombing & Gunnery School, Dumfries, March–May, 1941

An "air experience" flight in a Harrow (mentioned earlier) did not create quite the impression we imagined the instructors wished to convey. I presume the pilot on that occasion had actually flown before – but perhaps he thought we would be more at home if we felt that he too was a beginner! If you have seen one of the Laurel and Hardy films with an aviation theme, you may have some idea of the gyrations involved: with a Tiger Moth, or perhaps a Bristol Bulldog, OK – but with a Harrow? Suffice it to say that the experience did not calm our nerves in preparation for the trials to come.

First, (I'm skipping all the usual stories of parades, drills and P.T. – those agonies are the same wherever!) it was to learn bombing in Fairey Battles. Now there's an aeroplane to conjure with: the pilot in his own cockpit, a navigator and a wireless operator/air gunner crammed together into the rear fuselage. The W.Op/A.G. has a seat beneath a single Vickers M/G on a mounting in a mid-upper position; if he defends against an enemy fighter attacking from the rear, the most frequent occurrence, he must avoid firing directly astern for fear of shooting off his own tail. The navigator/bomb aimer has no seat; he lies down in a space 8 feet long, 2 feet high and 18 inches wide, above him the main fuel tank. To aim the bombs he has a bomb sight on a spiggot at the rear of a hatch in the aircraft's floor; approaching his target, he opens the hatch by sliding it aft, lowers the bomb sight through the floor with his head in the opening to see to line up on the target. We asked at first briefing what the goggles were for: that will soon become apparent we were told. You open the hatch, the purpose of the goggles is revealed: your face is directly behind the engine exhaust which ejects a constant stream of black oil into the slipstream i.e. your face. Ever tried lining up two wires focusing on an object a couple of miles away, when the whole machine and this contraption are bucketing up and down and weaving side to side and your vision is impaired by a film of oil? And in bumpy conditions, which is most of the time, every time you meet a down draft you rise until your back hits the fuel tank and then smack on your belly back to the floor!

Now, that was the mainstay of our air attack against the Germans from airfields in France during the early months of the war. The men involved all deserved medals – yet few survived to claim them. Is it any wonder that we failed to stem the tide before Dunkirk?

Next, we learn to shoot in the air. Now I enjoyed my visits to the firing ranges as a ground gunner and consider myself a fair shot with a rifle. In the air, from an aeroplane turret? Forget it – yet I once scored 16%, i.e. 16 out of 100 rounds actually hit the target; no-one told me what happened to the other 84! My worst effort – 1% – hardly bears thinking about!

This air firing was conducted from the Armstrong Whitworth Whitley, possibly the toughest of all the bomber workhorses of that era. But vulnerable? Bear in mind that we are talking here of airspeeds in the region of 100 m.p.h. and less. Shooting from the tail and mid upper turrets was a fun exercise; from the "dustbin" it was not! Roughly in the centre of the fuselage floor was a mid-under turret which, when retracted, sat three feet inside the aircraft. One climbed in, dropped into the seat, then powered the turret southwards. Seeing the floor of the aircraft rising above you was heart-stopping – would the damned thing never stop falling – what if it drops out of the bottom? Like your heart, it stops with a jolt – you wipe away the sweat and tears and start firing. Oh to get back to the drums!

Ground school represented a happy respite from that type of flying. Bombing theory, trajectories, mechanics, wireless and morse code, meteorology, aircraft recognition, with end-of-course exams all essential towards the coveted "O" brevet. This, with 21 training flights, was all compressed into 5 weeks; it left little spare time for other activities. Yet, I was able to enjoy several evenings in the Dumfries pubs with some of my old friends from the ground defence flight. The most raucous was in celebration of two coincident "Taff" birthdays. Six of us were in The Bull, on the first round of mild & bitter; a civilian, a stranger, invited us to a refill, continued staking us all for the next two hours, then invited us to his home to meet the family. Two daughters in their early twenties added greatly to the evening's enjoyment – and I was posted two days later – why could this not have happened during my previous sojourn in Dumfries?

One other incident is worth recall, I am walking along Dumfries High Street when a cycle shop opposite catches my eye: the name over the shop is William Conquer. Now you would hardly call my name a common one – could this be a relative? Calling in the shop I am told "Yes, Mr. Conquer used to own this shop but he sold it to me last month. He has bought a farm near Aberdeen". I had no time to chase it up then and the matter lay dormant until 50 years later when I became interested in Genealogy and began researching the family history. Yes, I found him – but that's for another book. Now it is May, the course is passed, and I get 7 days leave before reporting for navigator training.

No. 3 Air Observer Navigation School, Bobbington (later Halfpenny Green, near Stourbridge) May–August 1941

As the reader will have realised, we were not much impressed by our flying experiences so far but little did we anticipate the frights to come. Here, at Bobbington, we were introduced to the Blackburn Botha; this "operational" type had been diverted to navigator training as a priority – and we were to be the first lucky recipients of this bounty. Only later did we find out the real cause of this aeroplane's "relegation" to the training role – built as a torpedo bomber for coastal operations it showed a startling unwillingness to get airborne once a torpedo was loaded thereon. As it wasn't a great deal of use to the operators *without* a torpedo, the powers that be gave it to the training machine as "an opportunity to train navigators on a real operational type"!

We soon discovered that the Botha had several drawbacks in addition to its unwillingness to take off with a torpedo load. The first was its marked reluctance to take off period! I vividly recall the dour comment of a Scottish flight sergeant pilot when, concrete fast running out and barely 100 yards to go before entering the grass overshoot, he reached down to pull the undercarriage retraction handle: "Sod you, you bastard, now fly!" It did, just, taking a few twigs from the top of the boundary hedge.

Another minor problem was the terrible stench of petrol fumes which pervaded the cockpit at all times. I experienced only one flight in this aircraft in which that did not worry us: Flight Lieutenant Baker, (pseudonym) an ex-airline pilot with some 15,000 flying hours, loved his drop of scotch – the smell of petrol on this occasion was eliminated by the overpowering alcohol fumes.

Then, sadly, the worst problem soon became the last one for that aeroplane – it really hated the idea of asymmetric flight: engine failure proved fatal on so many occasions that replacement became essential. "Sadly" not because of the demise of the Botha but because it cost so many crews before the decision to scrap it was taken. After little more than a month of disasters we were back with the good old trustworthy Avro Anson – slow, ponderous, 138 turns of the handle to wind up the undercarriage, but oh so reliable. And, for those times, an excellent vehicle in which to learn the (fairly) complex business of air navigation.

From the "Anson days" to follow, one rather nasty incident, though humorous for some, led to my first serious argument with authority. As navigator/plotter in the Anson, one sat directly behind the pilot. The only facility for bladder relief on this aeroplane was a funnel alongside the exit door. (It led to a pipe directed into the aircraft slipstream for the dispersal of the liquid

– one infamous trick sometimes played by an errant member of groundcrew was to turn that pipe through 180 degrees, to the rather obvious damp distress of the user!). On this occasion, the pilot felt unable to trust another crew member to hold the stick, pulled open his side window and let fly in that direction, depositing his lunch time beer all over my chart table – and me! On return, I sought interview with the flight commander and stated my case – refusing to fly with that pilot again. "You will fly with whoever you're told to fly with", quoth he, rather ungrammatically. "I bloody won't", says I in an equally uneducated statement. Whereupon I was marched before the Chief Instructor: he repeated the flight commander's order, even more forcibly, but called me back afterwards to say that the problem would not arise in future, that pilot was grounded and posted.

Concentrated hard work is my main memory of this course – though I did start to learn contract bridge, previous knowledge being limited to much simpler card games – solo and auction bridge. This turned out to be a most valuable asset at a later stage in my training. Evenings were more concentrated study with the occasional beer in the NAAFI, but there were few visits to the delights of Stourbridge – there were some I suppose but for the life of me I cannot remember them.

For the first time in the Service to date, I was impressed by the officers on this station – at least those with whom I came into contact. Our course commander was an excellent teacher and thought nothing of spending endless extra hours in individual coaching where necessary. The Chief Instructor also would regularly check individual progress and provide extra ground or air instruction if necessary. The result was that all the pupils attained reasonable to good results and were able to qualify for their 'O' brevet. Early in August we received notice of our fate: I was to be commissioned on 24th August and, after 14 days leave, mainly to get kitted out at Moss Bros., (me – in a made-to-measure suit – such luxury!) posted to a Blenheim Operational Training Unit, with the log-book recording 52 flights to date with a total of 87 hours (of such experience was a wartime navigator assumed ready for advanced training!)

CHAPTER THREE

No. 13 O.T.U., Bicester, September–November 1941

Initial impressions are so important – and at R.A.F. Station, Bicester I was impressed! It was a well established peacetime station with the customary "H" type Officers Mess. Accommodation therein was perhaps more than adequate for a peacetime establishment but could not cope with the expansion of personnel involved in the transition to a wartime operational training station. Thus all student officers were accommodated in a country house directly behind the Mess – Brashfield House – and, though we were sleeping two or three to a room, the contrast to an airman's bed among 15 others in a Nissen or Seco hut was, to say the least, noticeable!

The next very pleasant surprise (though why it should have been a surprise I cannot recall) was to be awakened at 0700 on the first morning by a middle-aged civilian, my batman, bearing a cup of tea. You know, it takes some getting used to – the transition from a year and a half as a most junior ranker to the first day on one's new station as an officer. That batman, George, a local man, unfit for military service so he felt this was a way in which he could "do his bit", proved to be a godsend to the novice – and he treated me like a son! Perhaps that sounds corny now – but I cannot emphasise enough how important it was to me at the time.

But if you think that that was the start of feather-bedded days, forget it! I was now about to learn that a Pilot Officer pupil aircrew, though not the lowest form of life, could not yet feel any loosening of control by his instructors/superiors. Drills and route marches are no more (for the present!), guard and cookhouse duties will henceforth be done by others, one does not even have to clean one's own shoes (not boots!) any more; but the disciplines – strict adherence to timing, personal fitness, behaviour in the air and in the Mess whilst on duty – are, if anything, more strict. Now one has expectations and standards to live up to more than ever before.

This latter point was brought home to me most forcibly during the first three weeks at 13 O.T.U. That period was spent on refresher navigation and introduction to low-level flying, again in Ansons, at the satellite airfield – Hinton-in-the-Hedges. (We had airfields in the most marvellous places). The Squadron Commander, Squadron Leader Rotherham, was a peacetime officer of the old school and was determined to instil in his officer pupils all the best of Service traditions. To this end, we were introduced to the Dining-In Night, all officers dining formally at one table, every night of the week except Sunday. I know some found the ritual boring and unnecessary in wartime; personally I was fascinated by the whole procedure and, many years later, in the post-war years, considered it an essential feature in supporting the esprit de corps of Service life.

I received one very early, and costly, lesson during the first week of these evenings. As was customary, the port was passed immediately after the loyal toast to the King (in those days). Passed by right hand to your left, from the President back to the President – twice, that was the form. We pupils were appointed President in turn, mine came on the fourth day; the officer on my left, still being thirsty after the second glass of port, said "pass the port old man" – I duly complied. Port was a shilling a glass; there were 20 officers at dinner; my mess bill a few days later included an unexpected item – Port £1. My daily pay then was 14s. 6d. – an expensive lesson!

You will have gathered that the evening was stiff and formal. Regular officers wore Mess Dress, we wartime officers (emergency commissions in the R.A.F. Volunteer Reserve) were not expected to afford such extra uniforms (on a kitting-out allowance of £80) and so we wore No. 1 uniform, with white shirt and black bow. As our No.1's were also needed for squadron and station parades and for "walking out", we were exhorted to keep them in good order, but this became a major chore for the batmen following the severe drubbing they received (the uniforms, not the batmen) *after* the formalities of dinner: the antics from then until midnight, *every* evening, belonged more to the rugby field than the Mess. "High Cockalorum" was the highlight, usually preceded by gymnastic events involving most of the furniture and resembling the efforts of horse and rider at Aintree. After initially gaping at this spectacle in astonishment, it didn't take the newcomer long to get the hang of it – but why did I always find myself at the bottom of the ruck?

Now came the much more serious part of the course: back to the parent airfield, crewing of pilots, observers and wireless operators/airgunners, ground school on light bomber operations and associated subjects, followed by our introduction to the Blenheim Mk.IV. The pilots had already completed conversion on type whilst the "passengers" were otherwise occupied with their specialities. This was to be crew training for the real thing.

I remember the mixed feelings with which we all approached this stage. Excitement that at last we would have our chance at the enemy; relief from the frustrations of the "waiting time" (at least, in my case), but perhaps most prominent the fear of the unknown – after all, we were privy to all the facts of the 2 Group Blenheim operations and the "chop rate" was not encouraging; not all of us were the intrepid warrior type. But for the present we had our time fully occupied with working out as a crew: cross-country navigation and low level formation, bombing practice by both pilot and observer, air firing by pilot and W.Op/A.G. There was still time for an occasional beer, in the Mess or at the local, but not much – and certainly no question of more leave or days off.

My pilot, Sergeant Peter Crozier, was the "granddaddy" of the course – he was 28! I, and all the other lads, were just that – lads, 20 and under. Peter was a great chap, seemingly more experienced than his 120 hours would indicate, with down-to-earth common sense and what we now call "nous". For instance, on several practice bombing flights, with airtime to spare on return from the range, he would change seats with me to ensure that I could handle the aircraft, even on one engine, in case he should stop a bullet – "in which case my lad it will be up to you to get us home!" Whether a legitimate step or not, it made a lot of sense. Yet, in the event, it did not matter.

Within a month our operational postings came through: we were not destined for 2 Group, but for North Africa, to 105 Squadron, on Blenheim V's – the "Bisley". But it was not to be. On the afternoon of 11th November, 1941, we were briefed for our last O.T.U. exercise – low level practice formation – and so it proved to be – our last. We suffered an engine failure and flew straight into a tree at over 200 m.p.h.

I didn't feel a thing – then! I came to an hour or so later, lying in a field, legs doubled beneath me, but comfortable and warm. Slowly realisation dawned and, amazingly according to the experts, I did not suffer amnesia. I could immediately remember the whole episode, precise details of the few minutes between engine failure and crash, and could actually see the air speed indicator reading at the instant of hitting the tree. Consciousness waxed and waned until hands were lifting me on to a stretcher and into an ambulance. The ambulance ride to the Radcliffe Infirmary in Oxford was a nightmare; Peter was moaning on another stretcher beside me, Ron our w.op./a.g. was on a stretcher above me; some liquid was splashing on my face from above – blood – which was why, when in casualty later, it was at first thought I had serious head injuries. In fact, apart from a split eyebrow and cut chin, the damage was limited to my legs: fractured right femur and multiple fracture of left ankle.

Now came the first real pain – the nurses had to remove my flying clothing and boots and trying to cut off the boots with ordinary scissors was a scream a second! But a couple of jabs quickly stopped the noise and I remember no more until the following morning. During the night, my parents and sister travelled up to Oxford and were at my bedside when I came to. Then Peter's parents called to see me; in answer to my obvious question they told me Peter was fine and I should concentrate on getting well. Not long after I learned that both Peter and Ron had died; Ron was killed outright, Peter was badly broken up and died on the operating table. So much for Blenheim operations with 105 Squadron.

I have not herein revealed the full details of the reasons for the crash, though I was called to do so at a Court of Inquiry some months later. I do not think they are important for the reader to know. But I have felt it necessary to state the bald facts because that event, more than any other, coloured my whole future, both in the R.A.F. for the next 25 years and subsequently during the rest of my life. For one thing, I was not wearing my safety belts, just why is beside the point. The other members of the crew were: they were killed, I survived; is it any wonder that I now resent a law which obliges me to wear a seat belt in my car?

CHAPTER FOUR

Radcliffe Infirmary, Oxford, November 1941–March 1942
R.A.F. Hospital, Halton, April/May 1942
R.A.F. Officers Recuperation Centre, Palace Hotel, Torquay, June/July 1942

The above headings put my next 8 months in a nutshell. I could not praise highly enough the doctors and staff at the Radcliffe. Two surgeons controlled my life for that 4 months, 14 weeks of which was spent in bed in a Thomas's splint, with weights strung from a spike through my right knee, and my lower left leg in plaster. Sleeping in a laid-back sitting position was not easy to get used to, yet now I find it the most comfortable of all. The early days were painful, frustrating and madly boring, but I was not alone. Next bed on my right housed a corporal in the Tank Corps, similar injuries, tank accident; next to him Pilot Officer Peter Shields, pranged in a Wellington, both legs badly smashed – he never did regain normal mobility. In a bed opposite, another navigator, from a Hampden prang; on my left a middle aged sailor, rescued from a torpedoed ship. My, we were a happy crowd!

Needless to say, chat and laughter gradually gave way to practical jokes and acrobatic feats. The cleaning ladies, with their mops and buckets at 6.30 every morning, were the main butt of the jokes but, bless them all, they took it in good part. The acrobatics? When your leg is suspended in a frame from a horizontal bar, there grows on you the picture of some gymnasium exercises which might be attempted: swinging around horizontal bars could also be akin to aerial manoeuvres – loop the loop for example. But when your other leg is in plaster, and when strings from your knee lead to heavy weights at the foot of the bed, to swing over the top of the bar carried rather more risk than sense. The temptation eventually became too much – and it took the combined efforts of surgeon and nurses to recover the situation! Matron was a wonderful lady but a real stickler – for a while I was not her favourite patient.

After a couple of weeks in the Radcliffe, I had a visit from a Group Captain Medic from the R.A.F. Hospital at Halton. "Move this one to Halton" quoth he. My surgeon, Mr. Scott, a Canadian, was scathing. "He's in a Thomas's splint and there he stays for at least 13 weeks", says he. Hard luck Halton, this time. Mr. Scott's senior assistant orthopaedic surgeon, Mr. Masina, revealed later that Halton wanted them to plaster my leg and transfer me but they refused. After the "loop" incident, they rather wished they had acceded to Halton's request!

I had a wonderful 21st Birthday party in February, with all my family, a couple of friends from Bicester, and with doctors, nurses and fellow patients joining in. But what a place for such a landmark in a youngster's life!

After 14 weeks in the splint, I pleaded with the doctors to let me free; they thought it was still too soon, but I was so insistent, they finally agreed. Silly them, silly me. The femur immediately bowed and they had to slap me into a "hip-spiker" i.e. plaster from waist to foot inclusive, and with a walking iron on the foot. Fortunately by then the other leg was out of plaster so I could manoeuvre with two elbow crutches. Then there was no longer an excuse for me to stay at the Radcliffe and I was duly transferred to Halton.

I'm afraid I don't have much good to say of the Halton Hospital in those days. Immediately on arrival, the surgeon (that said Group Captain you will already have guessed) ordered an X-ray to check on the amount of "bow" in the femur. "Just as I thought", says he, "we'll put a couple of wedges in that plaster to force the leg to straighten." They cut the plaster with an electric saw all round behind the bend in the femur, and about 6 inches of skin and flesh as well, then, with one nurse's full weight pressing on top and pulling up the ankle (I thought they'd break the leg again in the process) inserted wedges and replastered. Three days of agony, then another X-Ray – no difference, not a millimetre! "We'll re-break the leg and start again", says he. "You bloody won't", says I. "You'll do as you're told", says he. "It's my bloody leg", says I "and if I say no, that's it!" Fortunately the rights of the patient still carry some weight, even in the Service.

In the bed next to me during these first few days at Halton was a Spitfire pilot. He had been shot down over the Channel and had belly-landed in the Thames mud at low tide. He was still recovering from the operating theatre, legs shattered and arms broken, and had an urgent desire to pass water – and couldn't. For three days the ward sister forced him to drink gallons of lemonade under the mistaken impression that this would cause the dam to burst. By the third night he looked pregnant, his belly was so badly swollen, and he was continuously moaning in pain. In the early hours I could stand it no longer, got out of bed to the ward telephone and called for the duty quack – emergency! All hell was let loose! Doctors and nurses came a-running, wanting to know who had had the audacity to awaken everyone – but then they saw the state of this poor sod next to me and carted him off to theatre for an emergency operation. His works had been damaged, of course, and he had to be relieved surgically – as any expert like myself could have told them! End result, a happier Pilot Officer, though still very ill, a furious ward sister, who got the reprimand of her life, and I was sent, still in my hip-spiker, home on leave!

Two weeks at home was agreed as the time needed for the femur to set firmly assuming I suppose that I would be resting as in a hospital. Some hope: from the moment of arrival friends and relatives rallied round and many wagers were laid in the time it would take me to get from here to there – and back again; firstly without the crutches – which was difficult because I was so lop-sided; then it was considered fair to allow the use of the crutches, with which I very soon became expert. My times rapidly improved, particularly between pub and taxi at around 11 p.m. What "friends" they were! One of their most frequent gags was to introduce me to one of their local girlfriends, encouraging her to be the seductive temptress: can you imagine the frustration when encased in half a ton of plaster!

Back at Halton, it was agreed that the femur was not yet set firm and that the plaster should remain for a further two weeks; but as Halton beds were urgently needed for more serious cases, I was sent to Torquay for recuperation in the Palace Hotel. What a splendid place to choose as an officers' convalescent home!

The first requirement was exercise, particularly for the left ankle which had become stiff because all my weight when mobile rested on the leg iron at the foot of the spiker – in fact, at that time, my plastered leg was some 3 inches longer than the other. Who should turn out to be in charge of physiotherapy at the Palace? None other than Dan Maskell of tennis fame. We began in the gym immediately on arrival – dear God, it hurt! My room mate was a Canadian pilot; from his prang he suffered a broken arm and severe neck whip-lash, so that he had a plastered arm and an enormous neck support, which made him look like one of the "Giraffe" ladies of the Pai Dong Long Neck tribe on the Thai/Burmese border.

You surely have seen that wonderful film "Reach for the Sky", the story of that great leader Douglas Bader? Then you will recall that scene where, just after he gets fitted with his artificial legs, he arrives at a country restaurant driving an open tourer; he and two other pilots, with an assortment of plastered limbs, limp their way inside to the astonished glances from the other seated customers – and to the great amusement of a waitress – Douglas' wife-to-be. Well that was the sort of reaction Scotty, the Canadian, and I quickly got used to on our daily sorties into Torquay town. The nearest bus-stop was only about 100 yards from the hotel entrance, now thoroughly used to the elbow crutches, I could make it in 20 seconds; with his head tilted back at about 30 degrees, it took Scotty double that! But he could take a seat on the bus – with my hip-spiker I had to stand!

This freakish behaviour soon ended – a week later the plaster was removed from my leg and the gym workouts began in earnest. A couple of days later, Scotty's neck band was removed – I walked right past him without recognition, he looked so different.

Unhappily, I thought at the time, my stay at the Palace was limited to three weeks, then I was declared fit to return to Halton. A few days after that the Palace was bombed by a lone FW190 and several of the inmates lost their lives. One really never knew what might be in store!

My return to Halton was short lived – just long enough for an X-ray to prove no further movement in the femur, a medical exam to classify me fit for ground duties only, and I was then sent home for a few more days leave before reporting back to Bicester. My homecoming this time was with eager anticipation, now that I was no longer handicapped by all that plaster – I'd teach those girlfriends not to mock the sick!

CHAPTER FIVE

No. 13 O.T.U., Bicester (again!), July 1942– March 1943

Fit ground duties only, to be re-assessed in 6 months – that was the verdict. What shall we do with him for 6 months? That was the question. Station Operations Officer was the answer. And that was a most enjoyable episode. The three shifts:-

       Day 1   1300–2000
       " 2   0800–1300; 2000–
       " 3   –0800.
       Off duty until 1300 on Day 4.

This was a most agreeable system, the only drawback occurring when one had a full flying programme during the night/ morning of Days 2/3; that did not happen too often – we were, after all, principally a day bomber outfit with occasional night familiarisation exercises.

The duties of an Operations Officer were not onerous, consisting mainly of flight planning, exercise and aircraft allocation, route clearances and liaison with other stations regarding their flying programmes. Many incidents during this period left lasting memories; some were highly amusing, some reprehensible, some potentially serious, yet all made great impact on an impressionable youth – yes, me!

In the early days of my return to Bicester, the Station Commander (as yet unchanged from the previous year) was that splendid Aussie "Digger" Kyle, later to become Air Chief Marshal

Sir Wallace Kyle and later still Governor General of Australia. But soon he was to be replaced by another – we'll call him Group Captain Alnutt. Soon after his arrival, the station was allocated one aircraft of a new type – the Albemarle – destined rapidly to sink into obscurity. I think the purpose of its assignment to Bicester was to assess its potential as a low level day bomber to replace the ageing Blenheims; it was certainly quite a bit faster and could carry a crew of four or five instead of the Blenheim's three. On the other hand, it appeared bulkier, heavier and underpowered, in a word vulnerable. The Station Commander, determined to give the aeroplane a thorough test under operational conditions, decided to make a daylight sweep along the enemy coast, from Cherbourg eastwards to the Dutch Islands, with the operational object of attacking any likely targets that presented themselves. For his crew, he planned to take the Chief Instructor (O.C. Flying Wing) as co-pilot, the Station Navigation Officer as Navigator, The Station Weapons Officer as bombaimer, the Station Signals Officer as wireless operator and the Station Gunnery leader as air gunner. For supreme confidence in his survivability he deserved first prize and one could only conjecture what the effect on our training machine would have been had this crew got the chop!

The Senior Operations Officer, my immediate boss, felt that this plan should be put to Group Headquarters for approval but the Station Commander considered secrecy to be the overriding factor and that details should not therefore be "broadcast". Fortunately, S.O.O., in discussion with the senior Flying Control Officer, knew that route clearance was required by normal standing orders and that meant that the proposed operation *had* to come to the notice of the appropriate Group staff. The resulting panic at Group led to the immediate cancellation of this fantasy.

During one of our night flying programmes, whilst I was on duty in the control tower, a Blenheim with pupil pilot took off in the early hours for his first night solo on type. Normal R/T procedure gave take-off clearance and we awaited the pilot's usual call "Downwind" signifying readiness for landing; the call did not come. Three times the controller called the aircraft – no reply. With that we hit the panic button – he must have pranged on take-off says Monty, the controller. He had.

The pilot was Chinese, Chang, a very tiny, very young, Chinaman, the only one I ever encountered during the war. The crash crew found the aircraft an hour or so later, badly bruised, on its belly in a field, engine failure – no sign of the pilot. Eventually, a very dishevelled Chang walked into the control tower – "Me plang that one, have another one pliz"! Until then, Chang had seemed rather a lonely figure, rarely joining in the hilarities in the Mess, just quietly getting on with his training. From that moment on, however, he became the toast of the station, the most popular chap in the Mess.

Brashfield House figured prominently in the "fun hours" at this time. The beautiful timbered floors of the main living rooms, well polished, were ideal for dancing and I had been fortunate in finding some musical colleagues to form a useful quartet – piano, sax, guitar and drums. This led to a regular Saturday evening function, we installed a bar and, hey presto, we had a night club. Most Mess members patronised the club, which proved a successful entertainment centre, often visited by VIP's and local "dignitaries". (Some 40 odd years later, when returning from a visit to the north country, I was passing Bicester and couldn't resist a call at Brashfield House. Now private property, the owners nevertheless were most hospitable when I explained my earlier connection with the property. Though they knew of the R.A.F. connection, of course, they had never heard the full story of the part played by the house during the war and were particularly delighted by the "night club" details. Funny thing – in retrospect I saw the House as a magnificent country mansion – but, whilst still a lovely property, it is nowhere near the memory I had cherished. The old adage is right – it often does not pay to go back!)

Members of the Women's Auxiliary Air Force filled many of the important administrative posts on the station and naturally, men and women worked together all the time. Needless to say, close relationships were, to put it mildly, discouraged – morals were much stronger in those days and – dare I say it – Service discipline was tighter also. The operations room was next to the telephone exchange and so there was a constant attraction between male staff and female telephone operators. I formed a close attachment to a young lady named Pam but we were always careful to stay at arms length, so to speak, whilst on the station. We met frequently in Oxford, where the Randolph Hotel was the favourite rendezvous. Even then, our relationship did not go beyond simple friendship. If that makes me look a prude, I can only say that the veto was strictly applied against all my efforts to break it. Unhappily, the relationship did not survive my eventual posting.

Such infuriating, though commendable, adherence to principle (and service discipline!) did not extend to one of my colleagues – we'll call him Flight Lieutenant Smith. During several weeks it fell to my lot to relieve him at 0800 hours at completion of his night duty; he was 40+, the girl just 20; several times they failed to surface before my arrival. I gave him full marks on two counts: age and experience was clearly a "turn on" (as opposed to the inexperience of callow youth); somehow that experience enabled him always to escape the attention of his seniors. Of course I was jealous – would you not have been?

The Court of Inquiry into our crash was chaired by a Group Captain from Group with one of the staff Blenheim pilots as member. Apart from myself, the only other witness was O.C. Servicing Squadron, Squadron Leader Ernie Fletcher, to give evidence of servicing record. The cause of the accident was attributed to engine failure and excused, I believe, by pilot inexperience. In November, just a year after the crash, I was called to the Central Medical Establishment in London to determine my medical fitness to return to flying duties (or otherwise!). Although still a bit "lopsided", I was passed "partially fit" – fit enough for non-operational aircrew duties, U.K. only, for a period of 4 months, then to be re-assessed. Interviewed by the Board Chairman afterwards, I was asked if I was prepared to carry on with flying: my response was blunt – "Yes, provided next time I prang myself!". "No dice, if you haven't the guts to continue as an observer, then you would be unsuitable for pilot training". I thought that unnecessarily crude, certainly unjustified, but persisted in requesting retraining as a pilot. "Tell you what we'll do" says the Chairman, "you do a tour of ops. as an observer and I'll mark your records to be retrained as a pilot then". "Done!" (but watch this space).

Returned to Bicester, I ceased duties as an Operations Officer and spent that four months as a staff navigator, flying as instructor with new pupil crews coming through the training machine. This meant good old Ansons again, now at the new satellite airfield of Finmere, alternating with Blenheims in the operational training flight at Bicester itself. During this time I enjoyed some very interesting diversions with other members of the staff.

On one occasion I was instructed to navigate O.C. Technical Wing, Wing Commander "Polly" Perkins (later to become an Air Marshal and Air Member for Technical Services), with Ernie Fletcher as passenger, to Newton, near Nottingham. Ernie and I were to bring back a Tiger Moth which had been refurbished there. Although it was but a short journey, I completed a proper flight plan (got to impress the Wing Co., thinks I) and on take off gave the pilot his course to steer. After about 15 minutes, in excellent visibility at 2000 feet, it was obvious we were drifting to starboard of track so I gave a few degrees alteration of course to port. Not enough I decided after another 10 minutes and requested a further few degrees change to port. Whereupon "Polly" drops the starboard wing and swoops down to 1000 feet and pointing to a building beside a country lane says "That's the Blue Boar. The barmaid there is Rosie and she's a smasher!". Back up to 2000 feet, then a few miles further on, down to port and at 1000 feet says "Look, there's the White Hart. The wife and I had a splendid weekend there last month!" I got the point: when you know the countryside like the back of your hand, you don't really need a navigator to give piddling little course alterations. However, perhaps not wishing to discourage a young "keen type" he followed with "But the weather might clamp down and then perhaps I'll be thankful you're aboard".

A little while later at Newton, Ernie and I collected the Tiger Moth, found it in splendid condition and took off for Bicester, he flying from the front cockpit, me behind. I figured he probably knew the way as well as "Polly", but nevertheless I gave him a course to steer and an E.T.A. (estimated time of arrival) but after five minutes he says "You fly her Norman, I'm a bit tired". What a nice gesture, thinks I, it's his way of giving me a crack at the controls. So, here I am flying and navigating myself – easier said than done, when all I'd handled heretofore was a comparatively stable Blenheim, straight and level.

Approaching Bicester some 50 minutes later I call Ernie on the intercom; now the word intercom, though appropriate enough, was perhaps a bit sophisticated for a Tiger Moth – it consisted of Gosport tubes, one in each cockpit, connected by a simple tube between them and the voices were not magnified in any way, thus speech was not easy in the open air at 80 mph. Getting no response, I shout through the tube – no dice. Leaning over and tapping him on the shoulder, I realise he is actually asleep. So he really was tired after all! Shaking and tapping the shoulder has no effect; as you can imagine, if you can sleep in the open cockpit of a Tiger Moth you're hardly likely to be awakened by a few taps on the shoulder.

So now what? Well, there's base, landing direction west, join circuit on the south side, no radio so we can't call Control for landing instructions – perhaps he'll wake up in a minute. No? Oh well, here goes. I'm saying to myself out loud "here we are on the downwind leg at 1000 feet, gradual descent, turn crosswind at 500 feet, 65 mph, slowly lose height on to finals, green from the duty pilot wagon, clear to land; over the hedge at 100 feet, 60 mph" – when suddenly there's Ernie "very good Norman, stalling speed about 50, hold her off at about 10 feet, alright I've got her now". He puts her down, we balloon 6 feet or so, bounce, bounce, she's down! Roll to the end, stop – from the front cockpit, "Now that wasn't too bad was it? I think we did well, don't you?" Frankly, at this point I'm almost speechless. "Yes, w-w-w-well done Sir", say I.

(I was reminded of this episode much later on when a navigator friend of mine, after retraining as a pilot, and then commanding a meteor fighter squadron, retained his "N" badge on his flying overalls. When flying in to another station, he delighted in the astonished gapes of the groundcrew when they saw a Navigator, apparently, descending from the cockpit of a single seater jet fighter. It led to several interesting confrontations with senior officers not in the know).

Perhaps at this point I should record a little hearsay about Ernie, a man I greatly admired. It is said that he volunteered for an R.A.F. war commission in August 1939 as an engineer. Asked about previous service, he revealed that he was a pilot in the R.F.C. during '14/'18, ending the war on Sopwith Camels. The recruiting officer asked whether he had kept up his flying since – "Yes, of course". He was accepted as an engineer with the immediate rank of squadron leader, complete with pilot's wings, and authorised to fly light aircraft types. In fact, he had not flown since 1918! I suppose the result could have been disaster, in fact nearly was on several occasions, but one couldn't help but admire the man.

There was then another occasion at Bicester, soon after our Moth experience, when an Anson needed an airtest following servicing in Ernie's flight, but no pilot was immediately available.

The Anson flight commander needed the aeroplane urgently so Ernie decided to airtest it himself – remember, qualified light aircraft only, and he had never flown a twin-engined aeroplane. The story of his take-off went the rounds for weeks afterward but regrettably I did not see it myself. At the first attempt he was all over the airfield – no runways, all grass. It seemed that he just could not co-ordinate rudder controls with two throttles and was swinging first one way, then t'other; he managed to stop before the hedge, turn her round and taxi back to the start, obviously learning by trial and error on the way, then achieving an almost flawless take-off on the second run. Landing? No trouble, a real kisser. Result: henceforth permitted to fly Ansons – only man I ever knew who went from singles to twins without a conversion course.

It was early in '43 when I got my first sight of the De Havilland Mosquito. This aeroplane swooped over the airfield at nought feet, straight up in a half loop with a roll off the top, a split-arse circuit and then finals with 45 degrees of bank down to 50 feet for a honey of a landing. Taxi to the tower and out steps a diminutive blonde lass in the A.T.A. (Air Transport Auxiliary). Could she stay the night? Could she – what a party.

CHAPTER SIX

No. 13 O.T.U., Bicester, March–June, 1943

Now my four months of "partial fitness" is concluded, I attend CME again for re-assessment and, now graded A3B fully operationally fit, I am fed into the stream for a new OTU course on Blenheims. My first shock is to be told that I must follow the full course – including the Anson flight syllabus – even though I had just flown as a "staff nav." through the two previous courses. Ah well, mustn't buck the system, what? Anyway, it's all good flying experience and having done all the cross-country routes twice before, I'm bound to shine throughout, am I not? That's the second shock: how would I ever live down that hairy three-hour flight around central UK which should have taken only two hours – I managed to get lost! Such over-confidence reminds me of the old pilot's adage: the most dangerous time in his life is when he completes his first 1000 hours – he thinks he knows it all; the second most dangerous time is at 2000 hours, because then he knows he knows it all!

However, no more boobs like that; the Anson course is happily completed (19 cross-country flights in 10 days), we re-enter ground school, meet the new Pilots and W.Op/AGs, and form our new crews. I find another "old man" for a pilot – he's 33, the grand-daddy of them all, and has just completed 2000 hours instructing. I hadn't heard that adage about pilots' danger points at that time but I can say with certainty that it didn't apply in his case. In the many experiences we were to share from now on "The Baron", as Flying Officer Hector Goldie was popularly known, never put a foot wrong in the air and I always had the utmost faith in his flying ability. Perhaps, as I had then also been promoted to Flying Officer (time promotion from Pilot Officer to Flying Officer was one year and from Flying Officer to Flight Lieutenant one further year), we naturally fitted together as the two seniors on the course. But despite the fact that we flew together for a year and a half, we did not really become friends; on the other hand, we crossed swords on only a couple of occasions which were soon forgotten. Trusting comrades, yes; easy-going pals, yes; real friends, no. Well that's war for you!

For the next six weeks, the Blenheim course went smoothly; all exercises were completed satisfactorily and I had my first experience of night flying. That came as another shock: when first taxiing out, the profusion of lights was confusion for me; fortunately Baron was the calm experienced one and my night vision eventually let me make some sense of the procedures. In the air, lights were no problem – in wartime there weren't any! Gradually one became accustomed to the contrasts of greys, browns and blacks at night compared to the colours of daytime and the way in which water features become so much more prominent at night. Another oft repeated adage comes to mind: it's only birds and fools that fly, and birds don't fly at night! However, we were destined for a day light bomber squadron, weren't we? I missed the posting to 105 on Bisleys in North Africa; would that be repeated or would it be a 2 Group squadron?

Before that decision was taken, let me recall a couple of interesting characters I was to meet during this time, gentlemen who were to figure prominently in my post war career many years later. We flew with a staff pilot on one of our practice bombing sorties – Flying Officer Ivor Broom. I had also done some course work with one of the staff navigation instructors, Flight Sergeant Ted Sismore. Both were highly decorated for their operational successes and, in their peacetime careers, attained Air Rank. There were to be several meeting points in later years, in the Ministry, on various stations, on one occasion in South Africa, then finally we were all destined to serve together in Germany.

Early in June, just before we were due for posting, the Station was visited by Wing Commander Sammy Hoare, everyone's image of the typical RAF fighter ace, large ginger handlebar moustache, wonderful sangfroid and "jolly good chaps" – one of our most successful nightfighter aces, and that with one eye! He was now Wing Commander Flying and Chief Instructor at the newly formed Mosquito training unit – 60 OTU, High Ercall, near Shrewsbury. He was seeking crews for night intruder squadrons; several of our course are interviewed and two chosen, including Baron and me. So now it is yet another OTU course before I reach a squadron, and then primarily in a night role (so much for day bombers) but what a lucky break – Mosquitos rather than Blenheims!

Farewell Bicester, Brashfield House (how I shall miss the band sessions at weekends), Oxford and the Randolph Hotel. Meanwhile a week's leave, in wonderful June weather, was a memorable interlude before proceeding to the next (and almost last) stage of training. Without the encumbrance of a leg plaster, and now with merely an impressive (?) limp, it was great to be home again with family and friends. All too brief of course, but notable for two events.

One young lady of my acquaintance was the daughter of a local builder, Bill Brough, who owned a splendid Wolseley Hornet tourer, four-seater, canvas hood, a delightful machine. It was laid up on jacks in his garage – petrol rationing (even for a builder?). Would he sell it to me? My own car, bought for me by my father when I reached 18 (for £10!) was a 1931 Singer 9, gate-crash gears. Bill offered me a straight swop! And he didn't even demand that I marry his daughter! Anyway, joking aside, it was a marvellous gesture and I accepted with alacrity. More of this car anon.

The other incident was a party attended by several old friends, in particular two young ladies: Peggy, a platonic friend going back many years, and Joyce, a once-upon-a-time serious girlfriend. Peggy had recently joined the WAAF and told me her brother Peter was flying Mosquitos; Joyce, still only 19, stayed home to nurse her sick mother. Both girls were to figure in tragic events soon to occur.

No. 60 O.T.U., High Ercall, June–September 1943

All too soon it's time to report to High Ercall for the conversion to Mosquitos – by now with the impressive total of 274 flying hours – don't knock it, many young aircrew were pitched into an operational tour with far less!

The Mosquito was, without doubt, a pilot's dream machine. It was fast, extremely manoeuvrable, a doddle on one engine, very reliable; just about its only vice was a tendency to swing on take-off – nothing to bother even an average pilot. Of ultra-light wooden construction, many thought it vulnerable to enemy defences, yet it proved more resilient to punishment than many other types.

Before leaping into the air, we absorbed a brief week's ground school, dealing with the mechanics of the aeroplane and the night intruder role for which we were selected. Put simply, the object of the exercise was to patrol the vicinity of enemy airfields at night, catch them in the air at take-off or landing if possible, denying them the use of their bases simply by our presence. This was an effective tactic, particularly applied to the G.A.F. night fighter airfields, often resulting in losses when their aircraft ran out of fuel searching for a safe place to land. Other tasks could be combined – bombing and ground straffing on the return run, trains, road transport, military installations.

While Baron took the short handling course, dual checks followed by air/air and air ground cine shooting exercises, I was enjoying half a dozen Anson trips with the then wonder of modern science, the GEE box. It was so hush-hush at that time that the receiver display unit was delivered to the aircraft immediately before each flight in a locked van under armed guard – and collected immediately on landing with the same rigid security. It looked similar to an early TV set with a small round screen and several control knobs. Twiddle a few knobs, read off a couple of figures from a scale, plot on a special chart and "Hey presto" you had your aircraft's position. With experience it took about 30 seconds and was accurate over most of the UK and surrounding seas to a mile or less. Wonderful stuff!

Then we were off on our full course of nearly 50 practice sorties – day and night, navigation, cinegun, live air firing (4 x .303 machine guns; 4 x 20 mm cannon), intruder practices, low level formation. With apologies to all the Blenheim fans I must say it – this was a great deal more exciting – "twitchy" at times, but a lot of fun.

During this time one incident badly marred the so far un-blemished record of the unit. A short aerobatic display over the airfield by one of the staff pilots started brilliantly and had an admiring audience of ground and aircrew alike, though senior officers were clearly angry that it should be happening against all the rules. The worst happened – in attempting a slow roll, much too low, he pranged into the runway intersection – a very nasty mess. I had only met the pilot again a couple of days previously – he was Peggy's brother!

At the funeral I met Peggy again; the loss of her brother, particularly in such a needless manner, hit her hard. Now a sergeant, she seemed content in the Service, stationed at that time near Bristol, We managed several meetings before my following posting and it began to seem as though our many years of platonic friendship was changing. But postings were to separate us for the next year and, though we corresponded for a while, such a lovely girl was not going to lack for male company. Inevitably, I lost out – is that not typical of so many wartime romances?

Several characters stand out in my memories of High Ercall, mainly because they were to follow Baron and me to our squadron/station in the ensuing months. Sammy Hoare, already mentioned as the man behind our move to Mosquitos, was O.C. Flying Wing and Chief Instructor: he was destined to be our Station Commander a year hence. Then there was Squadron Leader "Sticky" Murphy, another gungho type with a splendid huge moustache to match his wings; he had come from a "special" squadron, flying two very disparate aircraft – Whitleys and Lysanders – from the former dropping leaflets (or was this a cover for something much more important and sinister?) and from the latter dropping spies. And often switching from one to the other on alternate nights! He was to become first one of our Flight Commanders and then Squadron Commander. He and Sammy were already sporting both D.S.O. and D.F.C.

There was Squadron Leader Phil Russell, then Chief Flying Instructor, also later to join us, taking over from Sticky, first as Flight Commander and eventually as Squadron Commander. Also the Station Navigation officer, Flight Lieutenant Bill Gregory D.F.C. was to become a great friend – and join us as Squadron Navigation Officer.

Being one of the few officers lucky enough to own a car, I was never short of company on the occasional evening and weekend runs into Shrewsbury. A monthly petrol ration of only five gallons did not allow many such sorties, especially as I needed the car to get home on the few days leave allowed at the end of the course.

A favourite haunt was the Lion Hotel (but prices in our Mess Bar were so much more favourable!), the main interest, fairly obviously, being the parties given by local farmers – all of whom seemed to have such attractive daughters.

Bridge became my main diversionary interest at this point. The Station Dentist was my mentor and I believe that, under his tuition, I developed to a passable standard. But nothing had prepared me for the nerve-rending experience of a "friendly" bridge drive to which we were invited at a nearby country estate. Lady Jacquetta Williams was our hostess and was – or had been at one time – captain of the Great Britain Bridge Team. The house was large enough to accommodate 16 tables, so this was no minor or casual event. To say I was nervous among such a gathering would be an understatement but Lady Jacquetta's greeting only made it worse: "You are most welcome, dear man, and I hope you will honour me by being my partner this evening"! Dear God – me a beginner and a newcomer to the circle – what had Peter Simms, our dentist, let me in for? We played four rubbers at different tables, I managed to avoid any serious blacks, and milady and I finished the evening over 10,000 points to the good. Whereupon I was handed £25 plus; though I protested vigorously it was then explained that we were playing for five shillings a hundred! "But I can't accept it. Had I lost I could not possibly have afforded to pay that sort of money" (my pay as a Flying Officer was 18/6d a day).

"Nonsense" says Lady Jacquetta, "you couldn't lose as my partner!" What a pity it was that I was to be posted before the next drive was held.

One of the last exercises on the course was live air/ground and air/air firing off the Welsh coast in Cardigan Bay. Targets floated in the sea and drogues were towed by Miles Masters based nearby at Valley. For liaison purposes we used a small wartime airstrip at Llanbedr – one runway about 1000 yards long, east to west, from the foot of a mountain to the seashore. By day, the surface wind was invariably off the sea – so one landed from a near 45 degrees approach, throttles off, everything hanging, brakes on virtually from touch-down; overshoot and you got wet! For take-off, through the gate and haul her off at the beach! Engine cut on take-off? A serious ducking would be the least to expect. At night? Well, usually the wind was down the mountain which meant take-off towards the mountain – so forget it, not used at night. I suspect the strip was used purely to get us used to operation from a postage stamp – proved very useful practice for what was soon to be in store. And that news awaited us when we returned to High Ercall – we were to join 23 Squadron in Malta a.s.a.p.

Lyneham and Portreath, October 1943

Now to me "a.s.a.p." had always meant "get your skates on, do it yesterday!" But, even in wartime (or should that be *especially* in wartime?), a thousand and one things cause delays. First we were briefed to go to Filton to collect our "own" aeroplane and fly it to Lyneham (we'd heard Mosquitos cost about £30,000, great, we'd come into a fortune!); there we would be "prepared" for transit to Malta. It was now the end of August; I will not attempt to analyse September's delays, but the aeroplane was not yet ready, there was nothing for us to do at Lyneham until it was, so off we went on some more leave – much appreciated though when about to go overseas for an indefinite period. Eventually, we collected Mosquito Mk.6 HX813 on 4th October.

Now officially at Lyneham, we are informed that we must undergo a 4-days course, including 2 days of class lectures, to be taught how to navigate to Gibraltar! Well really – I mean – what could be simpler? You set off from Lands End at 1000 feet or so on course 210 magnetic for a couple of hours: you'll then see land ahead, turn right; if you don't see land ahead after two hours alter course 30 degrees port to 180 until you do; then follow the Spanish and Portuguese coasts for another couple of hours and you'll see this bloody great rock sticking out of the sea – that's Gib! But oh no, you have this lovely little gadget called a Drift Recorder sticking through the cockpit floor – you look through the lens, operate the pen on that little chart and that will tell you whether you've calculated the correct drift – you can then calculate the correct course to steer – it's the *only* navigation aid you have! The instructor was somewhat nonplussed when I pointed out that all our kit would be filling the cockpit in front of me and I wouldn't even be able to get at the damned drift recorder. Didn't matter though – still had to sit through the lectures and do a couple of Anson flights to learn how to use it.

Now, if you've read this far, I hear you say "But what about the GEE box?" No dice – doesn't work where we're going; anyway it's much too secret to take it out of the country.

Now at last that's over and we're as ready as we'll ever be. It's 15th October, so off we go to Gibraltar. Oh no we don't. We now fly down to Portreath, a staging post on the Cornwall coast, in order to refuel and get our flight clearance to Gib. "But we've got enough range with our two 250 gallon drop tanks to get to Gib. direct from Lyneham. Why . . . ?" Don't argue – it's procedure.

We fly to Portreath on 16th October, get refuelled – the Engineer puts the aircraft u/s and the Met. man puts the weather u/s. Some minor engine part needs to be replaced ("You have spares here?" "No, but don't worry', we'll get it from Filton"); clouds are on the deck all over the Bay of Biscay; and so another week goes by. During that week, two Beaufighters decided to go to Gib. direct over Spain, high level to avoid the weather; both were shot down by German fighters. Whoops – just as well we waited to go low level as planned!

Finally, a sigh of relief, a quick 15 minutes air test, all systems go, and we leave for Gib. on 24th October, 1943.

CHAPTER SEVEN

Gibraltar and Malta, October–November 1943

Weather was still poor, with low cloud over the Bay but, just as expected, there was the Spanish coast ahead after just under two hours, turn right, left at Cape Finisterre, left again at Cape Vicente and, after four hours there she is – Gibraltar. And you really can't miss it – in full view from almost 100 miles away – it's some rock!

Twice we had spotted a Ju88 in the vicinity of the Spanish coast; they turned sharply away at the sight of us but we were not prepared for a fuel-guzzling chase – our mission was to get to Gib.

The runway was, I believe, about 1400 yards long in those days (it's been more than doubled since), stretching east/west between the Spanish border and the Rock. Most notable was its 100+ yards width, with literally dozens of aeroplanes, of all types, stacked along the side – there was nowhere else to put them. And then the road from the border at La Linea passes right across the centre of the runway; traffic is halted on both sides whilst an aircraft takes off or lands and then, with a mad rush, it tears across both ways before the next air movement. It must have been an Air Trafficker's nightmare!

We were refuelled quickly after landing, a short visit to the Ops. Room cleared us for an early takeoff next morning, then beds were allocated in the Transit Mess – free time until 0800 so the greenhorns set off to savour the wonders around us.

Immediately noticeable, fresh from the U.K. after four years of wartime rationing, were the plentiful supplies of everything. For example, fruit of all sorts, especially bananas! An almost forgotten fruit, we bought whole bunches and ate them just walking around the town. From bananas, one's thoughts immediately turned to the indigenous population – so we climbed up the Rock and there they were – hundreds of them.

Even though there had never been a shortage of bananas in Gib. you'd be surprised how eager the locals are to steal yours. Someone might have told us not to go up there with a bunch of bananas – or alternatively to take up a barrow-load! All the family joined in, from Grandpa down to young junior – only there must have been 50 Grandpas (or Grandmas) and hundreds of young juniors, all of whom took an instant interest in us – or rather, our bananas. Too few to go around – that set off a mighty scrum – what a fracas! These Rock Apes (and I mean real apes – not the R.A.F. Regiment) are greedy, rowdy and aggressive creatures and we thought ourselves lucky to get away with limbs and clothing more or less intact.

There is much to see and marvel at on The Rock but with only a few hours to spare we managed no more than a quick tour of the harbour – Royal Navy in great form – some shopping for essentials to take to the squadron (cigarettes, chocolate, fruit, meat, whisky, – two more cases to choke up my very limited cockpit space!) and then a few hours over the border in La Linea. Now if I were writing a pornographic novel, I could find plenty of material from that night's experiences. Suffice it to say that a tour of the bars and clubs was very entertaining and our return through the Spanish frontier post in the early hours would read like an extract from one of Ian Fleming's best. Of course the Spaniards were not exactly on friendly terms with the British during those war years, especially there!

Amidst some panic on the morrow – there were literally dozens of aeroplanes awaiting the attentions of the servicing flight, the mechanics for minor repairs, the bowsers for refuelling, the armourers for re-arming – it was well on to noon before we could join the queue for takeoff. In fact it was rather like a major city airport of the present day – except that the aircraft and their crews had very different objectives in mind! In our case, Baron and I had but one aim – to get ourselves and our Mossie to Malta in one piece p.d.q. To that end we headed across North Africa, the mountainous region, staying just on top of cloud for most of the way; this layer cloud provides the ideal "bolt-hole" if you meet hostiles, but an awareness of the solid bits inside it makes a navigator's presence desirable – so nice to be wanted on occasions!

Malta was in the clear, both from weather and enemy action point of view – in fact the Island and its immediate area were no longer under German aerial domination – we and the Americans had supremacy in the skies over the Med. now. However, it soon became apparent to the newcomer that this change of situation was recent: evidence of the enemy's furious bombardment in the preceding years was everywhere, though the Maltese were hard at work repairing buildings and public utilities. I do not need here to repeat the stirling worth of that island race – they had borne their tragic lot with wonderful fortitude and we would now be able join in the task of supporting the allied push northward.

No. 23 Squadron, October 1943–September 1944

The Squadron were lucky enough to have the Meadowbank Hotel in Sliema as their Headquarters and Mess. Though billeted three or four to a room, it was now clear that we would be spending our spare time in considerable comfort – oh foolish boy, that's what you think – we had no inkling of what was in store in the so near future. However, let's begin with a few of the more bizarre happenings of the next few weeks.

When a squadron is operating on an airfield such as Luqa, with its aircraft dispersed all round the perimeter and with domestic facilities and accommodation several miles away, one of the essentials of life is adequate transport. Transport we had – but it was far from adequate. The squadron commander, Wing Commander Burton-Giles, had a car – of sorts: sometimes it started, sometimes not; occasionally, but rarely, it went three days without breaking down. But we all used it, serviced it, repaired it, and somehow managed to keep the CO mobile. Flight commanders sometimes had Jeeps; I say sometimes, because they were the mainstay of the movement capability for some 40 aircrews, around the airfield and to and from Sliema. And oh yes – we had a bus, and what a bus! The miracle was not only that it worked, but that it was by far the most reliable vehicle we had. Springs and shock absorbers were but a memory; seats were mainly just metal frames, devoid of upholstery, the driver's windscreen was the only glass left – all remaining "windows" had been replaced with gauze or simply boarded up. But this vehicle did stirling work, in constant demand to move officers, NCOs and men about their business on and off the airfield.

This bus was, in fact, one of the better examples of the primary means of transport on the island – for military personnel and civilians alike. The most remarkable fact was, not that the populace had to rely on such an obsolete, clapped out fleet of buses – there were several hundred in constant use – but that it had been possible to maintain them in working condition after years of constant bombardment and wreckage.

To augment this national transport system there was, of course, the Maltese version of the taxi – the "Garry" – a horse-drawn chaise, akin to a miniature stage coach. More modern versions still ply their trade but I imagine that some of those in which we frequently rode are lovingly preserved in memory of those not so graceful war years.

For us living in Sliema and frequently visiting the Capital, Valetta, or the Royal Navy dockyards, a much preferred alternative transport was the ferry, a ticket at that time costing 2d. i.e. less than 1p! Boats ran between the two towns continuously all day, every day. Or, of course, there were the much more expensive water taxis – really rather up-market rowing boats, something similar to the Venetian gondola, rowed by the standing oarsman with one oar. We were charged 2/6 each way (12p), but the boat carried five passengers!

On one memorable occasion, I borrowed the CO's car (with permission on this occasion) to take a party of five to the Officers' "Rest Camp" at St. Paul's Bay. Plenty of good Canadian beer (first decent beer since leaving U.K.) good swimming, met some of the Beaufighter chaps from the squadron at Hal Far. On return, the car conked out four times – choked carburettor – took two hours to cover 10 miles. Avoided the ignominy of a search party by just a few minutes – got back only just in time for the start of the flying programme.

Baron awoke one night in the early hours to disturb a burglar in the act of rifling his wallet. Leaping out of bed with a scream of rage, he grabbed his revolver from his locker drawer, and chased the would-be robber out on to the roof of Meadowbank and over several nearby roofs. The man was as nimble as you would expect a cat-burglar to be and, annoyed that he couldn't catch the man, Baron fired. He didn't kill him, thank goodness (what an international incident that would have caused!) and we never saw the creature again. But several weeks after we had left the island, we heard that the Malta police had arrested a man on a charge of burglary; he had a pronounced limp – a bullet was found in his leg!

From that point on, we all kept our handguns at the ready – the next interloper might not be just a thief. After a hectic party one night, when we retired three sheets to the wind, we had all just got to bed – and no-one had turned the light out. "Turn that bloody light out", from Pat Rapson. "Turn the bloody thing out yourself", says I. BANG! Baron put the light out with one shot! Dangerous things, guns.

One of our more interesting evening pastimes was a visit to a bar in Sliema – the Chocolate King. The Maltese owner had been in the Royal Navy for many years and had developed a soft spot for the lads of 23; his selection of drinks was better than most and his menu, though limited, was excellent value. I was at first puzzled by the number of pleasant girls who frequently accompanied his male customers, not because heterosexual couples were unusual, but because they always seemed to arrive *before* their boyfriends. The penny quickly dropped when one of them joined me at the table on my second visit. Whilst I managed to refrain from the natural sequel to this encounter, I enjoyed the conversation for the next hour: in particular, I was intrigued by the girl's philosophy – we are Roman Catholic, we sell our bodies from Monday to Saturday, attend church with Communion on Sunday morning and at the Confessional we donate one sixth of our week's takings to the Church and so our sins are forgiven; by Monday we have a clean sheet and are free again to follow our profession. I suppose that now, near the turn of the century, such morals would hardly be questioned but at that time it came as something of a shock – guess I was very naive for my age.

Meanwhile, the war continues! For some weeks, the "powers that be" had been investigating the possibilities of several advanced airfields to which the Squadron might move to give us a more effective radius of action, so increasing "on target" time and therefore stronger support for the armies on the Italian mainland. The first was an "airstrip" Sigonella, near Catania on the lower slopes of Mount Etna, Sicily; a section of "A" Flight moved there for a few days but the weather was constantly bad – and flying from a base at the foot of a 10,000 feet mountain was not the fun it's cracked up to be! So we abandoned that for a "much better" forward base at Pomigliano – on the lower slopes of Mount Vesuvius. Now, as everyone knows, that mountain is only about 4000 feet, so logic dictates that we had only four tenths as many chances of flying into it as would have been the case at Mount Etna!

CHAPTER EIGHT

Pomigliano, November 1943–January 1944

For an early reconnaissance to assess it as a potential base, Baron and I flew our Engineer Officer up to Pomigliano. Frankly it was a mess – smashed Italian and German kites cluttered the field, there were no available buildings to meet any of the usual needs – living quarters, messes, offices – the only buildings worth the name (all badly damaged) already being occupied by an American advance party. So it would have to be a tented encampment – and now it was almost November, with a light layer of snow already showing.

The three of us spent the night in Naples and accepted the offer of an Army major to get us back to Pomigliano by jeep; apart from losing the way twice, and getting us too close to the fighting for comfort, he managed to get us back in one piece and we returned to Malta that same afternoon.

Everything would have to be conveyed up in trucks – tents, camp beds, blankets, kitchen and mess gear, enough for 60 men, to say nothing of aircraft spares and ground equipment. It would be a major operation and the work of assembling and loading half a dozen 3-tonners began at once. "Kim" Kimpton and I were briefed to convoy the group – by ship to Salerno and thence by road to our forward base. I can imagine such a task taking weeks in peacetime – we did it in four days. Even whilst the convoy was en route, "A" Flight aircraft, plus a small ground crew section, flew up to Pomig. and were ready to operate even before their accommodation was arranged. The tented encampment was erected in no time and operations began before November was a week old.

Kim and I were lifted back to Malta and "B" Flight moved up to Pomigliano on 11th November. That night Baron and I did our first operation with the Squadron – an offensive patrol north of Rome, train and truck busting. On that night alone the Squadron destroyed 19 trains and what amounted to a mile or more of lorry convoys.

Thus was my triple coincidence complete: survival from a Blenheim prang – 11th November 1941; first flight after hospital in an Anson – 11th November 1942; first operational sortie – 11th November, 1943. Nowadays, for my family and me, Armistice Day is always a special occasion for a celebration dinner!

If I had felt that "life's hard" before – Nissen huts, marches, guards, trenches in Scotland, P.T. at 0630 on a Yorkshire beach in January – this perhaps was the most uncomfortable of all. Under canvas, in snow and sub-zero temperatures, is not funny; sleeping on a stretcher supported on 4 oil drums is not luxury; and whilst al fresco style barbecues in summer are wonderful, in snow on the side of Vesuvius they ain't! And yet my main memories of that month at Pomigliano are of the fun times, not the inconveniences. Firstly, there's the fun story of the stolen American Jeep.

In Naples, a city surely at its nadir at that time, there were few attractions – but the Arizona Club, established and run almost certainly by the local mafia, was notorious. Patronised mainly by American troops, with a few British Army, and now most of 23 Squadron, the premises rarely survived an hour without some major fracas. Fights, usually over girls of course, drunken orgies, even the occasional stabbing, were commonplace – rather like a "Wild West Saloon" really. For some time past, Sticky has been grumbling about his lack of transport – what a boon a Jeep would be. One day, Baron and I are shopping in Naples and decide to visit this den of iniquity – "Just for a drink ol' boy, just for a drink"! Outside at the kerb, a jeep is parked – and taking a peek we espy the ignition key in place. "Sticky wants a jeep – Sticky deserves a jeep – he shall have a jeep", so off we go. So much quicker to get back to camp this way, too!

Presenting his new toy to the boss, we noticed a certain lack of enthusiasm on his part – in fact he was torn between joy at the acquisition and concern about the possible inquisition. "There will be one heck of a row" quoth he. However, it was decided to hide the vehicle and try and ride out the storm if and when it should occur. It did – before nightfall telephone lines were busy and. though denying any knowledge of the theft, it seemed that a visit by the "brass" was inevitable.

We had stored the jeep in a tent. When it became apparent that our visitor (from the office of the Provost Marshal) intended to search the station he was escorted around the dispersal areas first, whilst we moved the jeep to a wood on the perimeter, then around all our tented encampment, (after which we moved the jeep back into a tent), and finally through all the wooded area. He may have suspected, but he had no proof and no sighting and finally left apologising profusely to the boss for all the trouble.

Nevertheless, it was considered too dicey to hang on to the wretched thing and by then Sticky's enthusiasm for the jeep idea had waned. The following day, Kim and I took the jeep to Pompeii to view the ruins, an impressive experience somehow heightened by the illicit means of transportation. We then drove back to Naples and quietly left it outside the Arizona Club where we had first found it. We always hoped that our escapade had not unduly lengthened the war.

In departing this airstrip, the Germans had littered the whole place with destroyed and damaged aircraft, mostly burned out. Bang in the centre of the field was the wreckage of an enormous German six-engined troop carrier, its heavy all-metal construction, all fabric covering burned off, for all the world like the skeleton of an aircraft hangar. We used the canvas of an old marquee to cover parts of this monstrosity and used it as our Operations Room!

Also destroyed by the Germans in their hasty departure were the Alfa Romeo works. Thinking of the war effort back home, where garden railings, old pots and pans, even discarded bicycles and old cars, were being scrounged and turned into war materials, the amount of scrap metal on view here would have delighted hearts at the Supply Ministry. Perhaps we should have spent our spare hours organising shipments to that end. As it was, we 'souvenired' many valuable items to improve comfort and amenities in our tented encampment.

On the morning of 12th November, when we'd only been back from our first sortie for three or four hours, we were awakened at "sparrow-fart" by a shattering burst of ack ack fire, immediately followed by a succession of bomb explosions – Jerry was obviously out for revenge! In 10 seconds flat, we were out in our slit trench in our night gear and with any covering we could grab. We were wet, frozen and frightened, it really wasn't funny; yet isn't that exactly what we'd just been handing out to the other side? Tit for tat, except that all our aircraft returned safely whereas two of his didn't. On this occasion no-one was killed or injured but shrapnel from some of their antipersonnel bombs put several holes in one of our Mossies – but it was repaired and fully serviceable before the day was out. Let's have no more of this – we thought we'd got him to the stage where he couldn't answer back!

A couple of nights later we put up a strong contingent into the Po Valley from Milan to Venice, taking in Villafranca airfield at the foot of the mountains in the northeast. That name regularly comes back to haunt me – Villafranca: it was then a G.A.F. night fighter base, mainly Me210s, the only enemy machine in the area to give us a run for our money. The place will figure frequently for the rest of our tour with almost daily signals from MACAF (Command HQ) to "Bomb Villafranca"; every time we moaned in chorus "Oh no, not again" – then sang it to the tune of "Glory, glory, hallelujah". But that night the whole of northern Italy was blanketed in thick cloud and, though we each spent a couple of hours cruising our allocated areas, the result was a lemon. But on the way back, with our airfield now also covered in thick cloud (and with no aids for letdown and landing!), Sticky Murphy was almost home when he was jumped by a 210 – tracers blazing past his cockpit window announced "near miss" and he dived into cloud to escape. One is a sitting duck when silhouetted against cloud, especially at night, and we navigators needed eyes in the back of our heads at such times; but Jock, Sticky's navigator, must have had his hands full at that moment working out how to let down through the murk over the sea, rather than into Vesuvius. At debriefing, Sticky was furious, not because he'd been attacked but because, having been airborne for over four hours, he didn't have the gas left to turn and chase the German. Dog fights at night? Come on! Besides, wasn't that exactly what we intruders were trying to do – catch them on their return short of fuel? Damned right – a case of the biter bit – almost!

Within a few more days the snow had melted, but the slightly milder spell brought a much worse hazard – rain and mud. It rained solidly for a fortnight; within a few hours we were living in a sea of mud and operating from this airfield became almost impossible. On the rare occasions a few got airborne, the weather continued to be most unhelpful over most target areas, particularly for ground attack targets. Sometimes this weather was more dangerous for our crews than anything the enemy could throw at us: for example, the occasion when "Rosy" and "Ritsi", our very experienced Polish lads, were caught in a massive CuNimb (thunder cloud), were thrown on their backs and regained control only when down to about 2000 feet. Very nasty! And one crew failed to return on that same night – also, we believed, caught in the same weather freak.

But by now preparations are already well in hand for yet a further move – to Sardinia. In the northwest corner of that island there is a small airfield, until recently manned by the Italian Air Force – Alghero. We understand that the Americans are also preparing to occupy it and have already established a small HQ unit in preparation. If we don't pull our fingers out we'll miss out on the allocation of available accommodation – but what's new about that?

Meantime, strapped as we are by this atrocious weather, let's make the most of what Naples has to offer. The situation here never ceases to astound us: most of the outskirts is in ruins, particularly the north and east sides, and the main approach roads are all but impassable. Yet the Via Roma, the heart of the city, and its surrounds are virtually untouched; crowds fill the streets all day long, reminiscent of Regent Street and Piccadilly on a Bank Holiday in peacetime – doing nothing, going nowhere and in no hurry to get there. Touts and pickpockets abound; shops are well stocked with clothing (unlimited nylons at 5/- a pair, and no coupons!), toys, furniture – but no food, sweets, chocolate and few cigarettes (very expensive). Money is virtually valueless – barter thrives. And amidst all this, the Arizona Club (previously mentioned – a real touch of the Wild West!) and, on the northern seafront, the Restaurante Stella.

We found the "Stella" quite by accident, whilst chasing a thief with stolen camera (got him and taught him a lesson). Not much to look at but homely inside with a friendly proprietor – in other words, an Italian more happy than most to sway with the wind! For three weeks, this became our haven of refuge, an oasis in the desert: despite all the shortages Toni could always produce steak, eggs and all the trimmings or a full range of their wonderful pasta dishes. All the best wines had disappeared, taken by the Germans we're told, but he could still find innumerable bottles of not-half-bad Chianti. After our third visit in a week, Toni reserved a 10-seat table exclusively for 23 Squadron.

In the midst of this duff weather spell we are visited by an official film crew, wanting some operational footage of the squadron's activities – briefings, crews manning aeroplanes, take-offs and landings, servicing crews at work. We understood it was a war propaganda film, perhaps also a recruiting aid for the Service. Though the team spent several days and miles of film, we did not see any results, nor did we hear any more of the matter at the time. (More than half a century later I met and befriended two brothers in the building business who had been RAF technicians and had maintained an abiding interest in matters aviation. By telephone one evening: "Norman, we've just seen you on film!" They had bought a tape entitled "Mosquito at War" – and sure enough, there was the gang of us at Pomigliano!).

I mentioned earlier, only briefly, my visit with Kimmy to Pompeii in the stolen jeep. It would be remiss of me not to include a few more comments concerning those remarkable ancient remains. Should you visit Naples, do not miss the chance to see the ruined city of Pompeii; the preserved sections offer an insight into the sophistication of the era, and the amazingly advanced state of the civilisation then existing. Two thirds of the city is excavated and houses, roads, gardens, utensils and furniture of 2000 years ago have been preserved under the mountain of lava. The public baths, the market square with its church, law courts, library and other public buildings, the arena and public parks – all are partly, or even mostly, destroyed but can still be seen for what they were. The house of the Vetti brothers, perhaps the richest in the city, is probably the most interesting of all, with a central courtyard and carved columns still largely intact, a fine example of a gracious residence – even though some of the artifacts are indicative of the debauched lives probably led by the privileged few (so what has changed?). In this, and several other houses to be seen, wonderful wall paintings in waxed paint have survived intact. A guided tour of Pompeii is a *must*.

Two more incidents during our thankfully short stay at Pomig.

are worth recalling. On the last day of November we received an urgent call from the Americans – a Flying Fortress was down near the Isle of Elba – could we spare an aircraft to search for survivors. My "driver" was away at the time but Alec Lawson was on tap navigator-less, so we were airborne within 20 minutes of the call. We searched the area for an hour, first line-ahead, then square, but failed to spot any survivors or wreckage; this was still enemy coast so we reckoned the crew may have been picked up by the Germans.

The final event was really bizarre: "Bilby" and I are driving back from the "Stella" one night around midnight when a man in what appeared to be army uniform thumbs us for a lift. As curfew in Naples is 1900, who is this guy? His uniform is American, but with a British Army greatcoat; he claims to be Free French but when we question him in French he doesn't understand – with my Frenchability that doesn't surprise but Bilby is fluent, so French he ain't! We haul him aboard – we're in a 3-tonner on this occasion – and march him into the American Military Police HQ. He was a Jerry, though where he got the clothes we never found out. I wrote in my diary "one confirmed"!

CHAPTER NINE

Alghero, Sardinia. Domestic Matters

It is 10th December and all arrangements are made for the transfer to Sardinia. The Pomigliano encampment is to be cleared up by a rearguard party, all we have to do is to pack our personal gear, this time including sheets, blankets and pillows, and fly away. Not knowing what supplies would be available in Sardinia we made our last visit to the NAAFI rations centre in Naples and, shooting the most horrible line about expected shortages of all commodities in an unknown area just abandoned by the enemy, obtained double rations of cigarettes, soap, chocolate and canned goods to take with us. One final farewell party that night in the British Officers Club ensured some thick heads for the early departure from Pomig. next morning.

First impressions of Alghero are not good. The runway is a dirt strip, though we are told that either wire mesh (as per Pomig.) or tarmac is to be laid. The Americans have commandeered the only buildings suitable as Officers' and NCOs' messes and briefing rooms/offices; we are to be allowed the hutted part of the station and our living quarters are a mile away at the seaside – buildings on the rocky shore previously occupied by the Italian military. Seriously miffed at their unceremonious evacuation (sorry Wops, you joined the wrong side this time!), the departing troops had done their best to make these buildings uninhabitable – no windows, no doors (not even the frames), damaged floors and ceilings, water supply system defunct, no heating – not a pleasant prospect. But what a challenge! It would be boring to spell it out stage by stage: suffice it to record that in little more than a month we had a working Officers Mess, Sergeants Mess and Airmen's Mess, barracks for all with fully functioning windows and doors, rainproofed, with running water in bathrooms and kitchens and, lastly, a fully operational hot water supply and central heating system. When a hundred men have time on their hands, when all necessary supplies are there for the taking, it's amazing how much can be accomplished in a short time. The results were most satisfying – and the Americans became envious of *our* superior facilities.

Weather-wise our move from Pomig. to Alghero was not "out of the frying pan into the fire" – more "out of one bog into an even thicker bog"! It rained for almost the whole month of December and the dirt runway became a mudbath, flying being impossible most of the time. Hence the temporary relief from the "war effort" allowing the man-hours to effect renovation of our quarters. Yet on one day early on the weather cleared locally just enough to allow A Flight to mount an operation to the Po Valley; there the weather was still too bad to allow of any successful attacks but gave one major victory to the enemy – our CO. Wing Commander Burton-Giles failed to return from Milan. This was a severe shock to squadron morale and made one wonder – could taking advantage of a short weather-break at base be justified at such a cost, unbalanced as it was by any success on our side? And how sad that he who made that decision was the one who failed to return – such is the dilemma facing all commanders in an operational theatre of war. Now "Sticky" Murphy assumes command of the Squadron and is replaced as B Flight Commander by Alec Lawson.

Though the island of Sardinia is mainly mountainous, with one peak rising to about 6000 feet, the coastal plains are very fertile and the many farms, even at that time, were producing adequate quantities of food, more than enough for the sparse population. Thus the orders from "on high" that we were not to "trade" with the locals made little sense – NAAFI food supplies consisted almost entirely of war-reserve cans of barely edible stodge called "M & V" (meat and veg.), bully beef and hard peas, occasionally tinned fish and hardtack (probably all been in store since 1918!), whilst fresh bread, meat, vegetables and fruit were entirely lacking, and yet we were supplied with enough tobacco, cigarettes, sweets and chocolate to satisfy ten times our number.

Another supply problem was the lack of decent "booze".

Official rations from NAAFI were one bottle of beer per person per *week*, spirits were occasionally allocated at one bottle "now and again" *per squadron*! Just try to keep 16 aeroplanes operational on those rations!

The solution to these problems was obvious – all children dote on sweets, women on chocolates and men on cigarettes and tobacco and the Sardinian population were no exception. Above all, the cigarettes were the main attraction, much more so than money, even though they were "Vs" (V may have stood for Victory but in the case of those wartime fags it could only have meant "Vile"); such was the shortage of tobacco on the Island that a carton of cigarettes was a bag of gold.

The Allied military presence was small, consisting only of the two flying bases – Cagliary in the south of the Island and Alghero in the north – occupied by three USAF and two RAF squadrons. No Allied army of occupation could be spared from the main assault forces then in Italy and so, despite the existence of a substantial part of the remaining Italian Army on the Island, the "powers that be" had presumably decided that they offered no threat following the Italian capitulation. Some of us were rather less than sure and for some weeks carried side-arms at all times.

Our barracks are at Fertilia, just across the bay from the town of Alghero, the sea lapping at the foot of the rocks barely 50 metres from the front door. Four of us now share a large room – Alec Lawson (B Flight commander), Pat Rapson (B Flight pilot and the "mastermind" behind our new plumbing and heating systems), the Baron and myself. Someone has to run the Mess so we four form the Mess Committee: nominally Alec is Messing Member (food) with Pat as his assistant, Baron is Bar Member (booze) with me as his assistant. But, whereas in UK officers filling these positions simply "administer", ordering being merely a matter of phoning the NAAFI or local suppliers to ensure delivery, we had to "find" and then "obtain" – which we did as a team.

We needed first to find an adequate supply source for fresh vegetables and fruit – several villagers on the edge of the town soon got to know of our "wealth" and were keen to barter eggs, fruit, veg. and eventually even chickens, in simple exchange.

By Christmas we had built a bar in the Mess, so we needed stock. This we solved by a visit to Sasseri, capital of the northern area. There bartenders were at first loth to deal, taking the view that, though Italy may have surrendered, we were still the enemy. It was then made plain to them that we came willing to buy for cash or barter for cigarettes OR, if they still wished to regard us as the enemy, then we were quite prepared to act as the "occupying power". Heaven knows how we were expecting to enforce this bravado, there being a substantial part of the Italian Army still armed on the Island yet not one soldier of an occupying Allied Army. Whether it was the fact that we all wore side-arms or that we maintained an outwardly pleasant manner we'll never know; suffice it to say that they found the immediate availability of large quantities of cigarettes (not interested in money!) more beneficial than the retention of their stocks of wine, vermouth, marsala and the like. Several such visits to Sassari soon resulted in adequate bar stocks in Fertilia!

During those early weeks we were almost continually grounded by the bad weather and a mud-packed runway and, whilst groundcrews had their work cut out to keep our Mosquitos serviceable in horrid conditions, aircrew soon became bored with the inactivity, constantly seeking new interests to pass the time. Keeping up-to-date with the war situation was hardly an arduous activity and aside from the regular morning and evening briefings there was little to occupy itching fingers once the refurbishment of our living quarters was finished.

The most sought after change from a dreary routine was the occasional trip to Sassari – a privilege and a delightful day out, regardless of the weather. Our transport on these escapades varied somewhat: favourite was Sticky's jeep or the flight 15 cwt. van, but an acceptable alternative was a squadron 3-tonner (you can pile in far more bods but in zero comfort), and on one memorable (perhaps for some I should say forgettable – but no names, no packdrill!) occasion with the Yanks in one of their many 5-tonners.

The mountain roads cross-country passed over steep hills, through narrow gorges, many hairpin bends, 500 feet drops to one unprotected side, demanding the constant attention of experienced and *sober* drivers. Suffice it to say that, though we often didn't deserve a clean sheet, none of these journeys were a cause of an increase in the squadron "chop-rate". But on one occasion crew stupidity was almost our undoing: returning after dark, Baron at the wheel asked for a cigarette – ready lit, of course. Fortunately his howl of agony as I thoughtlessly passed it wrong-end-first resulted only in him dropping the cigarette, not the wheel! His near-apoplectic response was not recorded.

Other non-operational activities indulged by most included cards – daily and nightly schools of bridge and poker were always in session – fishing, "shopping", rugby football (or an apology there for – no pitch, no rules!) and often, following a few evening drinks, the "egg-sesh". Fresh eggs were available by the hundred and several rooms boasted an electric or paraffin heater and a frying pan: a couple of dozen eggs made a super omelette divisible by four and acted as suitable blotting paper. Fortunately our M.O. had adequate supplies of senna and the like!

Now fishing – in Sardinia second only to farming as a food supply – but I don't think the professionals approved of our methods. An Alghero village local was always keen to hire us his dinghy but the fish, both in river and off the coast, were most unco-operative, turning up their noses at hook and line. We tried shooting, with .38 and .303, but somehow the water seemed to prevent the bullets reaching the fish. But then – Eureka! It is quite surprising what even a small explosive charge will bring to the surface. Thereafter, the daily diet was sometimes enhanced by a few fresh herring or their kin.

One great source of joy at this time was a small puppy; he arrived in the arms of a local youngster being toted "for sale". Within 10 seconds we had established a mutual bond (myself and the dog, not the urchin) and with the asking price only 20 cigarettes he was mine. I did not know the breed, if indeed he was anything but mongrel, but he was labrador-like, full of fun and frolic and soon became the Fertilia pet and the Squadron mascot. We built him a kennel (you can't keep a dog in a room you share with three others) and he remained totally at home during our time there, surprisingly never once showing a tendency to wander. I am not happy to record that I named him "Flak" – with hindsight how corny can you get!

With Christmas now approaching, the "Mess Committee" turned thoughts and plans to provisioning for the occasion and organising suitable functions. At this point, perhaps it is worth recording that our Committee was unusual in that, whilst on a traditional RAF station the three Messes – Officers', NCOs' and Airmen's – are managed and provisioned independently, in our case our Committee assisted in the provisioning of all three. Perhaps one should also say that the fairly obvious reason for this was that we four could readily acquire the necessary transport for the type of "shopping" expeditions necessary to obtain decent rations – and if there were to be any comebacks we were more able to "carry the can".

Food fit for a Christmas dinner was the first and foremost consideration – no way could one celebrate such an occasion on tins of "M & V". Turkeys there were none, but other fowl? Certainly, said our local contacts – a couple of dozen chickens, a few ducks and, as always, as many eggs as you wish. *And*, suggested one worthy, would you like a pig? Only one? Well three then. And so members of all three messes feasted on chicken and most excellent pork on Christmas Day and Boxing Day.

As already recorded, the problem of stocking the bar (the amateur "chippies" were well on the way with a superb new construction) had been solved. For once the NAAFI managed to produce some extra beer and spirits but such minor stocks were substantially reinforced with aquavite, vermouth (the staple local drink), marsala and other wines. Vermouth, drunk in half pints, I have never forgotten – and have never touched a drop of it since.

After Christmas our Mess Bar became very popular. First we had a visit from our Air Officer Commanding, Air Vice-Marshal Hugh Pugh Lloyd (affectionately known as "Huff-Puff"), who flew up from Malta in his Beaufighter to inspect the Squadron and see at first hand these renowned domestic facilities – seems the word had got around and, though there was some trepidation concerning the possibility of authority exceeded and rules broken, we need not have worried. The Old Man was highly chuffed with his visit, proclaimed 23 Squadron the "cream" of his command (what a flanneler!) and climaxed his day by a night in our bar – and what a night. Least said, soonest mended!

Then came the New Year's Eve party, to which we sent open invitation to the USAF squadrons. We thought they might send just a couple of representatives but were amazed and delighted to receive the Brigadier General commanding the Wing, both Squadron Commanders and some 40 officers – it seems they left only a skeleton section on standby – and those few were *not* volunteers. All were much impressed with the facilities and the refreshments but, by the end of the evening, highly critical of our near lethal games typified by "High Cockalorum" – the quickest and simplest way to break an arm or a leg known to man. The evening became the talk of the station for long thereafter.

Flying/Operational Matters

One flying incident which occurred just before the year's end is worth mention. The Baron and I were airborne on NFT (night flying test) prior to possible night operations; such a routine flight rarely lasted more than 10–15 minutes, requiring only tests of the aircraft performance and equipment to ensure reliability for ops. Navigation was not required, all tests being carried out in the vicinity of base, so all I had with me was a local map. How unfortunate then to have an urgent call from Air Traffic Control "American Marauder down in sea position 42N 6E – proceed and search for survivors". The position was some 250 miles north west of base and what follows is one of the biggest "lineshoots" you will hear from any navigator:

> "Gave rough course to steer. No pencil, fountain pen in pocket out of ink. Corrected course to steer by assessment of drift from windlanes observation. Estimated groundspeed and gave ETA. Commenced air plot by transposing ditched position to centre of map. On ETA started square search – height 200 feet, ground speed 4 miles per minute, estimated surface visibility for crew dinghy one mile – therefore first leg 30 seconds into wind, then 30 seconds right cross-wind, 1 minute right downwind, 1 minute right again cross-wind, et seq. for two hours. Regret no sighting. Fuel only enough for return to base with 30 minutes reserve. All turning points charted by using pen as pin. Estimated course to base by DR (dead reckoning), calculated ETA, grinned at Baron and offered silent prayer. Arrived over Alghero in sight of base 2 minutes after ETA!"

It was several years after the war ended before I learned the art (science?) of manning planning but one would have thought that there could be few more vital elements to the successful prosecution of a war. Yet now, out of the blue (so to speak!), eight new aircrews, with aeroplanes, arrived unannounced and unrequested as reinforcements for the squadron – and with the news that six more would soon be on their way and more after that in the training pipeline. No more groundcrew were forthcoming, even though we currently had too few of the essential tradesmen to keep our present 16 aeroplanes operational. So these new crews were promptly sent back to Blida, Algiers, whence they came – we were never told where they eventually ended up.

In one of the many wartime films about the RAF – Angels One Five – "Septic" left his R/T on transmit throughout his first operational engagement, thus screwing up Fighter Control's contact with their other Hurricanes. He wasn't the only one! Two of our new boys were on local flying and were attempting to land at the same time, one on a left-hand circuit, one right-hand. They arrived on the final approach simultaneously, one twenty feet above the other, neither, incredibly, aware of the other's presence. When they were almost at touchdown, with one now just ten feet above t'other, the controller gave up screaming at the R/T and loosed off a red Verey cartridge. It was fortunate that he had delayed – the "underdog" was now on the deck and only the "topdog" opened up to overshoot. What a prang that almost was and what a tragic start to the year it would have made – it was New Year's Day!

Despite our inadequate groundcrew manning levels, our tradesmen were the best. In often appalling weather conditions the task of servicing aeroplanes in the open was always our biggest headache: hangars? not on any airfield in the Med from which I operated. Yet the men regularly achieved a high average serviceability, on many occasions an amazing 100%. Even then, you could never be sure your kite wouldn't play you up in the air: sometimes these technical faults were not serious, merely causing the crew varying degrees of "ring-twitch"; on other occasions there were very serious, occasionally fatal, consequences (shades of Bicester and Blenheims?). Baron and I experienced several incidents in the former category:

A very dark night when both engines developed surging – increasing/decreasing revs, by 20% or more – just as we're over the Appenines with no room to spare; we got back by continuous throttle juggling, off-loading bombs on a railyard, wriggling through coastal ack-ack at 100 feet and wishing there were some nearer alternative to base.

Then the classic case of instant total failure of one engine – just as we were crossing the French coast at Perpignan, broad daylight, at 50 feet, heading for a German airfield, fortunately ample speed at about 270; essential to stay low to avoid the flak – but threading the port wing between the trees in a 180 degrees about turn did my digestion no good at all. Fortunately we were leading a loose four, so colleague Pat Rapson shepherded us back across the Med. (350 miles on one engine with Ju88s in the vicinity was no-one's idea of fun!) leaving the other pair to proceed to target.

There were several others but to record them would be merely repetitive – and already I feel that familiar "sixpence/half-a-crown" twitch as I write. But I must record one much more serious case: good friend "Kimmy" Kimpton was on take-off run and just as he attained flying speed his starboard engine threw out smoke and sparks and one could hear the thudding bangs a mile away. He got to about 200 feet when the port engine started playing up. Watching it from the window of our office it seemed that he was trying to reach the sea where he might have ditched safely, but half a mile short of the shore the aircraft stalled, dropped the starboard wing and went straight in. She burst into flames – crash vehicles and ambulance hadn't a chance. (My intention in writing this book was essentially to record the humorous side but perhaps the reader will understand that there are some serious and tragic events which I cannot pass over – otherwise one might convey a picture of a thoughtless and couldn't-care-less romp through one of our gravest times, without consideration for those who did not survive).

Though trying to avoid too much comment on actual air operations, one night in January 1944 is more than worthy of a paragraph – it was, one might say, a "red letter" day for the squadron. By our move to Sardinia we had opened up access to southern France and, as the Toulouse area contained a substantial element of the Luftwaffe in several roles, it was a splendid choice for our first visit. Sticky was first on the scene, found the airfield well lit, with a Dornier 217 on circuit presenting a tempting target; it soaked up a great deal of punishment but eventually blew up in his face! Next on target was Alec Lawson. The Do217 was still burning but all airfield lights were out. Alec cruised around, managing to avoid the probing searchlights; then the German ground defence helped him out – a searchlight cone lit up one of their own and the ack ack promptly blew it out of the sky. Thinking that they had destroyed the intruder, all the lights came on with several aircraft on circuit in clear view. Alec had a ball! He shot down three Ju88s before the enemy knew what was happening. A German cock-up for a change – well worth recording.

Sometimes even an operational sortie can contain a surprising mix of coincidence, incompetence, misery, hilarity and success. One such was one of our frequent "Bomb Villafranca" episodes. In poor weather conditions, especially unpleasant when operating near the foothills of the Alps, we patrolled what we hoped was the target area for half an hour, with only occasional glimpses of the ground through cloud, when a sudden break revealed the airfield barely a couple of miles away. A quick dirty dart, switches on, bombs released – and nothing! Did they go? Have we got a hang-up? No, they've gone alright, so why no flashes? Hit or miss? No idea – so, somewhat disconsolately, head for home. Oh dear, now I see it, my incompetence, omitted to fuse the bombs! I can't repeat what Baron said to me (many times) as we scraped our way through the murk back to base.

At debriefing much mirth and chiding from the gang as that navigator, tail between legs, retired hurt. But no-one could have foreseen the consequences: two days later, a message from Command ops/intell. – "Whose great idea was it to drop 'dummy' bombs on Villafranca? Great result – all flying there has been suspended for the past 48 hours – squads are searching for unexploded bombs. Do it again!"

Another incident with all the ingredients of drama and farce was our first attempt at "Operation Dolphin". Ju188s from Toulouse were operating down to the Straits of Gibraltar, attacking Allied convoys heading for Italy with vital supplies of men and materials. 23 Squadron to operate daily patrols down the east coast of Spain to attack and destroy. Briefing instructions: head for Cape Cruz and cruz (sorry, cruise) southward; no Allied aircraft will be in the vicinity. Baron and I form a pair with flight commander Phil Russell and Bill Gregory. Immediately on arrival at Cape Cruz, Phil spots a kite right down at sea level heading due south – "thar she blows" – we turn to give chase. Only the rear silhouette visible, very wide wings, high tailplane, he's weaving so he's spotted us, showing smoke so he's piling on the power, that's a 188 for sure – and is he fast! Phil's aeroplane has only Merlin 23s with +12 boost and he's falling behind; we've got Merlin 25s and are through the gate at +18, speed 330, yet only slowly catching up. Range now about 2 miles – watch it, tracer, he's shooting – streams of red balls pass harmlessly by. Maximum time on maximum boost is 5 minutes, we've already had her flat out for 8 minutes, temperatures are at danger and there are ominous rumblings from the port engine. Damn it, we're still 1000 yards behind and not going to catch him. Baron lifts the nose and gives him a quick burst, there's a flash on his starboard wing but it doesn't slow him. Give it up or we'll lose that port engine – no chance now – never realised the 188 was that fast. Set off for home nursing the protesting engine for our ground crew's sake. Back at base reported one frightened, possibly damaged, no other sightings. Phil had stayed around for a while hoping that Jerry might turn back, but no joy.

The following day we're called to the Ops. Room and asked "was it a 188?" Must have been, right silhouette, but right down on the deck, astern view only so from long range couldn't make positive identification. But anyway, no allied aircraft in the area (remember?), also he fired tracer at us. Must have been Jerry. Well OK, says Terry, our I.O., maybe, but it so happens that an American Marauder claims he was chased and fired on by a Ju88 at the same time and place. Tracer? He was firing off "colours of the day" cartridges as fast as he could load the Verey pistol – 3 reds! A week later we met the Marauder crew, enjoyed many a boozy laugh over the incident and left the best of pals.

Back to the Non-Operational

My diary reminds me of many more of the "ring-twitch" events which were crucial to our daily (and nightly) lives during that period but my stated intention has been all along to convey the "fun life" of the times, rather than the serious stuff. So back to the domestic, the amusing, and sometimes, the farcical.

We were by now getting rather fed up with our bar stocks of marsala and vermouth and were increasingly anxious to find a source of more popular supplies. The opportunity arose when our Army Liaison Officer was called to a Corps intelligence meeting – in Bari, on Italy's east coast. Surface travel for such a trip was out of the question so, with the Boss's approval, Baron promptly offered to fly him over. And what would Baron be doing while "Heff" was tied up at the conference? In a town full of shops and with a main NAAFI supply centre nearby, why, shopping – what else? They arrived back a couple of days later, I met them with a wagon at dispersal, and the sight of the baggage in that confined cockpit was reminiscent of our first arrival from Gib. Whisky and gin by the crate, *Players* cigarettes by the thousand, meat joints of this and that, cheeses – it was the Mess Committee at its best! I can't remember whether we ever bothered to find out what the ALO had to report – but I'm sure it came out at some of our operational briefings later. (Now we have Players for smoking and "Vs" for barter).

Looking back on those days from one's subsequent experiences of the Service in peacetime, I am reminded of the surprising degree of informality that was possible in moving about the theatre. The Royal Navy had established a leave centre/rest camp near Sassari and when visiting the town one day we met some of their officers in a bar. One said how much he would like to visit a Mosquito squadron – "Great – we'll take you back with us for a couple of days if you wish". Two days later, I ran him back to Sassari and brought another visitor back with me. It seemed so natural at the time and no-one minded a scrap. When I think of all the signals and approvals which would have been necessary in peacetime!

Yet, if visits to our Squadron were informal, far more notable were some of the visits we were able to make elsewhere in the theatre. Most remarkable was an occasion when two new Mosquitos arrived for us as replacements (without crews) – they are ready for you at Blida we are told. Well, from Alghero that was only about 500 miles away, wasn't it? Actually only 300 in a straight line – but we would be compelled to follow certain designated routes for identification – wouldn't want outsiders to think we were the enemy, would we? Method? Easy – two Mosquitos each carrying an extra pilot (three men in a Mosquito Mark VI was a bit uncomfortable but frequently resorted to for a swan such as this); this allowed for return in two pairs, each pair having a navigator in the lead aircraft. On arrival at Blida the first person we see is Sticky, our CO, there for an operations conference with our masters. "Do you want to go back today?" asks the Station Commander. "Er – well – er, if the aircraft are ready Sir . . ."

"I asked do you *want* to go back today." "Preferably not Sir, if we could visit Algiers?" "Right, consider it fixed". The new aircraft were suddenly found to have developed some minor faults which would take a couple of days to put right. So we shot off from Blida to Maison Blanche for a night on the town in Algiers, returning to Blida for another couple of pleasant evenings, then returning via El Aouina, where u/s electrics and poor weather necessitated a night in nearby Tunis, finally returning to Base with four fully operational aeroplanes and six fairly bushed, but very satisfied, aircrew.

The accommodation available on such jollies varied from the slum category to the luxurious, from a converted railway carriage outside Algiers to a single room with super-bed and en suite facilities in a Tunis hotel. But that was a minor consideration – the release of tension, the letting down of the hair as it were, was a very welcome perk much appreciated by all taking part, and undoubtedly good for morale and therefore for the prosecution of the war. Only in retrospect now does such freedom of action with our "personal aeroplanes", with full lawful authority let me add, strike me as extraordinary.

As a "thank you" for their great evening at the opening of our new mess, the Americans invited "The CO and Officers of 23 Squadron to a Dance in the Officers Club". A *Dance?* Now that was interesting! Women in Armies and Air Forces of today are an accepted fact – but in 1944, in wartime, in Sardinia? So we wondered, with whom shall we dance – each other? That may have suited a tiny minority of those present, but hardly likely to form the basis of an organised *dance*, what? Naturally we accepted the invitation, as much out of curiosity as expectation, but we reckoned without the ingenuity of the Yanks. We four members of our Mess Committee, the Messing and Bar officers, were asked to assist with the preparations of the food and drink: for the first time we saw some of the amazing foods provided by their support organisation (couldn't fail to make comparison with the M & V and biscuits supplied by our NAAFI), augmented of course by locally obtained meats and salads. But the eye-opener was the bar: dozens of bottles of just about every type of booze imaginable and then the centrepiece – a huge bowl of "punch". I watched as their man in charge emptied in several cans of fruit juices as a base, then added vodka, gin, brandy, whisky – several bottles of each – finally topping up with a small bottle of medicinal alcohol. Fortunately, I had time to get the message back to our chaps – whatever you do, steer clear of the punch!

So now we're ready – bring on the dancing girls – and they did! Two coaches arrived at the door on time, full of girls – all recruited from the streets of Sassari! The livening up process began immediately and most of the girls made a dash for the punch. I shall never forget one quite stunning blonde (unusual in Italy) who, after two glasses of punch, broke away from her partner and staged a solo in the middle of the floor, ending up naked and flat out. Fortunately, there was a doctor on hand to treat her in the time-honoured fashion. The function gradually disintegrated as more and more fell by the wayside and most of the guests became hors de combat. In the final stages, some amusement arose from a duo of American officers touring the bedrooms, one with a camera, one with a candle and torch. Many photographs were on show at breakfast the following morning and I am told that quite a lot of money changed hands in the purchase of the negatives.

In these early months of '44, during our constant recce of the countryside for more supplements to our food supplies, we came across the tiny village of Ittiri in the mountains 30 miles or so to the east of base. We four, the Baron, Alec, Pat and I, were driving a 30 cwt. truck, with ample supplies of cigarettes, sweets and chocolate, hoping for meat supplies – pork, lamb, chickens, whatever. When we arrived in Ittiri all was quiet as the grave; one lone hound, howling at our intrusion, but not a soul in sight. We parked in the centre, opened the tailgate and started munching a Mars bar. Within seconds the main street was full of jumping, laughing, eager children, quickly supplemented by several mothers and aunts, and our stock of sweets and cigarettes was rapidly depleted.

Then the men began to appear and finally we were very formally presented to the *Padrone,* Leonardo. He invited us to take coffee in his "humble" home: a drab looking plain adobe building in the main street – that is until one entered through the main door. Then what delight! A magnificent, almost palatial, house, beautifully decorated and furnished – an absolute goldmine in any country. Leonardo, it transpired, owned the village in toto and several miles of countryside all around. All the other residents worked his farms which were amply stocked with all the usual animals and birds.

To our total surprise, it was quickly made plain that here we were among friends, not enemies. Though politics and the war were never mentioned, either by us or by them, it became clear that they were delighted by our visit, wished it be known that they would value our friendship and would be pleased to see us often. Coffee was served by two young ladies in national costume, with great formality and much bowing and shaking of hands. On this first visit we stayed for only a conventional hour and, on departing, were presented with gifts of two pigs and two lambs, with the request that we return soon. That was the start of our most pleasant relationship with the *real* occupants of this beautiful but wild island.

Our visits to Ittiri became fairly frequent, particularly as Leonardo made it plain that he would welcome our regular business in the purchase of his animals and birds; and so pork, lamb, chicken and duck were often to be found on our squadron dinner tables. The highlight in our calendar of those days was undoubtedly at Easter, at which time we were invited to a barbecue and dinner. I call it a barbecue – really it was a fiesta! We foregathered at the house on the Easter Monday morning for an aperitif and then, some (including yours truly) on horseback, some on mules, the majority on shanks's pony, we set off up into the hills above the village. There the shepherds were already preparing the feast: an enormous bonfire had been lit, kids, lambs and piglets had been butchered and were roasting on spits, and large flat breadcakes had been baked. Dozens of casks of local wine stimulated the festivities. No formalities here – seated cross-legged on the ground, a leg of lamb torn from the roasting carcase in one hand, a flagon of wine in the other – who needs knives, forks, plates and tablecloths? What a session that was!

Dinner? Yes, well, the fiesta went on until around 5 p.m., we all trailed back to the village with much hilarity, Leonardo and his men joining in with our bawdy songs, to coffee in the main house. Then at 9 o'clock those same maidens in national dress entered the lounge to announce that "dinner is served"! We had been eating and drinking for some four hours that afternoon, yet here we were, faced with a six-course meal! I can hardly believe it now – I struggled my way through in honour of our host but the Baron (a big man, I may say) kept pace one-for-one with Leonardo, taking seconds with every course, accompanied by much burping and back-slapping – Leonardo and Baron were clearly meant to be brothers. Wouldn't it have been marvellous if Mussolini could have seen us all then!

CHAPTER TEN

Return From the Med.

Now it is early May and big news! The Squadron is needed back in UK to operate over Germany in support of the second front, due to be launched soon. Big planning session with the Boss, the flight commanders, crews and senior groundcrew NCOs; ground staff would have to return by boat, after max. effort to get all aircraft serviceable for the flight home. Navigators discussed best routes – preferably direct across France, nought feet all the way, in loose formation, max. cruising speed 260/270, following wind most of the way, time less than four hours, no more than a normal operational sortie (plus plenty of juicy targets en route!).

Initial approval given by Command HQ; but later that day – "Hold everything". The Planners at Air Ministry have decided that they want our aeroplanes to go to the Far East to enhance the progress of the war in that theatre. So, we are instructed to fly to Blida, leave our aeroplanes there, and return to UK by boat. All groundcrew are to be transported to Bari on the east coast of Italy to join a convoy there. The Boss went purple with rage and nearly blew a gasket. But the "powers-that-be" would not budge – that's it, do as you're told!

A few days to pack up, groundcrew conveyed to Bari, and we fly off to Blida to deliver and say goodbye to some great kites, await ship for home – not exactly how we foresaw the end of our Mediterranean tour.

"To Algiers to await ship" – now there's a phrase to conjure with. If we leave our aeroplanes at Blida then we have to find some means of getting ourselves and all our kit to Algiers – or to some accommodation at or near Algiers – after all, that is where the boat will go from, isn't it? And "kit" is a nice simple word which can hardly convey the impedimenta attaching to all of us after a year in and around the Med: personal clothing, flying clothing, service equipment (my navigation bag alone was an extra 20 lbs. of baggage), souvenirs (least said, soonest mended!) which none was prepared to abandon. Thank goodness that all the squadron records and other vital equipment had gone with our engineer officer and groundcrews to their boat at Bari; even so, thirty plus aircrew with that lot represented a fair sized load for the fifty or so miles to the coast – and in 3-tonners that wasn't funny!

Several hours later, arrived at the "Movements Office" in Algiers, we are not particularly chuffed to hear from the junior officer in charge "Where in hell have you lot come from?" The reader may recall that Sticky was not too happy in the first place to hear that we were to dump our aircraft at Blida but his reaction to that reception in Algiers really is unprintable – I almost felt sorry for the guy. But worse was to come: "We're not expecting a boat for about 10 days. We've only got hotel accommodation for three available – the rest of you will have to go into our reserve accommodation on the edge of the town". You'll love the next bit: that accommodation was in railway carriages on sidings outside the city's main railway station!

The waiting days passed slowly, eating and drinking in various restaurants in Algiers, but I have just one vivid memory of a day which stands out from dreary waiting times. That day was the Algiers Race Meeting: six races, alternately three flat and three trotting. Some twenty of us went along to enjoy the fun of the fair and were surprised to see that there were very few allied troops present – but the track was packed to capacity by the locals. To make it interesting we pooled our money, made six selections and put the lot on a "snowball'. The degree of excitement rose steadily as the meeting progressed: we had the winner of the first flat (three circuits), then the winner of the first trotting (two circuits); North Africa is damned hot in May I can tell you but the temperature soared steadily as our next two winners came up. When our fifth winner came up the excitement was intense – everything rested on the final trotting race. By the end of the first circuit, our man was two lengths ahead and it began to look as though we were going to pull it off; I can't remember the precise odds but I reckoned we were in line for something over £8000.

Then the whole atmosphere of euphoria evaporated in an instant: halfway round the second circuit the horse broke from trot into gallop and was automatically disqualified. The driver on the cart raved at the horse and lashed with his whip but I guess it was all for show – he'd been bribed to throw it, for sure. Immediately all the black looks we had been getting from the surrounding crowd, who obviously knew the score, changed to grins and much shouting of profanities (probably – none of us spoke Arabic!). Just as we were leaving we were approached by one of the race officials who, in fluent English, informed us that it was just as well we didn't win – he hinted that we would probably not have got far with the winnings!

In the event, the convoy arrived twelve days later, not ten. It was the same convoy our ground officers and airmen had joined at Bari – they were in HMT Strathnaver, we were to board the old P. & O. boat HMT Mooltan. After languishing in idleness (more or less) for two weeks, and so anxious to get home, the sight of these ships did not exactly excite us. And once aboard, the crush of hundreds of officers and men crammed into a modest 15,000 tonner – officers four or six to a cabin, NCOs, soldiers and airmen packed into every available corner, some had bunks but many slept out on deck – this was not exactly a morale booster! And to think, here we were, squadron separated into two ships, aeroplanes left behind, effectively barred from the operation of the war for at least a month (it totted up to two months in the end), and for what? Ostensibly so that our aircraft could be taken by others to join the "other war" in the Far East. Only much later were we to learn that those aircraft never did get to that other war – they rotted at Blida!

With the convoy limited to the speed of the slowest ship, the journey home took a tiresome 12 days. One felt almost sorry for the two destroyer crews who raced round the perimeter at their 25 knots or more whilst we all plugged steadily on at about 6 knots. Of course, this was wartime, and these were "dry" ships, weren't they? Well that was the theory – but none will be surprised to know that bottles of booze oozed out from all sorts of hiding places. You didn't think all those "souvenirs" I mentioned were just for the mantlepiece, did you? But, for us, the trip was memorable for just two things – bridge (the card game, not the eyes of the ship) and the nightmare in "U-boat Alley".

With the threat of a boring fortnight on the "slow boat to Scotland" (our destination was Gourock), the six of us in our cabin spent the entire voyage playing bridge. We took meal breaks in turn, keeping the four going, two pairs on one pair off, all the daytime hours. We played for "daredevil" stakes – penny a hundred – and after 12 days I had won by the respectable total of 1500 points for the prize of one shilling and threepence! No-one had won/lost more than half a crown.

But the excitement came about halfway home – bang in the middle of the Bay of Biscay – U-boat Alley. Our ship suffered a broken rudder shaft, we hove to, and were stationary for repairs – for 24 hours. As was standard practice, the safety of the convoy as a whole being paramount, we were left solo; one destroyer circled us for an hour then, sounding off, she dashed after the convoy. My, it was quiet! The only sound was from many suffering the proverbial "ring-twitch". I'd prefer to take my chances in the air any time! Hundreds of us lined the rails on U-boat watch; false alarms were frequent yet, would you believe it, we got away with it. The rudder gear was fixed, huge cheers for the engineers, and then we were off at a rare old lick – 25+ knots – and we caught up with the convoy abreast the Brest peninsular.

We finally docked at Gourock on 2nd June and (after kicking our heels there for 3 days – we never found out why) then endured a wearisome train journey to our new base at Little Snoring (yes, honestly) in Norfolk. Now, all we had to do was to collect some new aeroplanes and get on with the job. I'm kidding, of course. "Your new Mossies won't be available just yet – grab a few days leave while you can" – so who's objecting to that! Meanwhile, D-Day has happened and we are cooling our heels wondering whether we are grounded for good when suddenly we're given the "go, go, go" – over to Filton to collect the new kites. It then took a couple of weeks to "work up", absorb the necessary intelligence for operating over a very different territory, then finally beginning operations again early in July. So much for the planners' edict that we were wanted in time to operate from the launch of the Second Front!

CHAPTER ELEVEN

Little Snoring – June–September, 1944

Little Snoring had been aptly named – quiet, "nothing ever happens in this neck of the woods", converted farmland. And then 23 Squadron arrived to join the recently established 515 Squadron, both armed with a dozen or more new Mosquitos; the peaceful countryside was peaceful no more. The war was now at its height, with the armies struggling to secure and advance their foothold on the Continent; the "locals" very soon got used to us and the associated racket, and were supportive both visually and vocally. One such supporter, Tommy Cushing, then aged 12, son of a local farmer, spent many hours (we learned much later) sitting in his field just off the end of the main runway, enthralled by the constant activity, day and night. (Shades of my own youth – many hours with members of our "aeroplane club" sitting just inside the perimeter fence of Hornchurch aerodrome watching the Bulldogs and the Hinds). Several years after the war, when the RAF had abandoned Little Snoring airfield, Tommy *bought* it and built a beautiful house there as his new farmhouse.

One of the "greats" of the Mosquito world soon arrived to take command of Little Snoring. He was Sammy Hoare, a fighter ace who had an even more impressive moustache than our Squadron CO, Sticky Murphy. Both sporting DSOs and DFCs earned from their extensive operational experience, they represented the finest example we could have wished for – great leaders, both of them. As previously mentioned, Sammy had been the Wing Commander Flying at High Ercall when we went through the Mosquito OTU course the previous year. My own stay at L.S.

was to be limited to only three months, but this short period was not without some memorable experiences, both serious and light-hearted. First then, operational matters.

My main memory of that period was of the weeks of unbelievably bad weather. My logbook records frequent cases of 10/10ths cloud over most of northern France and Germany, fog, storms, you name it, resulting in little enemy nightfighter activity and thus few sightings and "kills" on those sorties. Or dare I say that it could have been our constant patrols on their airfields, regardless of the weather, which made sure that they stayed down!

Then there was that night of 31st August/1st September: brilliant moonlight, totally clear skies over the whole of northern Europe, as bright as day. Bomber Command stood down in anticipation of possible massive losses to enemy nightfighters and gave the Mosquito squadrons carte blanche to create mayhem. The word was "patrol such-and-such group of airfields for your one hour, then the roads and railways on the way back are all yours"! The result was a massive "cull" of German road convoys and goods trains; one of ours must have been an ammunition train – never seen a series of explosions like it. Our reward was the biggest scare of the day: although almost at ground level, taps fully open, we were "bounced" repeatedly by a twin-engined job, immeasurably faster than our 320 mph, yet he didn't open fire. "What the hell was that?" we both yelled in unison. Back at the Ops. room on debriefing we're told that must have been the Jerry's new Me262, the first known jet fighter, clearly on trial and as yet unarmed. It's not only cats that have nine lives!

So much for the operational – I prefer to recall the more amusing aspects of those L.S. days. The reader will remember that beautiful Wolsley Hornet tourer I acquired from my girl friend's father a couple of years back, open four-seater in British racing green. Upon our return from the Med. I spent most of my leave getting that car into shape. Now I didn't actually have any enemies on the Squadron but you'd be amazed at just how popular I then became! Have you ever seen a Wolsley Hornet carrying 14 jovial bods on a night out? How the springs on that car survived the following three months I shall never know. (The end came suddenly when Dave Atherton and I were driving home on leave that September in heavy rain – the canvas hood split right down the middle from windscreen to boot. We were soaked and so was the upholstery – and in view of the excessive wear and tear (literally) from the numerous maxi-passenger journeys it had suffered as the "Squadron hack", I sold it at the then very impressive figure of £110! Its replacement? A sedate Morris 8 saloon).

In the early stages at L.S. our nights out were spent at our then favourite pub "The Feathers" at Holt – until that night of the "big black" in July. Following a small birthday celebration in the Mess bar, two carloads, the CO's wagon and the Conquer hack, trouped out to The Feathers in high glee. We were surprised to find the pub not yet open – we were perhaps five minutes early – but the top half of one of the ground floor windows was open. "What are we waiting for?" cries Sticky and heads for the open window; half way in he's stuck, struggles to squeeze through and – *crash* – foot through the window. "You're barred!" snarls madame, as if she were the proprietor of the Rovers Return in Coronation Street. Not to worry, let's try "The Star" just down the street. And that, Duke, is how we came to regard your pub as our very favourite local!

'Duke" Buck was the great-hearted licensee of The Star and we became good friends. Our visits to his pub became virtually routine every night we were not on the flying programme. I never had less than six in the car and frequently a dozen or more, and Duke and his wife Rosie treated us as family. If we arrived a bit before opening time he opened up immediately. Unlike some pubs in those days, he rarely ran dry of anything – on the rare occasion when the brewers were unable to resupply immediately he would borrow from another pub in Fakenham. And when closing time was nigh, it was "psst. no need to rush chaps", door locked, "carry on, Rosie's just making us some bacon and eggs". One evening, five minutes after locking up, there's a rap at the door – the local bobby; oh dear, we thought, now Duke'll catch it. "Come in George" says Duke, introduces us all to his friend and a great supper party was enjoyed by all!

One night as we were leaving, I told Duke we would be unable to come again for a couple of weeks because my petrol ration was exhausted – the Hornet did only about 20 to the gallon so the ration of 5 gallons a month was a severe limitation. "Have you got enough to get you here tomorrow?" asks Duke. Well a nod's as good as a wink, so we returned next evening. By the end of the evening I was getting fidgety and told Duke I might have to leave the car there and call for taxis for the party as my tank was empty. His reply – "it isn't now!"

Station life at L.S. was pretty basic; most buildings were Nissan huts, including the messes and quarters, but facilities were adequate for a wartime station. At Luqa, Pomigliano and Alghero I cannot remember any serious breaches of discipline and certainly no call for harsh counter-measures – occasional charges for minor offences were easily handled by flight commanders. Back in UK however, more serious crimes began to appear for which sterner control became necessary. One such case resulted in a District Court Martial: one lunchtime, in the Mess bar, Sticky called me over to say "The Boss has got a job for you Norman – hope you're all britched up on Courts Martial". "Never attended one in my life", says I. "Then you'd better get the books out PDQ".

I reported to the CO that afternoon. "Ah Conquer. We've got an airman who's a bit of a bastard; I've been hoping to catch him out and this time I've got him banged to rights. A Court Martial is convened and I want a "patsy" to defend him – you're it!" "What's he done?" "He came back to camp at 0100 the other night (all airmen were required to be back in camp by 2359 hrs, as I'm sure the reader will remember), woke up the Duty Sergeant and demanded an early call at 0600 hrs. Said sergeant began to tear him off a strip when Smith just thumped him and stalked out. When the sergeant had dressed and gone to Smith's billet he found him fast asleep, drunk, and threw him in the brig. He's charged with drunk and disorderly, late in camp and assaulting a SNCO".

The adjutant then told me that the Prosecuting Officer would be Flight Lieutenant Simpkins of 515 Squadron. I sought him out and discovered that he had no experience of courts martial either, so we both grabbed copies of Air Force Law and started sweating – no rush, we had all of three days before the court would assemble.

At the trial Simpkins presented the facts of the case, with the sergeant as the only witness, and then my interview with Smith went something like this:-

> Were you drunk? – Well, I'd had a few but I wasn't incapable.

What time did you return to camp? – Not sure, probably about midnight.
Why didn't you check in at the guardroom? – Forgot.
Did you thump the Duty Sergeant? – Course not.

There was no entry of his booking either in or out of the guardroom, no-one in his billet could (or would) say at what time he got to bed, no-one witnessed his "interview" with the sergeant. Though convinced he was guilty, I merely suggested to the court that it was one man's word against the other and there was no case to answer. Much to my surprise the case was dismissed.

I cannot repeat what Sammy Hoare said to me at the bar that evening – but he bought me a drink to celebrate what proved to be my first court martial experience of many. This case proved to me one of the main drawbacks of the Courts Martial system (or of our normal civil trial system for that matter): the need for firm prosecution evidence without which the case fails and dismissal means the slate is wiped clean. If only this matter had been dealt with by Squadron or Station Commander, within his normal disciplinary powers, where the word of the SNCO would be accepted in evidence, then even a nominal punishment, such as 14 days c.c. or a reprimand, would have ensured that the case was entered on the airman's service record. This could then be taken into account in dealing with the inevitable future misdemeanours committed by this particularly odious character.

September has dawned and now the end of our operational tour with 23 Squadron is approaching. On the night of 3rd September Baron and I complete our 35th Intruder sortie with a "no activity" report. Would we like to continue for a second tour after a spot of leave? No Sir, I have fulfilled my promise to the Re-selection Board in March last year, completed a tour as a navigator, and now I want that pilot's course if you please. "Absolutely right my boy", says the Boss, "and I will back your request to Group forthwith." He did too – and I was off for the re-attestation board within the week. Passed, fully fit A1G1, and strongly recommended for pilot training; meantime, posted to 51 OTU Cranfield (Mosquito operational training unit) as Chief Navigation Instructor.

Well, I expect you know what's coming. You're right – end of the war in sight, all transfer training for existing aircrew stopped until further notice. And that's not all – after a few months as CNI my old chum Bill Gregory is posted in with acting squadron leader rank to take over as CNI and I become just one of the nav. instructors. But that's how the cookie crumbles and in the service you smile nicely and get on with it.

CHAPTER TWELVE

51 OTU Cranfield, September 1944–May 1945

Cranfield was a peacetime station with a splendid Mess just like Bicester. Furthermore, being a non-operational training station, life was somewhat more relaxed than at Little Snoring and, even though days were far busier than in squadron life, it provided more interest, with administrative secondary duties appearing for the first time (apart from that dreaded court martial). There was still plenty of flying and instructors were clocking up as many hours as accrued on a squadron, sometimes more.

In between courses I was given leave to visit 23 Squadron at Snoring when I wished. Keeping in touch with friends there helped when teaching new crews on the OTU. On one such occasion I was returning to Cranfield from Norfolk and, on my way through Bedford at lunch time, decided to stop at a pub in the High Street for a beer and lunch. Directly outside the pub the road was full of parked cars but the opposite side was clear so I parked there for about an hour. The following day I was off home for a few days leave. On return to Cranfield there was panic – "Where have you been? Half the police force of Bedfordshire has been hunting you." (Had they heard about that bank robbery I wondered, couldn't have done, it only happened yesterday, in any case it was the bank that was robbing me!). It was a summons for an unpaid parking fine – court attendance the very next day. "Did you know you were prohibited from parking on that side of the road on that day?" "No, I saw no sign". "Well your car was parked right alongside a large notice – parking this side on even dates, t'other side on odd dates. You were there on an odd date".

"Sorry Sir, didn't see it. I had been to my Squadron in Norfolk on operations the previous night and I was rushing back to other duties at Cranfield and just needed to stop a moment for refreshment. – and there was nowhere else to park." "Do you mean to say you were flying over Germany that night?" "Yes Sir." "Who decided to bring this case? Case dismissed!"

One day early in January 1945, I'm summoned to the Wing Commander Flying's office. "Got anything on tomorrow, Conquer?" "Only routine lecture programme Sir." "Right, get a stand-in for that – you're navigating me to Acklington (Newcastle), we're going to a late Christmas party." It was appalling weather: 10/10ths cloud up to about 18000 feet all the way, a Mossie bare of nav. aids apart from radio. So, dead reckoning all the way, let down over the sea, turn in at nought feet to find the airfield, split-arsed turn and straight in. Only an intrepid aviator would have stuck with it and Johnny Topham was that sort of ace. The motivation? His girlfriend was a WAAF officer there. I didn't want for female company that night either.

As far as the Service was concerned, there was little but the routine of navigation instruction for the next few months but my personal life took some dramatic turns. My father, still a comparatively young man, died in hospital from his long-term complaint stemming from W.W.I – bronchitis and asthma. On that same leave I met again a young lady whom I had known briefly before the war when she was engaged to the elder brother of a close friend. She had been heard to remark to her then fiance, after one Sunday meeting "I feel sorry for the girl who marries that little upstart!" She was now in the ATS, we meet again at a party in Romford and are married three months later – I expect she has been sorry for herself ever since.

So now the Service presented me with a new problem: where to start married life. Joan got immediate release from the Army and we moved into a local hotel in Bedford for a weekend after our honeymoon (which I had to sell my car to pay for – a Flight Lieutenant's pay at that time was 22/- a day = £400 a year!). Reporting to Cranfield on the Monday morning – "The Adjutant wants to see you". Adj: "You're posted to 54 OTU Charter Hall (Scotland) as CNI forthwith." Joan goes back home to await my call.

54 OTU Charter Hall, June–September 1945

Talk about "back of beyond" – this really is it. My billet is in a seco hut on a dispersed site; so my first move is to draw a bicycle from the stores. My appointment carries no special perks – no Service car, no chance of married quarters (Newly married, no children? Then you've got zero points!). And then the same thing happens as at Cranfield: old mate Pip Orange is posted in a week later with acting rank as CNI and I'm just a nav. instructor again.

"So, Adj., advice please – where can I find accommodation for my wife?" "My dear chap, you'll just have to search around, like almost everyone else." It was to take over two months before I found a "bedsit" – 15 miles away in Kelso. As bedsits go, it wasn't too bad I suppose – one small but pleasant room, limited daily use of kitchen, very limited use of bathroom, but at least it made possible a start to married life.

The Operational Training Squadron (Mosquitos) was commanded by Squadron Leader Jock Brown, who had been "A" flight commander on 23 Squadron the previous year. Naturally we had identical views on the subject of night intruder operations and so were able to co-ordinate closely the pilot and navigator crew operating procedures. Of course, we had just seen the end of the war in Europe but it seemed more than likely then that the Far East war would take some time to "wrap up" and more Mosquito crews would be required to that end. However, after six years of urgency in turning out trained crews, there was a noticeable relaxation of pressure, with more time for sport and "free days".

My main interests then were tennis and cricket. Turning out for the station cricket team on one occasion, we didn't draw stumps until 2015 hrs. and so, with about a mile to cycle to the Mess, I knew I'd have no time to go to my billet and change before dinner, which would be "off" at 2030. So I took a chance and went to dinner in cricket flannels and blazer (open-necked shirt!). Unfortunately, who should be one of the last diners present but the Station Commander, Group Captain Bobby Burns. The ticking off was delivered the following morning when I was summoned to his office – my "excuse" was deemed to be pathetic and certainly no occasion to buck the Mess Rules! This incident had some amusing repercussions some 13 years and nine postings later when I was appointed President of the Mess Committee by that same officer, once again my CO (and a personal friend).

Charter Hall time was short and sweet: I arrived there at the end of June 1945, moved Joan into the Kelso bedsit at the beginning of September and, arriving for duty on the Monday morning following just our second weekend there, again received the now dreaded call to the Adjutant – you're posted! Put Joan on the train back to London and her home and I'm off three days later to join the specialist navigation course at the Empire Air Navigation School, Shawbury, Shropshire.

HALF-WAY NOTE

It is now the autumn of 1945 and World War II has ended. The Japanese have surrendered under the shock of the first ever atomic bombs. Two "small" airburst weapons have obliterated the cities of Hiroshima and Nagasaki and that has persuaded the Japs that, even if "hara kiri" with the traditional samurai sword might still be on the cards, they can't fart in the face of that type of thunder! (I say "small" – those bombs were each of 20 kilotons, against the very much more powerful multi-megaton weapons with which the world has been threatened throughout the latter part of the 20th Century).

And this is where I had intended my musings to end. But if the reader has been entertained by some of the less serious of my experiences so far, the silly happenings and daft decisions were by no means confined to the war period. Each subsequent posting, to both flying and ground appointments, contained similar elements – annoying, frustrating, exasperating at the time, but seen as funny, even hilarious, in retrospect.

So let the tale continue until my retirement from the RAF in 1968.

FOREWORD TO PART 2

VE Day was 8th May, 1945. On 12th May, 1945, Joan and I were married.

There are, therefore, two factors which will explain a distinct change from Part 1 in my recording of events for Part 2.

Up to this point my record depicts events as seen by a youngster at war: apart from regular letters to my parents, my concerns were almost solely with my rather limited contribution to the war effort and to the fun and games we had en route. But from now on I also have the responsibility and concern for a wife, eventually family, and principally the constant difficulty of housing – at least for the next ten years.

The RAF "rules" discouraged an officer from marrying before age 27 (unless permission be Granted by his Commanding Officer) – and even then, payment of Marriage Allowance was denied until age 27. Thus for those three years (I was just 24 when we married) I was obliged to keep two persons, plus housing, on an income barely adequate for just one living in Mess. For a young married couple, married quarters on stations were non-existent for many years and so I have felt obliged to record many of the family problems in addition to the normal (and sometimes far from normal) Service matters.

Furthermore, whilst in no way belittling the vastly more dangerous business of flying in wartime, post-war service became a more serious matter – it became a career, as opposed to a temporary job. Also one was getting older and rather less likely to get into "madcap" schemes!

Thus, in Part 2, somewhat more attention is paid to the detail of the unit and the task itself, perhaps less to the fun and games. I certainly gave more than half my time to duty, but now not all of it – say 70/30!

Blackpool – our delightful landlady, with daughters and lodgers. Author at top.

ACRC Corporal and his squad. Author second row, far right.

Above:
The Albemarle.

Centre:
Not 'Scotty' – but my remembered image of him.

Below:
YP-D over Malta.

*The Baron and
Alec Lawson.*

Ittiri.

*Aviators of 23 Sqn. – that
1500 ft. hill on the Alghero
circuit.*

'Flak'. *Kit Cotter.*

The Baron and Atherton.

23 Sqn. at Little Snoring.
Front row (from left): 5 – Sammy Hoare, 7 – Sticky Murphy.

EANS Shawbury – Onethirsty (130) Staff Navigator Course.

Left:
Author and Joan with that Lanchester coupe.

Below:
Aries II at Baragwanath

Right:
Picnic at the rondavel – centre right Air Commodore Jimmy D'Aeth.

Leeming. Army officers visit the Brigand training flight.

Watton. Air Commodore Sandy Rogers, Author and Ladies at the Summer Ball.

Gliding at White Waltham.

Staff College Bracknell. No. 46 Course, 1956.

Wahn. HQ 83 Group Staff, 1957.

Harry and Gwen Coates, self and Joan – Summer Ball, 1957.

Sundern. 'The Murkey Mere' – ready for launch.

. . . that sinking feeling!

Staff College DS. Tennis team 1961. Bill Threlfall – front, second left.

Continental Tour. Visit to AAFCE Fontainbleu, 1961.

Left:
End-of-course Concert –
'Clueless'.

Right:
Bruggen. AOC's Inspection –
Ivor Broom second right.

Left:
Royal Visit – the Planning Room.

The Parade rehearsal – fair weather.

Dress rehearsal – bad weather, Jesse Broom as HRH.

*The Parade – **HRH** returns from inspection.*

Joan's 'Ladies Room'.

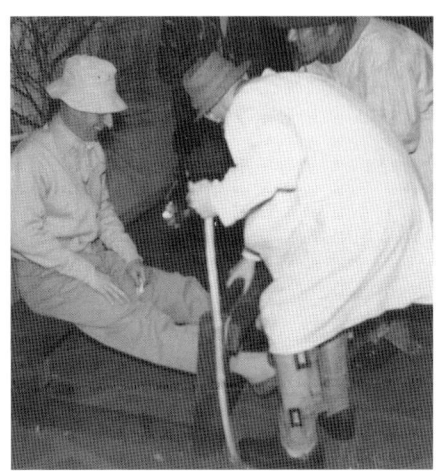

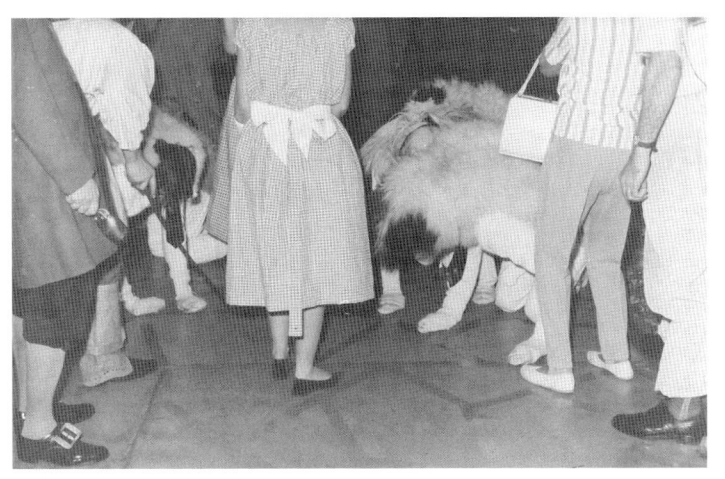

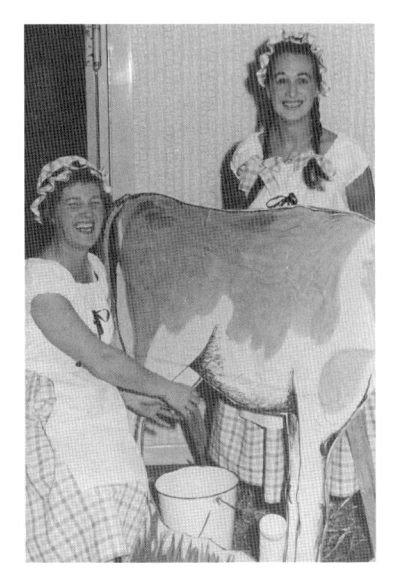

The 'Farmers Ball'.

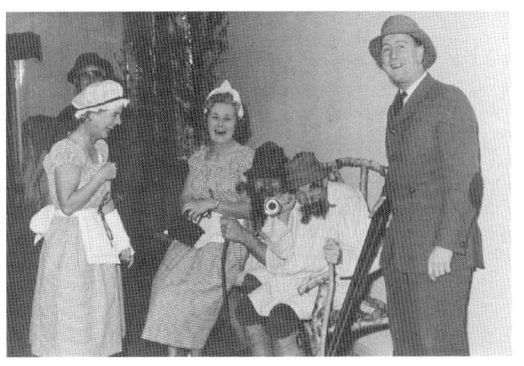

*Left and below:
Ivor's Farewell –
with mast and
de-masted.*

*Left:
AOC at the Police
Dog School.*

PART TWO

CHAPTER THIRTEEN

E.A.N.S. Shawbury, September 1945–July 1947

This was to be one of the happiest, yet at the same time most eventful, periods of my Service career. At this time, of course, I did not yet have a "career" – merely a wartime commission which could be concluded virtually instantly at the wish of their "Airships" at the Ministry. And it was to be a further three years before I was established in a permanent career.

No. 130 Staff Navigation Course – soon known by all and sundry as "one thirsty course"! "So, you thought you could navigate? Well you're now here to learn how it's really done!" So much for all those "by the seat of the pants, low-level, day and night, no nav. aids, dead-reckoning" sorties which our masters had the apparent audacity to proclaim as successful! Ah well, let's sit back and enjoy being at school again.

You know, most of us hadn't realised until then that this navigation business is so complex – it had all seemed so simple and basic in the Mosquito. Now we had "Instruments', "Radar", "Astro-nav", "Meteorology"; we were back to basics with Maths., Mechanics, Physics; we learn to construct maps, build radar systems, weapons theory; finally we learn to speak and teach! A comprehensive four months, both on the ground and in the air. By the end of the course, there was not one of us who did not wonder how we had ever survived for so long in such abysmal ignorance!

The final course exercise was a triple cross-countries flight in a Halifax, with a team of three navigators, each taking it in turns to be "1st Nav-plotter", the other roles being radar operator and instrument "basher", the latter including star shots with sextant. The first leg, with yours truly as 1st Nav., was from Shawbury to Pomigliano, Italy – of all places! And how changed it was since I had left it two years before – it now boasted a runway, a hangar, a control tower and refuelling facilities. We had left Shawbury in the early hours, arriving at Pomig. for breakfast; the other crew members couldn't believe that we used to find it at night-time – without any navigation aids! They were even more sceptical after I introduced them to the Arizona Club in Napoli.

The return legs were Pomig. to Gibraltar (where we wangled a two nights stopover – never did find out what was wrong with that No. 2 engine!) and thence to Shawbury.

There was great rivalry for first place in our end-of-course results. The exams were held over a three day period following our return and the main subject – three hours on DR Navigation – was a total nightmare for me. We had two French officers on the course and our end-of-course party had been held in the Mess the night before that exam. The Frenchmen made one of their "special" potato pies for that evening, to be shared by all. It was heavily laced with garlic and, in case we found it not spicy enough, they supplied a dozen garlic cloves, sliced, in separate dishes for adding as required. My great friend "Midi" Midlane had consumed two enormous portions of this pie, with added garlic slices, and for dessert had polished off the remainder of the sliced cloves. He was to be at the neighbouring desk for the exam: he arrived late and you could smell him from the second he entered the building some 20 yards away. And frequently, throughout the exam, he would turn to me and ask "Hhhh-o-w are you getting on, Norman?" I mean – how can you concentrate on a tricky nav. plotting problem through a veritable haze of garlic?

When the end results were announced I was pleased to have recorded second place – ruined by the fact that first was Joe Dalley – a pilot! This announcement was immediately followed by another – our postings: I was to remain at E.A.N.S. as an instructor.

Ordinarily I think I might have been disappointed not to be going back to a flying appointment but the news was in fact a great relief because we had found, early in the course, the most delightful accommodation – on a farm at Preston Brockhurst, just two miles from the airfield. The farmer, Fred Embrey, his wife and their son Derek, had made us very welcome. Lighting was by candles and a paraffin lamp, heating was a single coal fire, cooking by paraffin stove, and we carried the hot water (heated on the paraffin stove) by bucket up to the shared (and unheated) bathroom! Yet we loved every minute of it and fifty and more years later we still recall with amusement climbing the stairs to a very cold bed by candlelight – but when you're young and newly married who cares?

Neither of us had even visited a farm before, let alone lived on one, so we were rather taken aback at some of the then standard practices – particularly in the manner of animal slaughter. Our mouths watered at the sight of the delicious fresh hams and sides of bacon which hung from the main kitchen rafters but, offered some ourselves, and invited to see their "production", were taken aback to see the chosen animal "hog-tied", strung from a rafter in the barn, then deft application of carving knife to throat and left to bleed to death: "bleeding thus provides the whitest and best meat" we were told. We kept away from such scenes thereafter and Joan restricted her farm activities to "dipping" the lambs, which she enjoyed.

The activities I enjoyed most were shooting – pheasants and rats. As for the pheasants (lovely grub!), you cannot eat them straight away, says Fred – they must "hang" for four days before plucking. So, after my first kill, I return from work four evenings later, with great expectation to pluck and prepare our first bird for the table – it no longer hangs in the kitchen. "The bird," I ask "where is it?" "Oh that smelly thing – I've buried it" says Joan. She's never been allowed to forget it!

The rats? Hordes of them, an absolute menace in the chicken run. Derek solicits my aid in the cull – he has a spade and a torch and arms me with a 410 and a pocketful of cartridges. We block up all the holes in the wire and leave the gate of the run open at dusk; an hour later, wearing thigh-high boots, gloves and mufflers, we enter the cage and close the gate behind us. Torch on – there are dozens of them: the gun was fun but the spade was far more effective. And I confirm – when cornered they attack, the fight was not all one-sided!

Our two years at Shawbury were memorable for so many things, affecting both my personal life and military career. On the personal side, we frequently recall market days in Shrewsbury: meeting Fred and his farmer pals, watching the canny deals at the livestock sales, lunching at the Lion Hotel (excellent two-course meal for 3/6 – 17p!), cinema seats for 2/6 (or if a bit short, 1/9!); but then my pay as a flight lieutenant was but £1/4/0. a day (including first increment after two years of 2/- a day). Then there were my cars: the reader will recall that I was compelled to sell my Morris 8 to pay for our honeymoon so I *had* to buy another to live on the farm – it was first a Wolseley Hornet saloon, purchased at auction for £117 10s 0d. It was a runner, after a fashion, but I managed to make a profit of £25 a few months later when I found a beauty: a 1934 Lanchester Special Avon Coupe. This I bought from another RAF type who resided at the farm during the war and had returned to see his old friends, the Embreys.

On the matter of career, two events occurred almost simultaneously. First I received a letter from the Secretary of my pre-war employers, Sedgwick Collins & Co., insurance brokers: would I be returning to my old job? Now I must here offer a sincere vote of thanks to that firm (Now "Sedgwicks"), who had supported me on half-salary throughout my RAF service to date, It was only £60 p.a. but it was a Godsend to an airman recruit on 2/- a day (and for all the years thereafter) – and how many employers made that gesture in recognition of an employee's war service? Anyway, I was invited to an interview with the Company Secretary on my next leave; it was an interview I could never forget. "We would be very pleased to have you back, Conquer. Of course, you have been out of touch with the insurance world for six years now, but I expect you could soon catch up, and so we would be pleased to offer you the same position which you left, and at the same salary." I had then been a junior clerk in the Accident Renewals department at a salary of £120 p.a. Now as a flight lieutenant, on nearly £450 p.a., there didn't seem to be any alternative to an apologetic but regretful "thanks but no thanks"!

It so happened that only a few days before this interview I had been offered an Extended Service Commission for 4 years, with perhaps a further 4 years thereafter. With the possibility of a Permanent Commission looming, the offer from the Company Secretary merely served to make my decision for me.

Whilst accepting this Extended Service Commission, it seemed to me an opportunity to re-apply for the pilot's course which was cancelled owing to the training "rundown" at the approaching war's end. I received an unexpected holding reply: "Not at the moment but there is the prospect of increasing targets for aircrew intake, especially pilots, and your application will be kept under review". Ah well, at least it was not another definite "no" like last time – fingers crossed, note in diary "remind same time next year".

The winter of 46/47 was a b . . . For a time we were well and truly snowed in on the farm. Walk to work then . . . what, through 8 feet deep drifts? "No problem", says young Derek, "I'll take you on the tractor – hop on". After all the stunned looks as the instructor, in full uniform, arrives riding a tractor, who got full marks for initiative? Great fun!

Of the various air exercises involved in my term as an instructor at Shawbury none merit comment here – all were routine, rather dull, medium to high level navigation exercises, flown by experienced staff pilots and navigated by experienced navigators learning specialist techniques. But in April '47, I was detailed to be one of a three-man navigation team, taking Aries II on a month's tour of South Africa, Rhodesia and Kenya – and this trip contained enough calls to "panic stations" to suffice for any one posting.

Aries II was a specially converted Lincoln – nose and tail turrets replaced by fairings – the whole almost "civilianised" – and called a Lincolnian. E.A.N.S. has operated several marks of "Aries", starting with a Lancaster (Lancastrian) as Aries I, then after Aries II a Canberra and later more modern types. The object of all Aries flights was to tour the world enhancing navigation techniques, lecturing to other Air Forces on those techniques and latest equipments, and generally spreading inter-service goodwill. But this South Africa sortie carried one more aim – the Commandant had obtained approval from AOC-in-C Flying Training Command to go for the Cape record, then standing at something in excess of 35 hours, I believe.

Recently posted in as Captain of the Aries we had a Canadian Wing Commander, for some inexplicable reason given precedence over our own Wing Commander Flying, "Blackie", who then crewed as co-pilot. The "record" rules required us to start from Manston so we flew there a.m., refuelled and got airborne for Cape Town early evening, with one planned refuelling stop at Kano, Nigeria. All went as planned until well into Algeria, by when all radar aids were no longer available. No problem – drifts and map-reading will suffice – except that we hit a broad blanket of low cloud. OK – wireless op., bearings please: sorry, no radio bearings – dawn effect! Never mind, astro – second nav. get me some astro sights please. It takes perhaps three minutes to locate the stella body required and take a sextant sighting; two of those for a fix, or preferably three for triangulation; but no information forthcoming. So I watch the "sight taker" – standing in the astrodome, with star in the sight he's gradually turning first to the left, then to the right. What the hell . . . ? The aeroplane is wandering all over the sky, the pilot making no effort to maintain "straight and level", essential for this exercise. Big row navigator/pilot, latter tells me to shut up, Commandant from the rear "Do as the navigator tells you Captain", woops! One astro fix puts us 60 miles port of track, second one puts us 100 miles starboard of track; fat lot of damned good that is. Just then we hit 10/10ths cloud cover overhead; now we're between layers so no ground sighting, no radar, no radio, no astro; the most professional team of specialist navigators is *lost* over central Africa! What to do? Stick to flight plan and Dead Reckoning, ignore all side issues, one hour and a half later, all cloud disappears and there is Kano, dead ahead, two minutes after E.T.A.! Which just goes to prove . . . what? Who needs careless pilots?

What the crew had not foreseen was that this, comparatively minor in the event, lapse of concentration by the pilot was but a forerunner of things to come. Refuelling at Kano took barely an hour and from there the next leg was due south direct to Cape Town. Blackie flew her most of the way, no problems; I had handed over the plot and was map reading from the rumble seat. Shortly before reaching our destination the captain took back control and on joining the circuit was given landing clearance – runway two zero, i.e. landing towards the south. (This should have been obvious: it was night time, when a katabatic wind down Table Mountain to the south of the airfield would have necessitated landing into it, i.e. to the south). Circuit completed, captain calls "Finals" – I happen to look out of the starboard window and see Table Mountain directly beneath us – with not too many feet to spare. "Thinks: we're slipping down the southern flank of T.M. on finals – he's landing to the north. He's obviously taken runway 20 (i.e. 200 degrees) as 02 (i.e. 020 degrees, the exact reciprocal) and he's landing *downwind*!" I yelled this to him and urged "Go round again" but he waved me down. Then came the air traffic controller in panic "Aries, you're landing the wrong way – go round again – go round again". "Oh shut up" says our wonderful pilot – and switches off the RT.

We're over the end of the runway at about 110 knots with everything hanging, and we float – and we float – and we float – "Switch off all engines" says the captain, and Blackie throws the switches. All engines silent – and we're still airborne. I happen to glance towards the rear and the Commandant and other "resting" crew members are on the deck, backs to the main spar, heads between legs, anticipating the "inevitable", but finally we touch down with barely 100 yards of runway remaining, brakes full on, and we squeal to a halt in the over-run, a few yards short of the hedge.

The Commandant, Air Commodore N.H. 'Jimmy" D'Aeth, was none too pleased with this performance when it was realised that practically the whole of the Cape Town Establishment plus our own Diplomatic Corps were present as a welcoming party. Headlines in the Cape Town Express next morning – "ARIES ARRIVES!!"

In addition to all the officials present, I was astonished to see two old friends of mine, still in flying kit, in the foreground – pilot Micky Martin and navigator Ted Sismore. Our surprise at seeing them was as nothing to the reason for their presence: it transpired that Transport Command, intending to deliver a Mosquito to the South African Air Force, had decided, quite independently of our project, to go for the Cape record – and to do it on the same day! Mick and Ted were the selected crew and had taken the East Africa route, landing three times for refuelling, and had landed at Cape Town not long before our "spectacular". Worse: our official flight time was 26 hours 57 minutes and would have beaten the previous record comfortably. Mick and Ted's time – 21 hours 35 minutes!! Well, that's the Mosquito for you!

Soon after our arrival we met Jan Smuts, the then South African President. He expressed his pleasure at our visit and, assuming that our time would not be wholly occupied with meetings and lectures, offered the crew the use of three cars, with drivers, to take us for a three day tour of the Kruger National Park. For pure enjoyment, this was the undoubted highlight of the tour: three nights in "rondavels" at the visitors' camp, with daily tours of the park. Warning from the warden: "Don't get out of the car in the presence of lions, elephants, rhino, etc.". We thought he was joking, of course. "No", quoth he, "it's not dangerous – but if you get out of the car the animals will run away and you will miss so much"! Yeah, yeah, a likely story! And we saw the lot – white rhino, lion, hippo, elephant, to name only the obvious. I suppose it's "old hat" for some of today's holidaymakers but to us it was a whole new world.

But back to the hazards of aviation with a certain pilot, who wasn't finished by a long chalk. We were asked to take part in an air display being held at Baragwanath, Johannesburg. As an RAF exhibit and the largest aircraft at the show, we had merely a static part to play, whilst the South African and Rhodesian Air Forces provided all the action. That was until the late afternoon when, apparently as the "piece de resistance" of the show, Aries would take off, departing for Zwartkops, Pretoria. Now, Barag . . . was a grass airfield, with only a few hundred yards of level ground from the takeoff point, after which quite a steeply sloping area led to some thick woodland on rising ground – not an easy takeoff run for our aeroplane. So our dear pilot, the crowd hushed and expectant to see this large modern machine get airborne, slams open the throttles whilst holding on brakes, then releases brakes on full power for maximum acceleration. The result: a screaming ground loop! Fortunately, the undercarriage held, no props got bent, and we staggered gently back to the starting point to try again. At that stage, no-one was offering any odds on our probable survival from this tour. But second time lucky, we breathed a sigh of relief, wondering what tomorrow would bring.

The remainder of the tour, with Blackie driving, went without further incident. Pretoria to Durban (to No. 21 Squadron, S.A.A.F.) to Langebaan (SAAF Navigation School) to Salisbury, Rhodesia (R.R.A.F.) to Heany, Bulawayo to Thornhill (R.R.A.F. Navigation School), thence home via Eastleigh, Nairobi, and Castel Benito.

By and large, the fundamental purpose of the tour was fulfilled, though we failed to get the record (not our fault) and left a few bad impressions on the way round. But we all knew whose fault that was and no-one was surprised when a certain officer left Shawbury rather rapidly and Blackie was appointed as Aries captain for future occasions. (The navigation team soon got over their "ring-twitch" and have enjoyed many a laugh since).

Following the excitements on the African Continent, the return to the directing of course studies was rather dull but there is a great sense of achievement in graduating young students and sending them out into the wide blue yonder (to use a favourite Americanism). But by the time yet another Advanced Navigation Course had passed through the machinery and the African adventures had been documented, discussed and lessons learned, the Air Ministry wallers who constantly move the pieces on the chequerboard found that I had been in stable employment for almost two years and so it was time to move me on.

Summoned to the Adjutant's office in the usual way, I was asked how I would like to go back to the Mosquito fighter role – would I? just try me! "Well you're posted to Leeming, No. 228 O.C.U. (Operational Conversion Unit) as Chief Navigation Instructor". "Oh yes – I've heard that before. I was posted to 51 OTU Cranfield as CNI and a month later Bill Gregory arrived to takeover. Then I was posted to 54 OTU Charter Hall as CNI and a fortnight later Pip Orange was appointed over me. So don't tell me the old old story!" "No, no, this time it's definite – you're getting acting-squadron leader rank for the post". Conflicting emotions: pleasure – back to an operational appointment (well, almost); satisfaction – a step on the promotion ladder; sorrow – we have to leave our splendid billet on the farm. But then service life is all about frequent change and one must take it as it comes. So – to Leeming.

CHAPTER FOURTEEN

228 O.C.U., Leeming, July 1947–October 1949

The first thing to become apparent on my arrival was that my newly advanced status would not give us the slightest chance of married accommodation on the station. Aged 26 and no children? Not a chance. There were just 10 officers' married quarters: one Type 3 for the Station Commander, two Type 4's for the Wing Commander Flying and the Wing Commander Admin., and 7 Type 5's, of which three were allocated "ex officio" for the Wing Commander Tech., the Senior Air Traffic Control Officer and the Senior Medical officer. That left four for allocation on the points basis – and with several quite senior officers (in both age and rank) having several children each there was no prospect for a junior such as myself.

Thus, my first task was to find local accommodation so that we could move from the farm; for this I was awarded 7 days leave. I was fortunate to find, fairly quickly, a couple of rooms in a house five miles from the airfield and well within my leave we had moved from Shropshire to Yorkshire. But this was but the beginning of the constantly moving saga which marked our two years at Leeming – six moves in one posting – unheard of, before or since!

This house was not only five miles from the airfield, it was also five miles from any other habitation; no shops, pubs, garage or any normal amenities existed nearby. So Joan would need the car during the day – I must find alternative transport for commuting. Now, how about an ancient motorbike, square tank, cracked saddle, bald tyres, one working brake, 1929 OK Supreme, £15?

Never a keen motorcyclist I found this machine a frightful (and frightening) form of transport, more so even than the Fairey Battle! There was one bend in the road near the house I never did fully master – ended up in the ditch several times.

Money was always a problem at this time. Though not enthusiastic gamblers, we did try a regular small flutter on the football pools – just a few lines each week on 10 homes and 4 aways. Checking the coupon one week in my office, I found I'd come up on one line of 10 homes and hopefully awaited the published news of the payout. A colleague phoned me the following day: "You've won £1500!" After the second beer in the bar, I thought I had better check the paper myself – colleague had mis-read, it was £150, and that was for a full shilling stake, whereas my stake was only sixpence, so the win was only £75. Though that was a lot of money then (about six weeks' pay), the point of the story is that the figure of £1500 shot round the Mess like wildfire; though I protested it was all a mistake, "Pull the other one" they laughed. Before I knew it most of the £75 had gone – I never knew I had so many friends!

Whilst on the subject of money, it was at about this time that I received an unexpected (and uninvited) visitor to my office. "Good morning Sir. Your good friend the Wing Commander has suggested I call on you. My name is Smith, I'm from the Sun Life Insurance Company of Canada. Would you consider buying one of our nice Endowment policies? For just £4 a month, £4.10.0 to include flying risks, you could have £1000 cover for 20 years etc. etc.". I had a simple philosophy then – if anything happens to me, the Service would provide (such innocence!). However, perhaps a bit of protection for my wife would not be a bad idea, so I bought it. I mention this here only because it was such a pitiful provision and because it was to be a further 15 years before an ex-navigator friend, retired from the Service and well into his second career in the insurance business, showed me what Smith should have done at that appointment. (See Bruggen 1964).

For the first 6 months of this tour, my job as CNI was of minor significance. Although it was a Mosquito OCU, the Intruder role was but a small part of the training; the main role was night fighter using A.I. (Air Interception) radar. The Wellington was the workhorse for AI training and that half of the course was run by another squadron leader navigator, AI trained and experienced, which I was not; only in the final stages did the intruder training role figure. So for that period I was seriously under-employed. Thus it was with some relief that early in 1948 I was detailed to relieve the 12 Group Navigation Officer (at RAF Newton, Notts.) for three months whilst he went on a course (Shawbury – where else?).

Relief from the point of view of the job, yes, but upsetting from the domestic viewpoint. We had quickly grown tired of the old problem of shared bathroom and kitchen, and restrictions on when and where we could hang washing to dry, so had left that house and the strict landlady for a splendid flat in a nearby country club, literally just on the airfield boundary, an ideal situation. And then there's another problem – my wife is pregnant. Following two miscarriages whilst we were at Shawbury, she has been warned that "next time" she may have to spend much of the time in bed resting, if the pregnancy is to run its course. So clearly, I can't go away for three months and leave her in the flat. So, once again, Joan is shuttled off home – this time for what was to be a longer separation.

What can I say about that shift at HQ 12 Group? Not much – a routine staff appointment, with an interesting insight into the conduct of Group exercises and the Fighter Command training machine, several interesting visits to Fighter Command HQ at Bentley Priory and the chance to meet again several of my old squadron friends. It was also a useful apprenticeship for other appointments to come.

At the end of the Newton attachment, Joan was pronounced satisfactorily through the initial pregnancy stages and was considered fit to travel and join me again. A close friend who resided at the farm near Shawbury with us, Dusty Miller, was now CNI at Dishforth, just down the road from Leeming, and he and his wife Barbara had a bungalow nearby. They offered us a bedroom and to share the house with them for a couple of months, until the baby was due and for which Joan would return home. So, the fourth move of the Leeming saga.

By this time there had been a significant change in the role and establishment of Leeming. The Mosquito night fighter element remained but we now had the added light bomber role using the Brigand, just a heavier version of the Blenheim really. So now I had a more demanding part to play, with my earlier Bicester experiences helping considerably. After the Mosquito, the

Brigand was ponderous and vulnerable and, despite the fact that it carried a reasonable payload, had limited range and thus a limited life in the role. But it was fun while it lasted.

One nasty accident deserves mention for several reasons: an aeroplane destroyed by a silly mistake (of which we're all guilty from time to time), no lives lost, the heroism of the navigator, the impeccable reaction of the emergency services. The "mistake" and the "heroism" deserve explanation.

The pilot concerned, (who shall be nameless), was one of our most experienced operational Mosquito pilots. Since the arrival of the Brigand, he had developed a fondness for flying it, at the expense of his normal practices on the Mosquito. In the Brigand, the fuel supply has merely to be turned on at the start and from then on it flows automatically from all tanks throughout the flight. On the Mosquito, the pilot selects "Outer tanks" first, then switches to "Inner tanks" after takeoff, then usually back on to "Outer tanks" for landing. In this event, having flown the Brigand frequently and not having flown the Mosquito for a couple of months, our pilot followed the usual routine of takeoff on "outers" but forgot to switch to "inners'. The "outers" normally give about half an hour's endurance and it was shortly after that when he returned to the airfield to practice a "roller"; needless to say, he ran dry and "landed" powerless in a field beyond. The pilot was a big man, perhaps 15 stones; the navigator was Ray Follis, perhaps 5'4" and 9 stones. The pilot was knocked out and unable to move – but Ray, having leapt clear immediately, climbed back on to the wing and *hauled* the driver from his seat and clear. I refrain from commenting further on the outcome – except to say that the pilot was subsequently promoted and the navigator wasn't – but perhaps they blamed the navigator for not reminding his pilot to change tanks!

All readers will be familiar with the term "secondary duties" – Orderly Officer, Station Duty Officer, Mess Committee Members, etc. One such duty which had not come my way before was Chairman (or was it President?) of a Trade Testing Board. All airmen were subjected to progressive trade testing to ensure their continuing progress and suitability in their trades and on this occasion I was required to supervise such tests over a 3-monthly period. In every trade, the Officer in charge of each section was, of course, responsible for arranging and conducting these tests – my task was merely the overall co-ordination and supervision and to ensure that they were carried out and properly recorded.

However, at this particular time, the M.T. officer was facing a problem – several of his NCOs were either sick, on leave or away on courses and so he was short of qualified examiners. Well, I'd been a qualified driver for 10 years, I had driven RAF vehicles, cars, jeeps, 3-tonners, 30 cwt. vans during the war, can I help? I much enjoyed, on several days over the following few weeks, riding various vehicles, with both airmen and airwomen drivers, over much of the A1 and the Yorkshire countryside, combining testing with many routine MT duties, and even a few non-duties, dare I say. All drivers enjoyed themselves, passed their tests – and I wasn't frightened once!

By the mid-summer of 1948, Joan is approaching the last three months of her pregnancy – she has been pre-warned that she must spend this period mostly in bed to avoid a repeated miscarriage. So now she must go home – and I move into the Mess until the birth draws near. Where can we live thereafter? All accommodation in the Club is taken; we can't go back to house-sharing with a baby – local landladies always insist "no kids!" OMQ for us is still out of the question; and she refuses to stay at her home without me. Only one answer – a caravan!

Easy to say – but far from easy to arrange. Firstly, finance: to buy we need at least £1000–1200, an unimaginable sum on my salary. Try the bank – flat "NO", £500? Again "NO". Then how much will you lend an RAF Squadron Leader? Nothing – bad risk! My Mother eventually solved the problem, though she had very little money of her own, and I had no chance of repaying her whilst still in the Service on (then) 35/- (shillings for those who have forgotten) a day (i.e. about £650 a year).

Then, where to park it? We had a disused wartime site of Nissen huts just off the station where water and power could easily be reconnected – so a sympathetic CO gave permission to park the caravan there. After a few weeks and several mishaps that site became impossible – and so we moved the van to a field adjacent to the OMQs. But though caravanning may be fun for many, it was not our idea of heaven – not with a newborn babe. And then, not long after, I was appointed to the board of a Court Martial at another station which lasted for four days; during that time, an escaped convict tried to get into our caravan one night – scared the wife . . . less! Fortunately, our Wing Commander

Admin, who lived in OMQ only a few yards away, heard the kerfuffle and intervened – the escapee ran off to be detained nearby the following morning. That ended our 6 months of caravanning!

As luck would have it, our Senior Air Traffic Control Officer (SATCO) was about to be detached on a course for three months and offered the use of his MQ for that period – we moved in the next day – sold the caravan at a substantial loss – but that's life!

You, the reader, might wonder, while all this "switching" of family accommodation was going on, when was any work done? Well, the job of CNI at an Operational Conversion Unit (OCU) at that time was not arduous: courses comprised three or four crews (pilot and navigator) at most, all the spade work in setting up the briefing room, lecture syllabus, flight planning facilities and operational route training plans had been completed in my first six months, so the task thereafter was but to progress the small courses to qualify for posting to squadrons. With my able assistant, Flying Officer Ron Parfitt, my job, though always interesting, was routine.

So now, is my family finally settled for the remainder of this posting – still perhaps nine to twelve months to go? Sorry, no! SATCO is due back from his detachment rather sooner than expected and, naturally, he wants his house back. So where to now? A birdie whispers that a flat in Leeming village has just become vacant – a smart dash to see the owner and it's on offer at three pounds a week. But what a dump – above a transport cafe at the side of the A1 – two tiny rooms plus a bathroom-cum-kitchen – the latter containing a bath (of sorts) with a hinged board over for a kitchen worktop/draining board and a washbasin doubling for washing up; the cooking facility was an ancient coal fired range in the living room. Oh well, beggars can't be choosers; we move in forthwith.

Not long afterward, our Accountant Officer, after coming for tea one afternoon, suggests that such rent for such a property is outrageous – we should appeal to the Rent Tribunal. But would that be wise with nowhere else to go? Once again, "Guardian Angel", aware of our plight, comes to our aid with the news that a widow lady in Bedale, alone in a very large house, would welcome the company of a young officer and family from Leeming, she had ample accommodation to spare. Lady Mabel Beresford-Pierce, widow of Admiral Sir Charles Beresford-Pierce (God bless her!)

was a most charming and generous lady; she immediately fell in love with our baby girl Gillian, and said we would be most welcome to move into her house whenever would be convenient to us.

Two beautiful large rooms, a sitting room and a bedroom, were reserved for our exclusive use, plus our own kitchen, or share the main kitchen with Lady Mabel if we prefer, plus permanent invitation to share all the main rooms of the house and her lovely garden – sheer heaven on earth, especially compared to our present hovel. Could we perhaps afford two pounds per week?

I referred the matter of the flat rent to the Rent Tribunal, gave the owner a formal week's notice plus a week's rent and we moved into "Bedale Haven" that very day. Lady Mabel even raised no objection to Bruce, our bull terrier, who incidentally loved cats – and Lady Mabel had three! (Bruce slept in a kennel in the garden and when we opened his kennel door in the mornings it was often one of the cats who was first to emerge).

As if this most fortunate move had swung the luck in our favour for once, it was now that I received a formal letter from above to say that I had been awarded my permanent commission; at last I could look ahead to a full career in the Service. I was immediately tempted to remind their Airships about my pilot's course but, anxious to enjoy our new-found home for as long as possible, decided to extend my patience on that subject for a bit longer. And yet . . .

Our joy was to last but a couple of months: the dreaded call from the Adjutant then proclaimed once more "You are posted" – to 115 Squadron, Mildenhall as "B" Flight commander, Flight Lieutenant post, losing my acting rank. The pendulum swings, luck goes out of the window, thanks for nothing, a drop in rank, a reduction in pay, and we shall now shortly lose our delightful home in Bedale. Is there a silver lining? Well, yes, a return to an operational flying appointment and my first flight command. But Lincolns, Bomber Command, not really my scene, as they say. Will there be a MQ available? Not a hope, so the family must stay here until I've sorted out accommodation there – what's new? But wait a minute – as we have to move I'll re-apply for my pilot's course after all – this could be a real opportunity. Ha ha! Nothing has changed – maybe after your next tour!

Note: I wasn't particularly proud of myself over the "rent tribunal" business – but I felt much better about it when I learned that a young new arrival on the station who had followed me into the flat had benefited – the rent was slashed by half!

CHAPTER FIFTEEN

115 Squadron, Mildenhall, October 1949–March 1950

My posting to 115 Squadron, Mildenhall, was the nearest thing to a "non-event" in my RAF career – and I was thankful it only lasted for six months. This period 1949/50 was probably the nadir in the post-war affairs of Bomber Command. There were four squadrons on the station, 35, 87,115 and 207, each equipped with Lancasters and converting to Lincolns. The latter were just a larger version of the former – similar crew, longer range, heavier bombload, better defence armament.

A Unit Establishment (U/E) of 12 aircraft per squadron appeared to be shrinking daily; we had eight when I arrived, six when I left. General serviceability was no more than fair, poor in the case of the radar equipment. What flying we did was mainly local test flying, radar navigation and bombing exercises, interspersed with night sorties (3 to 5 hours) with simulated bombing runs, plus the occasional max. effort from all Bomber Command Stations to exercise the defence services – searchlights, radar reporting, ack ack units, etc. Most of us managed to get airborne no more than three of four times a month (compare this to our activity on 527 Squadron at CSE Watton in 5 years time). Squadron morale was not good – and a weak CO did not help.

Once again, the accommodation problem was a nightmare! The family were safe and content in Bedale still but it took me three months to find one room with shared mod. cons, in a small house some 10 miles from the airfield. It wasn't quite the case of the "landlady from hell", but at times it came close to it. She accepted us with a child only with the greatest reluctance – and I was only a flight lieutenant; "My dear, I am used to Brigadiers and equivalent in my house, not *junior* officers". Babies cry – but in this lady's house that was not allowed. "Put her in the pram out in the garden, dear – no, not at this end of the garden, down at the bottom if you don't mind". "Hanging out washing on Friday/Saturday/Sunday? Really dear, only on Mondays – if you must!".

We stuck it for two months and were just about to give notice and move back to wife's home when I got wind of a semi-detached house in Bury St. Edmunds: the owner was prepared to rent it to the RAF as a hiring and we leapt at the chance – absolute Godsend. It took a month to organise it and we moved in – a whole house to ourselves – in December 1949.

We were now just 15 miles from base; I had sold my car in order to buy the caravan at Leeming – so – another motorbike. This time please, not an ancient putt-putt like the last one – so a brand new BSA 250, just about viable on HP.

What more could we want – a house to ourselves, garage, nice little garden for vegetables, a bike for transport and flying (sometimes) for the day (or night) job. We are set for a while – or are we? Oh not again, surely! Damn me, we hadn't been ensconced for more than a fortnight when we are told that the Squadron is moving to Marham, Norfolk, immediately after Christmas, to convert to Washingtons (B29s to those who remember). Well now I'm bolshie and feel inclined to tell the Adj. where he can stick his posting – if forced, I'll resign my commission – enough is finally enough!!!

But, would you believe it, the fates are once again on my side. I tried the "pilots course" ploy again but this time, so sorry are they to refuse me yet again (oh yeah!) they just happen to need an experienced bomber navigator (me? experienced on bombers? oh well, if you insist) to be Station Nav. Officer with the Yanks at Lakenheath. As Lakenheath was almost exactly the same distance from Bury St. Edmunds as Mildenhall, we would be able to keep our hiring for the foreseeable future. (You say you detect a fiddle? I heard that reader).

RAF Lakenheath, March 1950 – March 1951

At that time, Lakenheath was still an RAF Station, even though the operational squadrons ("groups" in USAF parlance) were all

American, flying B29s. The RAF contingent consisted of a Group Captain (Station Commander), Wing Commander (Admin.) and about a dozen other officers. My appointment was, ostensibly, Station Navigation Officer; very early on it became quite apparent that the USAF Groups all had their own navigation kings, briefing rooms, maps and charts supplies, training rooms and so on. But we did not have a Station Briefing Room/Operations Room, expected to be required for visiting or back-up squadrons – so I commandeered a suitable room in the Control Tower and built it. This then added Station Operations Officer to my job spec.!

It further became apparent that there was a requirement for photographic workshops; we had an NCO and several airmen in the photo trade but no officer to organise. So now I was obliged to add Station Photographic Officer to the list. And then, for the next step, Station Intelligence Officer, to deal with photo-interpreters.

Our Station Commander and the USAF Commander were also at this time becoming very concerned about security. Aircraft on the dispersal pans were at constant readiness (two at "immediate", fully armed); the main road had recently been diverted around the enlarged airfield, passing close by many of these pans, and we were now beginning to receive frequent warnings of possible IRA activity.

Armed American service police and group airmen patrolled their aircraft day and night, yet we all felt this defence inadequate against the possible threat. We were now, therefore, to be heavily reinforced with defence personnel: a squadron of RAF Regiment, an officer and about 60 men, plus an Army company, Royal Ulster Rifles, an officer and some 100 men.

Conquer – organise accommodation! Yes SIR. So now I am also Station Security Officer and Station Defence Officer and to think that when I was drafted to this appointment it had been suggested that I would probably find very little to do! Tented encampments was the only answer of course – and who more used to that task than the Army and the Regiment; all I had to do was to organise the sites and the necessary admin. support. I became quite adept at press-ganging some of the other officers into lending a hand.

One potential problem in all this tight security was co-ordination between armed and jumpy USAF guards on the dispersal pans, RAF Regiment armed patrols inside the airfield and RUR patrols around the outskirts, especially along the fringes of the main by-pass road. It didn't need too much imagination to fear "friendly force" clashes at night – so tight plans for patrolling limits, passwords, signalling were arranged in conference between all the involved parties.

In my more sober moments I could not help wondering what a Station Navigation Officer was doing getting mixed up in the security and ground defence of his station – but then, of course, it became blindingly obvious! That's why the fates had decreed that I spend my first year in the Service on guard against the expected German hoards and the Luftwaffe – good training for this year of protecting the Americans from expected attack by the Irish Republican Army! (You know, you really couldn't make it up!)

Not long after the soldiers in blue and khaki "took post", the CO received warning from "authority" that a certain retired Group Captain (we'll call him Hector Dunnit), now working as a correspondent for the Daily Telegraph, was likely to visit us "to test our security measures". I was instructed that he was not to be allowed to reach any of our aircraft in dispersal and (one most useful piece of information) he drives a green Rolls Royce. Suitable instructions were given to the patrol leaders: if he parks on the main road and even attempts to move towards one of the pans, he is to be apprehended, handcuffed and brought to the Guardroom. Sure enough, within 48 hours, he was seen to arrive, park near one of the pans and start to walk rapidly towards the aeroplane. He was immediately picked up by one of the patrols and brought to the Guardroom suitably manacled, protesting volubly the while.

My first visit to see him was rather unpleasant, plenty of shouting and bluster of the "Do you know who I am?" variety – yet surprisingly he carried no positive ID. So we let him cool off for a few hours after which the Station Commander sent him off with a flea in his ear. "If there's a next time" quoth the CO "I'll keep you in a cell for a week". Subsequently, a single paragraph in the D.T. mentioned tight security at Lakenheath.

As previously mentioned, the airfield was at this time still designated "RAF Lakenheath" but halfway through my time there, in the late summer of 1950, the overall responsibility changed and it became "USAF Lakenheath". Operationally the change of title made very little difference: the "Base

Commander" was now a USAF full colonel and all operations were American; the RAF contingent was unchanged but responsibility limited to administration and housekeeping support; Air Traffic Control remained joint RAF/USAF; I remained the "General Duties" dogsbody. Operational readiness was, if anything, increased – no doubt for the reasons I was to learn about in my (as yet unknown) next appointment to come (March 1951). But, in one particular matter, the effects of the change were quite dramatic.

The "Officers Mess" became the "Officers Club"! After my experiences with the Americans at Alghero, I was pretty sure that this would go down like a lead balloon with the "Boss" – and we did not have to wait long for the full effect to be felt. Cigars at the breakfast table! Bar "open all hours" for those not on duty; bar "closed all hours" during operations and exercises; ladies to have full access to lounge, dining room and billiard room at any hour.

Soon after the start of the "new regime", the new Club Committee decided to hold a Celebration Dance. Could this be a repeat of the Alghero "Dance" I wondered? It was! Formal invitations were sent to the RAF officers and their wives but there was much conjecture among my colleagues as to the choice of function; only a few of the American officers lived with wives in quarters or in nearby towns, there were no servicewomen stationed here, surely a "Dance" would be a bit dead without a supply of partners, would it not? You've guessed it – an exact repetition of the Alghero event. The Yanks sent a couple of coaches down to London and pulled several dozen "fun girls" off the streets with the promise of a rewarding weekend. The coaches arrived soon after the party started and by 10 p.m. the Club was rocking to a cacophony of sound and the sight of more and more clothing being discarded as the pace, and temperature, built up.

Now our CO, Group Captain Huxham, was a grand chap of the old school. A long time career officer from early Cranwell days pre-war, he was, perhaps, what the youngsters of the war years (like me) would probably call a bit "straight-laced". He and his wife were quite obviously embarrassed by the "goings on" and the reality of what was happening and who the "lady guests" were, was only just dawning on them. They left in a hurry after a few words (of thanks?) with the Colonel; my wife and I, with most of the other RAF members and wives, followed very shortly thereafter. I understand the party went on well into the early hours, though many of the American officers and "ladies" disappeared to quarters in great voice and high spirits, not to reappear. I have only vague memories of the few days which followed, except to say that the Club was very quiet, coach services back to London were discreetly arranged; the Colonel offered most humble apologies to the Group Captain and then disappeared very smartly back to the States – that must have been some bollocking from above!!

Of the only three RAF GD (i.e. flying branch) officers on the station – the Group Captain, the Wing Commander Admin, and myself – I was the only one in a flying appointment, yet apart from a few occasional jaunts in a Tiger Moth with the CO, I had no opportunity for productive flying. Unlike our willingness to offer experience flights in our Mosquitos to the Americans at Pomigliano and Alghero, the Yanks were not too keen on us participating in their flying at Lakenheath. However, on one occasion, after I had lobbied some of the lads in the bar one evening, I was offered a trip as an "observer" on "Operation Emperor" in October. The pilot, Captain di Salvo, was a quiet, seemingly unexcitable, man of undoubted skill and talent, with whom I felt totally at ease from the off. The route took us to Shetland, Malmo, Sylt, Heligoland, Channel Islands, Portland Bill, Birmingham, I.O.W., London, Lowestoft, Base (in that order, believe it or not) and included air refuelling, bombing practice and fighter attacks. Flight time just over 11 hours and, just like the South Africa trip and my few Lincoln sorties at Mildenhall, boring, boring; and the necessity of crawling through "the tunnel" between the front and rear of the aeroplane impressed me not one bit! I take my hat off to the guys who regularly flew such missions in that aeroplane but it made me more thankful than ever that I had not stayed with 115 converting to B29s at Marham!

One last memory of the odd goings on at Lakenheath: in view of the number of VIPs frequently visiting the station, the CO instructed me to form and command a regular guard of honour to receive them. (This must have been the result of my attendance a couple of years previously at the Junior Commanders Course at OATS [Officers Advanced Training School], Hornchurch). Just one minor problem: three Services with very different military styles now occupied Lakenheath, the USAF, the RAF and the British Army – which one should supply the guard of honour?

Why, all of them of course. Of course! The USAF – yes, their admin officer would provide 18 privates, properly drilled by an NCO. The RAF – of course, the RAF Regiments speciality, wasn't it? And the Army – all ready any time, Sir.

After some discussion, it was agreed that the three guards (18 men each) would form a hollow square, each with a junior officer in command. If the VIP visitor was American then the Americans would form the facing guard with the others on the flanks; if an RAF VIP, then the RAF guard facing, British Army or politician VIP, then Army guard facing. I would be Guard Commander and would give all the usual orders, following which each individual guard officer would repeat the order. It would go something like this:

(Assume visitor is American)

Me:	GofH	Atten-tion.	
Yank:	Guard	tenshun	slither.
Army:	"	SHUN	Bang
RAFR:	"	A-tten-tion	Bang

Me:	GofH	Slope Arms	
Yank:	Guard	Shoulder Arms	1,2
Army:	"	Sloooope HIPE	123
RAFR:	"	Slope Arms	1pause2pause3

Me:	GofH	Present Arms	
Yank:	Guard	" "	1 ~2
Army:	"	Preeeesent HIPE	1 slap
RAFR:	"	Present Arms	1pause2

On the first few occasions we practised this I thought it was crazy, unmilitary. But we soon tightened it up, retained the format, and then the first two visiting VIPs commented favourably, so much so that the word spread and we thought that several subsequent visitors came just to see this spectacle. It least, it was different!

The one feature of the parade that really got me going, had me almost in hysterics on the first few occasions, was the "march off". On the order "Guards march off independently", first the RUR would step away smartly at their fast 140 to the minute with much stamping of boots; then followed the RAF Regiment at the slower pace of 120, also boots stamping in unison; finally, the USAF guard would "Forward march" at an even slower pace, in their "soft shoe shuffle"! The comparison caused some hilarity – which then turned to enthusiastic applause on one occasion when they swung into an orderly trot singing one of their training songs as they continued for a couple of miles round the airfield!

This tour at Lakenheath had been a settled period for the family – a very welcome change after our two previous postings. But, in the ways of the Service, it had to end soon and, after a little more than a year, I was warned that I was to move to a staff appointment in the Air Ministry in April '51, with the return of my acting rank. From the career viewpoint this was good news but, naturally, there would be a down side – our hiring, that very nice semi-d. in Bury St. Edmunds, must be vacated within one month of the posting date. Inquiries at the A.M. revealed no prospect at present of available Service accommodation in the London area – we must make our own arrangements. Thus we had to fall back on the good offices of family and so we eventually arranged to move into my pre-war home in Essex, albeit temporarily, but with the almost inevitable friction that such arrangements often cause. Beggars can't be . . . etc.

CHAPTER SIXTEEN

Air Ministry, April 1951–February 1954

Most G.D. officers (i.e. aviators) probably regard the move to a desk job, especially in the Ministry, and even more particularly in the "Personnel/Manning" departments of Adastral House (as then was), as "the end – the backwater" of all postings. But an RAF career cannot be built on flying jobs alone, at least not for the majority of us, and so sometimes "flying a desk" became inevitable.

I had no idea what I was getting into and approached the appointment with some trepidation. I was instructed to report to the Director General of Manning (DGM), then Air Vice-Marshal Norman Allinson, who conducted the usual "getting to know you" interview and then directed me to report to the Director of Manning (Policy and Plans) (DMPP), Mr. Roberts, a Civil Service Officer of Air Commodore status, who then, after another "pleased to meet you" type interview sent me to the Deputy Director of Manning (Plans) (DDMP), Group Captain E.J.P. Davy, who was to be my immediate boss, a delightful man of whom I have the fondest memories. He explained that my appointment was Manning Plans (Air) and my task would be planning the future aircrew manning of the RAF.

Said quickly that sounded a fairly simple matter; after all hadn't I had evidence at Leeming and Mildenhall of smaller OTU courses and reducing numbers of aeroplanes – so surely the fewer the aeroplanes the fewer the aircrew needed and smaller numbers should simplify the planning task. Then I remembered a paper by Air Chief Marshal Sir John Slessor, circulated by C-in-C Bomber

Command in 1949, urging the need for a strong bomber force, and the seriousness with which the Americans at Lakenheath were facing the threat from Russia, and thought again: perhaps the "run-down" is over and we're facing expansion, not reduction. But I guessed this would all become clear in due course (it did – very shortly – in spades!).

Now Group Captain Davey introduces me to the man I am to replace – Squadron Leader Ted Sismore! Well I'm damned, we were at Bicester together in 1942, since when Ted has had a hectic and very rewarding war, winning DSO and DFC; and, of course, as previously mentioned, we had met briefly at Cape Town in 1947 when he and Micky Martin, (his pilot during the war also winning DSO and DFC), had flown in on the same day in the Transport Command Mosquito in record time. Then he really spins me a shaker – he's off on a pilot's course! When I'd just been turned down for the umpteenth time despite all previous promises. Obviously I didn't have Ted's clout – but just wait till this tour is over!

So now to the job – Manning Plans (Air). At the end of the first week my mind was in a whirl – how on earth can I remember all this detail, all these figures? By the end of the month I thought this is really impossible, I shall never get the hang of it. Let's not mince words, I remained in a daze for almost six months. Fortunately, my No. 2 was a first rate lad, Flight Lieutenant John Smith (yes, really): he was a Cranwell graduate, a pilot, had suffered a temporary medical problem which affected his flying category, hence his posting into this job a year before, and his temporary misfortune was my godsend. Smithy really knew his stuff and virtually held my hand during that early period; he led me to progressive understanding and eventually to total comprehension.

My first attendance at an Air Staff conference in Whitehall (one month into the job) completely blew the concept of a declining air force and reducing aircrew figures. Quite the opposite in fact. Previous post-war plans ("E", "F" and "G') had made front line reductions (as I had thought) but now we were presented with Plan "H". The Korean war and the worsening international situation, especially the onset of the "Cold War", was necessitating rapid expansion. We were also now faced with the introduction of the "V Bomber force – the Valiants. Victors and Vulcans. Thus I was introduced to the phase of "midnight oil burning" – everyone in the Ministry was demanding to know how many pilots, navigators, signallers, radar operators, flight engineers will we need next year, the year after, et sec. – for the next 10 years! The numbers involved were phenomenal, over 4000 pilots, 3000 navigators, 3000 other aircrew to enter training *per year*. This meant increasing our recruiting rate ten-fold, expanding the training capacity similarly, almost impossible in the timescale required by the Air Staff. More training aircraft needed, reopen airfields recently closed down (no mean task – ask anyone engaged in the "Works and Bricks" department), massive increase in instructors, need I go on?

One of the early results of this rapid expansion requirement was a policy decision to seek help from the USA and Canada for more training capacity, especially pilots. To this end the Assistant Chief of the Air Staff (Training) (ACAS(T)), Air Vice-Marshal Theodore McEvoy (about whom more later) led a team comprising Group Captain Operations, Wing Commander Ops. Plans and myself to conferences in the Pentagon and RCAF HQ in Ottawa. We flew from Heathrow in a BOAC Stratocruiser to Washington in January '52, a memorable flight for two reasons: it was the first (and last) time I sat in a "downstairs bar" drinking on an aeroplane and Theodore McEvoy and I "took over" the aeroplane in mid-Atlantic!

About an hour after takeoff the Boss suggested we visit the "pub"; I thought he was joking, being unaware of the bar on the lower deck – a bit different to our aircraft, what? Our modest session was soon interrupted by one of the stewards: "Air Marshal McEvoy, the Captain requests the pleasure of your company on the flight deck". It transpired the Captain was on Mac's squadron flying Spitfires in the "Battle". About half an hour later the same steward returns: "Squadron Leader Conquer, the Navigating Officer would be glad if you would join him on the flight deck". Said Nav. Officer was, I then discover, at Shawbury with me in '45/46; after a brief recap on old times, he introduces me to his equipment, showing current chart position, and suggests I might like to take over for an hour while he has a rest. So there was Mac, thoroughly at home at the controls, me navigating (sort of) and the crew back in the bar. I often wondered what the hundred or so passengers would have felt had they known. Needless to say, the aeroplane flew itself on "George" on its preset course without much interference from we two – and the authorised crew were back in control long before our destination.

The Pentagon conference, USAF General Disosway in the chair, an RCAF Air Commodore, several staff of both Services and two French officers, plus our team, was an eye-opener for me. I had been in my job little more than six months, had been somewhat overawed by the mass of detail I was expected to know and now, I nearly had a fit – the Boss, asked by the Chairman to set the scene, stated our urgent need for more training spaces, and invited me to make the case. Many of you "old hands" will know the phrase "ring twitch" (sixpence/half-a-crown – remember?) – that was me now. As I made my way to the lectern, notes in my hand, I felt what I can only describe as a heaven-sent flash of intuition – and everything fell into place. For the very first time I realised I had control of my brief and, as I began, the entire picture of the RAF front line for the next ten years, all the training machine and the sequence of feeding through the necessary recruits, became clear in my mind. I have never been a particularly bright scholar, but that flash of total knowledge of my subject, coming as it did at that vital moment, was one of the most satisfying experiences of my career (I've often wondered about the "guiding light", the "guardian angel" – but in this case I think the credit goes to Smithy).

The result of the conference? Both pilot and navigator training spaces for the RAF in the States and Canada were considerably increased. Oh, and a nice compliment from General Disosway who told Mac that he was going to apply to have me transferred to his staff in the Pentagon (I wish!).

All comparisons are odious but one could hardly not be aware of the glaring differences between our MOD (Adastral or Whitehall) and the Pentagon. May I mention just one – the eating facilities. Of course at that time we still had rationing in the UK but, it was not only the food and drink range, it was the whole approach to providing a service. At one main restaurant in the Pentagon, the service area was a huge "horseshoe" of tables, laden with the widest variety of dishes one could want. For example:

Soups, prawns, crabs, smoked salmon, salads.
Fish, steaks, chops, curry, vegetables, rice dishes.
Puddings, pies, flans, fresh fruits.
Ice creams, assorted, by the bucket load.

I can't remember the price but a meal was certainly inexpensive. I do recall seeing one American officer carrying two trays (self-help of course) taking more than one (or two) portions from each section ending with enough ice cream to feed ten starving children! I assumed he was carrying one tray for himself and one for A.N. Other – but no – all for himself! One would never starve in the Pentagon.

On our third day, conference concluded, the team were invited to visit Wheelers Field to see the new F100 fighter, an enormous machine for a single-seater, or so it seemed to me. Following a brief display (beat-up) over the airfield, the Colonel commanding the Base instructed his squadron commander to give "Mac" a helmet. Squadron Commander: "You wish me to show the Air Marshal the cockpit, Sir?" "No, just give him a helmet. He can find all the bits for himself." "But, Sir!" This is where I must tell you a little about "Mac". Before the war he had a very nasty accident on a motorbike – he broke his back. (That was the story I was told; I believe others hold that his condition was due to a serious illness). The surgeons told him before the operation that his spine would never again be fully tractable – either they must fix it so that he could stand vertically, in which case he would be unable to adopt a normal seating posture, or they could fix it in the permanently "bent" position, where he could sit normally but never stand upright. His response: "Fix it so that I can fly again!" He then flew Spitfires throughout the war, unable to turn his head to watch his tail, so flew with mirrors strapped to his wrists for backward vision. And so, ever since then, he had walked permanently stooped forward, almost at a right angle. Now you can see this squadron commander's dilemma: how can the CO permit this old cripple to fly one of my brand new aeroplanes?

But the Colonel knew Mac of old, they had served and flown together – and he had already given Mac a thorough briefing on the F100 behind "closed doors". Mac took off and gave the boys a display they talked about for years afterward.

Mission completed in Washington, the group were flown to Ottowa for our planned liaison visit to RCAF HQ and to firm up details for the increase in pilot and navigator training facilities. Our transport? The good old "workhorse", the Dakota, courtesy of the RCAF. Whilst in Washington the weather had been damp and muggy, mild for January; on arrival in Ottawa the temperature was 30 below zero – after walking from aircraft dispersal to the Control Tower I could have snapped my ears off at the root!

We were soon ensconced in the Chateau Laurier in which the central heating system produced a comfortable summer temperature. Retiring to bed under two or three blankets, all windows tightly closed, the heat gradually rose, and rose, and rose – blankets were discarded, then sheets and finally pyjamas! The hotel staff were horrified to discover that I had thrown all the windows open in an attempt to cool down – the external temperature had gone from –30 to +15! 45 degrees increase overnight – the streets were awash!

After a day of conference on future training plans, some lavish entertainment (lobster as I'd never seen it!) and some more worthwhile shopping, the group returned to London to begin, in great haste, more conferences in Adastral and Whitehall to advance the essential expansion of the training machine and, thence, the front line.

Sometimes one receives an unexpected insight into the peculiarities of the career ladder in the Service. Soon after my return to Adastral I ran into a new arrival in the Manning (Policy) department – none other than Micky Martin, last seen in Cape Town five years before. "Hello, Sir". "Norman, I saw your recent substantive promotion, congratulations". "Thank you – good to see you again, Sir". "Why are you calling me Sir? They've taken my acting rank – we're both Squadron Leaders now". This was a man with two D.S.O.'s and three D.F.C.'s, who had commanded his squadron as a Wing Commander at the end of the war, still had that rank until recently, and now was back to the substantive rank of Squadron Leader. What on earth were they thinking about at these promotion boards?

However, it seems that someone finally got his finger out not long after this: over the next 10 years, Micky Martin was promoted five times at successive appointments, attaining the rank of Air Marshal in a top NATO post and awarded a "K". So when we next met my emphasis on the "Sir" raised a big guffaw.

One of the lasting memories from my tour in Adastral is of the Globe – a tiny pub in Covent Garden, right opposite the main doors of the Opera House. I lunched there daily for over two years – always an enjoyable two course simple meal. Apart from the food, there was also the pleasure of good company, which was virtually unchanging day by day, and numbered a maximum of twelve. The proprietor had adopted a unique charging system which ensured the regular attendance of his customers: the cost of your meal depended solely on the length of your "membership"! For example, I paid 2/9d for my lunch for the whole of my stay in Adastral; one delightful chap at my table – the local Lloyds Bank manager – had been eating there since before the war and he paid 1/3d; the most recent "recruit" when I left early in 1954 paid 4/3d. I never did quite understand the economics of that system but it certainly resulted in many happy regular customers!

(N.B. Whilst on the subject of pub lunches, such memories return whenever the Government puts out phoney figures on the rate of *inflation* – a two-course cooked lunch in Dowlings, in Leadenhall Market, (1938) 11d = say 5p; ditto in the Globe, Covent Garden, (1951–54) 2/9d = 14p; similar today (2004) at my local £10.00! Inflation in 66 years 20,000%, in 50 years 7100%).

Fearful of the possibility of getting totally out of touch with the flying business (flying a desk is very necessary for some, especially in planning the flying of others, but one can very quickly get out of practice – and I hadn't been in a flying appointment now for over three years), I asked the boss for some "aviation leave". I had not been totally out of touch recently – local flying in Chipmunks, Proctors and Ansons from Hendon, Redhill and Hornchurch – but I needed a return to some productive crew work if possible.

What about Coastal Command – long flights to get back the "hang of it"? An attachment to 201 Squadron, Pembroke Dock, flying Sunderlands, was the answer. First, in January '53, two typical Coastal sorties – rendezvous with H.M. Ships in the Atlantic – provided some good navigation refresher work. Then a second attachment 3 months later provided not only a few hours air activity but also a delightful 3 days in Gibraltar – always a favourite. On our return to P.D., there was a panic call for me to return to work pronto and the Squadron Commander, Sqn. Ldr. McCready, flew me back to land on the Thames at Chatham, most convenient!

On return to the office my immediate question "What's the panic?" The Air Staff require your comments urgently on this paper! Now I must be a bit careful here because "this paper" was on the subject of "The Manning of the V-Force" and had been produced by a "think-tank" directed by an old adversary of mine, a certain Group Captain who shall be nameless. The proposals therein were, not to put too fine a point on it, the most ludicrous ever in my experience – either before or since. Based upon the experience considered necessary to fly one of these "big beasts", it was seriously suggested that all captains of "V" bombers should be squadron leaders; two aircraft should form a section to be commanded by a senior squadron leader, two sections (i.e. 4 aircraft) to form a flight to be commanded by a wing commander, two flights to form a squadron to be commanded by a group captain. "So, would the Station Commander be an Air Marshal?" I ask.

Bearing in mind that a very large force of "Vs" – Valiants, Victors and Vulcans – was to be built up over the next 5/6 years, where on earth did these "air staffers" think all these senior officers were to come from? With the approval of the Director General of Manning, and supported by the Air Secretary no less, I collected a small team from "Establishments", "Aircrew Postings", "Promotion Board" and "Finance" and conferred in Whitehall with the authors of this infamous paper. We pointed out in no uncertain manner that the number of active pilots with the experience and seniority suggested just did not exist: we could grant numerous "acting ranks", not only one rank but two ranks above substantive, but how would the grant of such acting promotions increase their *experience*? Point taken, paper cancelled! Five years hence we were feeding young pilots direct from basic training to Operational Conversion Units on V-bombers! And why not? It was only another aeroplane after all.

The incidence of that paper was a typical example of the battle we, in the Manning departments, constantly fought with the Air Staff behind the scenes – to get Manning Planning in the forefront of all Operational Planning. Length of flying training courses, expansion of Flying Training Command schools in time, training wastage rates (sometimes in excess of 50%!), recruitment and selection problems, all needed to be synchronised if we were to get anywhere near the huge and rapid expansion of the front line then planned. This was not, of course, a problem peculiar to that time in the '50s or, for that matter, solely for the RAF. It must be a principle applicable to all military planning for all forces in any age.

The above arguments led to the production of another Air Staff paper, this time thoroughly endorsed by all the Manning departments: subject "National Pilot Training". Why should all three Services operate their own pilot training schools, in addition to which there were separate civilian schools for the training of airline pilots? Would it not make sense to have one *National* flying training organisation, syphoning off pupils at the "wings" stage for their selected operational training in the Services and the Airlines? Of course – but there must have been some very powerful self-interests affected – the paper dropped out of sight – a lead balloon!

If the reader thinks that "stress" is just a modern sickness affecting the workshy, I have news for you! Two and a half years in the Manning Plans (Air) seat had got to me and I was feeling "punch drunk". Solution? A solo fortnight in Jersey, flown there by Anson from Hornchurch, courtesy of Home Command Communications Flight. In that two weeks I walked the whole circumference of the island – take my tip, that's a wonderful tonic and clears the head a treat!

So, my final gambit in Adastral House: now we are recruiting nearly 5000 a year for pilot training, what about *my* pilot's course? I have applied and re-applied umpteen times since I was first recommended for it in 1944 and have been fobbed off every time for different reasons. Sorry again, no! But why – you gave it to Sismore at the end of his tour here? Ah yes, but he was 30 then – the cut off age is 31 – and you're now 32. So that's it – I've had it! (Some 10 years later there was a sequel to this saga; it greatly amused two pilots but infuriated me!)

Well if I'm not to be allowed to retrain, I'd like a Squadron. What about my old Squadron – 23? But that's a fighter squadron – and you're a navigator. Exactly, but it's a Javelin squadron – two-seater pursuit ships – right up my alley! Sorry old son, the present C.O is a navigator and we can't allow that twice running; tell you what, would you like 527 Squadron, Central Signals Establishment, Watton – very busy outfit – 18 aeroplanes? Splendid. (When I eventually get there I'm taking over from another navigator!)

CHAPTER SEVENTEEN

Interval

I purposely have not interrupted the Adastral House saga to mention family detail but, before pressing on to events at Watton, I feel compelled to record our two years sojourn in the most delightful property in New Malden, Surrey. We had been grateful for temporary accommodation at my family home in Upminster but some three months after my posting to Air Ministry, I was offered another hiring – this time a detached house on a corner right opposite a small public park; the road named, fairly obviously, Park View.

Not only was the location pleasant but extremely convenient for all our needs: five minutes walk from the railway station (16 minutes to Waterloo, 4 trains an hour), in easy reach of shops and a good primary school nearby for my daughter, then aged four and a half. Frankly, we thought we could never be so fortunate again, yet, when my posting to Watton came up I was informed that, as a squadron commander, I would be entitled to ex-officio married quarters on the station. And those pre-war OMQs were, and still are in my opinion, the peak of luxury for the limited few – only ten per station.

Mention of the New Malden to Waterloo trains brings to mind one of the horrors of modern day commuting. Though I had regularly commuted to an office in London from Upminster during the immediate pre-war years, I had not previously experienced the intolerable bad manners and selfishness which now was so much a part of that appalling method of travel. As a train neared a station, occupants for whom this was their destination would stand, collect belongings from the rack, and the person nearest the exit door would grab the handle in anticipation. As the train passed the near end of the platform, he (sometimes she) would throw open the door without regard for any prospective passengers standing too close; then, one after the other they would jump off whilst the train was still moving, sometimes crashing into a passenger who had jumped off from the next compartment, or even one who was waiting to board! On one visit to us in New Malden, my mother was almost decapitated in one such incident.

Determined to help put a stop to this dangerous behaviour, I would attempt always to grab a seat nearest the exit door – sometimes when such a seat was unavailable, I would wait for the next train to be first into the carriage. On approaching destination, and disregarding standing passengers, I would grab the door handle and forcibly prevent any other from so doing. I would hold the door closed until the train stopped, then open it, sit back and signal "after you, *gentlemen*!" I put up with the stern looks and grunts from fellow passengers at first; eventually many of them (often the same people who travel at regular times) approved and actually thanked me for a contribution to safety.

Now, about to depart for Watton, I am told that I must first go to Swinderby for a short navigation refresher course. Is this really necessary I ask, citing my fairly recent "swans" on Sunderlands. Yes, it's policy, I'm told. Oh well, if it's *policy!* Just 20 hours or so on Varsities was certainly no hardship and I had to admit afterwards that it did wipe away some of the rust that had accumulated over the previous three or four years.

Other navigators on this course were going on to the "V Force" and so they were to undergo a "decompression" test – a physical check under high level low pressure conditions. "I must have a go at that," say I. "Not really necessary "at your age" (all of 33!)", quoth the instructor, "and anyway, you're not going on to 'V' bombers". "No, but I shall be engaged in high flying so I think I should take part". (Of all the stupid, idiotic . . . Didn't I learn the hard way many years ago that you should never volunteer for anything?)

I'm sitting in this damned cylinder at the standard pressure of 37,000 feet (with oxygen of course) when I begin to suffer the "chokes" – low pressure causing the lungs to clog up and impede the breathing. Panic – rapid descent to surface pressure (never mind the earache!) – and a very embarrassed squadron leader undergoing medical tests checking for lung damage. Though found not to have suffered unduly, I'm ordered to report to CME London (Central Medical Establishment) for checks and assessment as to future flying category (currently A3G1 = fit navigator flying anywhere in the world without restriction).

Now, if I lose that category, I lose the squadron! There is talk of downgrading me to A4G2 (limited, UK only) but I appeal. "If you do that, I lose my squadron and virtually my career. I shall not be on "V" bomber operations, required to maintain height at all costs, but on variable peacetime flying duties. Any explosive decompression at height (the fear in "chokes" cases) and I can make a panic descent to safe altitudes". (What a bit of foresight that was – it actually happened a year later). My plea was accepted by the Review Board Chairman and my current medical category retained. A note was added "Not recommended for the 'V Force'" – thank heavens for small mercies!

No. 527 Squadron, C.S.E. Watton March 1954– January 1956

So now – what was this Central Signals Establishment all about? C.S.E. Watton had two main elements: a research and development department for future signals and radar equipments and four squadrons forming the flying arm of 90 Group, Signals Command. Several flying roles covered test flying for the development and evaluation of current and new air and ground navigation equipments, the routine testing and calibration of all ground radars and Royal Navy signals equipment and some more highly classified roles not to be mentioned herein.

No. 527 Squadron was tasked in the "calibration" role, supplying aircraft as targets to enable specialist signals teams on the ground to calibrate the accuracy of ground radar equipments. Two main types of radars were involved:

a. *The NATO Early Warning System*. Some 28 radar stations were sited around the circumference of the British isles, on the Continent of Europe from North Cape to the eastern Mediterranean, and in Gibraltar, Malta and Cyprus. Their task was the detection and warning of possible enemy air attacks on the West.

b. *G.C.I, Units.* Ground Controlled Interception radars were situated in many areas of Fighter Command in the UK and in the areas of the 2nd and 4th Allied Tactical Air Forces in Germany and Italy. Their task was the control of defending fighters and directing them to intercept the enemy.

Three factors were needed to position any incoming aircraft or defending fighter: direction, height and range. Aircraft of 527 Squadron were flown in set patterns from the radar station outward, at varying heights, maintaining rigid course, speed and height, constantly recording position and time, thus enabling the ground crews to check the accuracy of their plots, both during the flights and by subsequent post-flight comparison with navigation logs.

When I joined the Squadron in March 1954 (following that refresher course at Swinderby) it comprised three flights: A Flight with 6 Lincolns, B Flight with 6 Varsities and C Flight with 6 Meteor NF11s and NF14s. The Lincolns and Varsities were employed on the calibration of the CH and CHL early warning stations and the Meteors on the GCI stations. The Varsities in addition served as transports to convey the ground parties to the applicable radar sites.

Johnny Tipton was my predecessor, a colleague from two previous postings; all tasks were 100% up-to-date so I was privileged to start with no "catching-up" problems. The handover was brief, consisting mainly in introductions to my Flight Commanders and other officers and the SNCOs responsible for the maintenance of the 18 aircraft – this was, numerically, the largest squadron in the Service at that time. Arthur Stroud commanded the Lincoln flight, John Dean the Varsities and Dick Ferre the Meteors. Serviceability was then, astonishingly, 100% and remained so almost the entire time of my command; such a creditable situation was a pride and joy, virtually unheard of in my previous experience and would be regarded I imagine with incredulity by most of today's commanders.

There were some who mocked us as "non-operational hacks', "routine dogsbodies" and many worse epithets applied to a mere adjunct to the fighting arms of the Service. Perhaps – but it didn't take me long to realise just how important (and enjoyable) was this "adjunct" to the efficient operation of those two essentials in our country's, and NATO's, defences – early warning and fighter control. All the early warning stations needed to be tested and calibrated at least once per year, the GCIs every six months. Thus we were regularly on detachment to other airfields, not only in UK but over much of Europe. What better way to enjoy a flying tour than on detachments to Orkney, Ireland, Germany, Gibraltar, Malta and Cyprus!

Naturally, the CO could not always participate in these "jollies". Whilst the organisation and the operation of the Squadron was well established, largely automatic and well controlled by three excellent flight commanders, plus a junior but fast-learning adjutant, there was of course the constant flow of "bumph" and the routine administration which occupied so much of a squadron commander's time; reports after every completed task, annual reports on all officers and personnel, normal station affairs (accommodation, messing, leaves, sickness, etc.), and, in the case of this squadron especially, planning and organising frequent detachments to all those places just mentioned.

A Station Commander's inspection of our airmen's barrack block I have good cause to remember. Air Commodore "Sandy" Rogers was a fair and easy-going boss, but he was also strict on detail – especially where airmen's welfare was concerned. On this occasion, a couple of the lads had legitimate moans about the state of some of their furnishings and there were problems in one of the bathrooms; complaints had not been attended to by my officer i.c. the block and of course the boss took me to task on the spot. Very foolishly I moaned that I'd been too busy running a flying machine to attend to such minor matters – and I got the "bollocking" I deserved! In the Station Commander's office afterward to which I was "invited": "Never forget that a squadron commander's responsibilities are total – covering every aspect of his men's welfare, as well as his operational commitments!" Well-deserved admonishment and words of advice which I never forgot – a worthwhile lesson in duty and manners!

And then, soon after this event, as if to remind me of an officer's duty to his Station as well as his Squadron (remember all those secondary duties I acquired at Lakenheath?), Sandy called me to the Officers Mess at noon, bought me a beer, and then "Conquer, I want you to take over as PMC (President of the Mess Committee)". Shock, horror! The task of PMC is no sinecure – one of the most important "do well" jobs on the station, continually under the eye of all the other officers, to say nothing of frequent VIP visitors. This time I told the boss I wouldn't invoke my earlier plea of "busy with flying responsibilities", much to his amusement thankfully. In fact I think I also actually said "Thank you, Sir"!

Perhaps before going on to describe some of the more important and enjoyable events of my two years with 527, I might mention a few incidents on the "downside", even embarrassing, worrysome and "should have been avoidable'. Soon after my arrival, Johnny Tipton not yet having evacuated our married quarters and therefore I am resident temporarily in the Mess, John Dean invited me to a cocktail party in his house to meet several of the officers and their wives. During the party I was chatting to some of the ladies when one bemoaned the lack of good looking young men on the Station (she was single, a WAAF officer). "You surprise me", I said, "there is one particularly handsome young pilot living in the Mess – tall, dark, named David". A few seconds ominous silence, then, from another lady in the group "That is my husband!" Whoops! Apparently, they actually lived in married quarters but had temporarily separated after a blazing row – because of his gallivanting. But how was I, a newcomer, to have known?

On joining my first squadron detachment, to Orkney on this occasion, John Dean and the crew invited me to join a planned visit to a local distillery. I had, until then, never touched whiskey, and was completely ignorant of the distillation process. During the rounds I was invited to sample a tot from a barrel; "This colourless liquid is early in the process and quite harmless" quoth our guide. In with both feet – it was moreish, so I drank that and then two more "samples" further through the process. Didn't feel a thing – until we hit the fresh air outside. I didn't feel much then either, except a BF in front of my lads! "Don't ever do that to me again" I moaned, quite unjustifiably.

I loved the Meteor – my first experience of jet flying. It was our custom to arrange a night flying programme once a month to ensure all crews were kept in night flying practice; necessary because it was the nature of our normal tasks to be limited to daylight flights. On this occasion I had all six Meteors serviceable but only five crews in the flight available to fly; we had no spare pilot so I suggested that the Flying Wing Adjutant, Brian Boundy, a qualified Meteor pilot, might care to join us and I would navigate. All six took off on a first sortie, some on circuits and bumps, some on cross-country, some on practice radar work. Brian and I did a couple of GCI interceptions and practice landings, then all crews reassembled in the crewroom for Met briefing for the second sortie.

The Met. forecast was gloomy: we had already found lowering cloud in the circuit when we landed and the forecast now was for total overcast at 1000 feet by the time we returned from a second sortie. The flight commander was in favour of cancelling but we had assisted landing aids and I could not accept that cloud at 1000 feet was too hazardous for landing, so it was "press on chaps". The forecast was accurate but all the other five landed without mishap. We seemed happy on the approach but on finals, just before reaching the runway, there was a loud "bang"; we touched down but did a "roller" to test all controls. Landing gear intact, flaps OK, all control surfaces working – let's try again. No problem this time, smooth landing, but a bit late and halfway down the runway; then, immediately "No brakes!" Up undercarriage, slide down on belly, into the overshoot, stop just short of hedge, leap out pdq!

Bags of panic, fire engine and ambulance soon on the scene, plus Wing Commander Flying and Station Commander. "Anyone hurt?" "No, Sir. Only the aeroplane!" In the Mess, tucking in to night-flying supper of bacon, sausages, eggs and chips, Brian Boundy was discussing the event with a couple of his chums; I couldn't help overhearing his remarks: "As soon as we touched down I realised we'd no brakes and then, plain as a pikestaff, I heard this angel voice say 'Up undercarriage!' I reacted to it immediately and as soon as we had stopped I heard this voice again 'Switch off, get out fast'. I switched off ignition and fuel, reached for the canopy toggle, but the canopy had already gone. Looked round for my navigator but he was gone too!" Too darned right, I had the top off and was 20 yards away whilst Brian was still thinking about it. First time I knew I had a voice like an angel!

Embedded in the undercarriage and wing root were leaves and twigs. The following morning we observed the origin of that woodwork: some three feet of the tops of several trees just off the end of the runway had been shaved clean – it became known as "Conquer's haircut"! The collision had sheared the brake cable – hence no brakes. There was some suspicion of carelessness and, although I was convinced that no blame could be attached to the pilot, it looked as though a court of inquiry could lay blame on the Squadron i.e. on me. But luck was with the devil on this occasion. I borrowed a theodolite and measured the angle of those tree tops from the end of the runway – it was 13 degrees, and airfield rules stipulated there should be no obstruction at either end of a runway exceeding 11 degrees. Had that ruling been observed, and those trees pruned accordingly, we would not have hit them and there would have been no accident. Yours truly exonerated – but I never did discover whether anyone else carried the can.

Last of the "down-side" incidents, and by far the most worrying to occur during my tour at Watton, also concerned a Meteor – and its loss. Two crews of C Flight and their aircraft were on detachment to Ahlhorn, Germany, on GCI calibration flights. One of them, Sgt. Coleman the pilot, had flown several legs at varying heights, at night, all above cloud, and at the fringe of radar navigation cover. On the final leg, and unsure of exact position, he requested a "homing" – course to steer for base. He was instructed by the controller to "switch to Channel C-Charlie". This he did and was given a course of 090 – due east.

After steady descent to below cloud and failing to spot Ahlhorn, he again requested a homing; again he was given 090. After a further 10 minutes, including yet a further course 090, he was running very low on fuel. Twice more he appealed for position information or course and 090 was further repeated. Fuel now gone and engines spluttering he spotted what appeared to be an Army camp ahead, with sufficient grass for a belly landing, which he safely executed. Crew were uninjured but aircraft was a write-off. Turned out they had crossed the "iron curtain" and were in a Russian military base!

It is perhaps unnecessary for me to enlarge on the serious panic which ensued – at Ahlhorn, at Watton, at Headquarters RAF Germany, and at Air Ministry in London. (In Government circles too, I imagine – though I was not privy to the sparks at that level). Within minutes I was airborne with Dick Ferre to Ahlhorn to try to sort out 1. how we get the crew back 2. *can* we get the aeroplane back? 3. how the hell did it happen?

To cut a very long story brutally short: 1. we had the crew back in 24 hours. 2. we got the aeroplane back *eventually*, minus some of its equipment. 3. Ahlhorn's Channel "C" frequency differed from the aircraft's Channel "C" – the controller should have passed the frequency itself, not a button letter.

It seems that the pilot on "C" was actually speaking to a controller in PARIS, who further confused the issue by assuming the caller was an American aeroplane flying in from the Atlantic – obviously EAST was correct for him but it was disastrous for Sgt. Coleman and his aeroplane – and was not exactly good news for me!

My reader may think that several heads should have rolled following this incident. Fortunately, my crew was absolved, as by inference was I, as squadron commander. Blame should have been placed firmly on the shoulders of Air Traffic Control in my opinion but, as far as I was able to ascertain, no-one was punished and the whole incident was forgotten. (Except by me!)

Some three months after I took over the Squadron I received advance warnings of changes to come in our aircraft establishment. First, my Lincolns were to be withdrawn almost immediately and the C. & R. (Control and Reporting) calibration tasks were in future to be carried out by the Varsities alone; yet there would be no reduction in the operational task – the calibration programme was to continue unabated. Thinks: if we previously required 12 aeroplanes (Lincolns plus Varsities) to meet the C. & R. calibration task, how am I expected to achieve the same work volume with half those facilities? So, the first question to Group: what is to happen to my strength of aircrews and groundcrews? Well, all your A Flight personnel will be posted! So that means my B Flight personnel will henceforth have to *double* their flying hours/work time, does it? And I have to keep 6 Varsities serviceable whilst doubling their flying hours, is that so? Ah, I see the problem, saith the Staff man! Result – 50% of Lincoln air and ground crews can stay, short conversion courses will be arranged. Not an ideal solution but it sufficed for the next year, by when the second change was to happen.

The second change – the Meteors were to be replaced by Canberras in the spring of '55. With much higher speed than the Varsities and much longer endurance than the Meteors, this would allow a total revision of the method of calibration flying and technical crew operation at the radar sites.

Until then, the flying task had involved a "semi-spider's web" of tracks, centred on the Radar site and extending out at various heights to specified ranges. For example, assume a radar station on the east coast of, say, Lincolnshire; any enemy threat, and therefore the required radar coverage, would be in the arc from north-east, through east to southeast. Thus, tracks would be flown on, say, 045, 060, 075, 090, 105, 120 and 135, at 2000, 5000, 10,000 and 15,000 feet, out to perhaps 50 or 60 miles or until the "OK enough" call from the ground. Obviously, not all those "legs" would be required on any one sortie.

Now, with the onset of the Canberras, faster, higher and longer endurance flights enabled us to provide a regular daily method of position checking for all radars in the C. & R. role. The routes planned were dubbed the "North and South Milk Runs":-

a. *North*: Watton – Valley (Anglesey) – Stornoway (Outer Hebrides) – Stavanger (Norway) – Watton.

b. *South*: Watton – Scillies – Paris – Island of Sylt (Germany) – Watton.

These routes were to be flown daily, one morning, one afternoon, north and south alternating, each of about four hours duration. All these sorties were flown at high level, varying from 45,000 to 52,000 feet. Technical ground crews would still visit all sites periodically, both to assess the practicality of the new system and to ensure that the station's regular operators could make full use of those daily flights. Position calls were made frequently by pilots, navigators operating on continuous radar and radio fixing. Copy navigation logs were made available to stations on request. After two months experience of this new system it was proclaimed a success and preferable to the previous more cumbersome method. Calibration of the GCI units continued, employing Varsities for the low-level runs, Canberras for the high level.

It was whilst navigating one of the northern "milk runs" that I experienced for the first time the phenomenon known as the "jet stream". We turned short of Stavangar, about 100 miles east of John o'Groates, heading south for base, height 52,000 feet; radar fixing was poor and shortly faded altogether. R/T calls for fixes produced doubtful results – doubted by me, anyway. This uncertainty continued for 30/40 minutes by when it became clear that we were way off track to the east. A few minutes later, we pinpointed the island of Sylt – only some 200 miles out of our route! Plotting this result when we landed showed a Westerly wind well in excess of 200 knots! So even our sophisticated systems failed on that occasion to cope with the foibles of the weatherman.

One other Canberra incident deserves mention – remember the "skin-of-the-teeth" escape at the medical exam, the year before? Returning from Malta, 50,000 feet over the Med., a sudden loud *"Crack"* – the canopy split from top to bottom! I was about to emulate the submarine commander "dive, dive, dive" – quite unnecessary – young David Swift already had her on her nose, throttled right off and, after barely a minute strap-hanging, we were straight and level at 10,000 feet. The wings and tail didn't come off, the engines didn't flame-out and in 10 minutes or so we had landed at the French Air Force base at Istres. The canopy had not blown, fortunately, and we did not suffer explosive decompression; this seemed to justify my appeal at the medical and my retention of full rating. Of course, the effect on my nervous system was another matter – the "sixpence/half a crown ring twitch" was most noticeable!

John Dean flew down to collect us the next day with a new canopy and a fitter and the aeroplane was repaired and recovered within a couple of days.

By early 1955 it was becoming the "norm" that if something needed testing, if trials of a new idea or system were needed, 527 will handle it. Thus when Command hoped to extend the coverage and effectiveness of the "Gee" chains we were allocated the task. "Gee" was a very successful concept in its time: produced during the war, Top Secret for years, it gave navigators in aircraft fitted with the special gear an immediate fixing facility of high accuracy. When we first had it installed in our Mosquitos in 1943, the "magic box" was brought in a locked wagon, under guard, to the aircraft to be fitted just before takeoff – and then removed immediately on landing with similar tight security.

Three ground transmitters emitted pulses which could be received by the aircraft receiver, which gave simple readings for plotting on special charts. In good areas of coverage and in the right height brackets, position accuracy could be to within yards close in, reducing to a mile or two at longer ranges. The main advantages were speed and accuracy, the main limitations were range and height.

By 1955, the system was rather "old hat', yet the "powers that be" wanted to improve it, especially at short range and in extensions over Scotland and Germany. These trials we conducted with both the Canberras and Varsities. I see from my logbook that I personally flew some 50 hours on eight sorties on these trials alone which was certainly less than 10% of the total effort expended. I take leave to doubt whether it was worth it as that aid was soon superseded by more sophisticated computerised systems.

One other trial proved very worthwhile. I was allocated the task of launching the first BBC airborne television trials. One of my Varsities was modified to contain special TV cameras/transmitters to link with ground broadcasting stations. A crew of technicians was drafted in, for whom we provided living and working accommodation; they were given daily access to "their" aeroplane. I appointed John Dean, O.C.B Flight, to be their "regular" pilot, and they conducted several sorties until they proclaimed their equipment to be working satisfactorily. We then welcomed Raymond Baxter who was to be the first airborne BBC commentator. The two programmes which he devised were then broadcast and, on 28th August 1955, viewers caught their first sight of television pictures from the air of Buckingham Palace, the Houses of Parliament et al. Today, when TV stations broadcast news worldwide and we receive pictures from beneath the sea and from space, it is hard to realise that airborne TV is still barely 50 years old!

So, whilst all this aviating was going on, interspersed by "jollies" to Gibraltar, Malta, Cyprus, Idris, Castel Benito, even Blida (Algiers again!), what about a few words on the domestic front. After all, there was still the family to consider. First I must say again that living in one of those pre-war married quarters was extremely pleasant. They were spacious, comfortably furnished, with garden and garage and, of course, so convenient for all aspects of service life. But then, there is the rub – the one obvious disadvantage for the family, though not for yours truly, was living, literally, on the job! It was absolutely essential that a squadron commander, and his flight commanders, be constantly available – living miles away off the station was just not acceptable. That had been the main problem with my Mildenhall posting, being a flight commander yet living up to 20 miles away from the squadron.

However, being now PMC, it was also necessary that I could be "on hand', at least most of the time, to control and assist all the normal Mess activities. I do not intend to dwell at length on the many functions we enjoyed during my two years there but perhaps just one event merits a few words. Our Summer Ball in '55 was a most joyful occasion. The four squadrons each had a marquee in which they developed their special themes: one was "Wild West", one a "barn dance", one had a "space" theme (with two barmen in home-made spacesuits), and one "aboard ship" (the Royal Navy, of course). My wife had developed a passion for flower arranging and made the several table arrangements in the Mess itself. One notable event of the evening: our delightful, rather elderly, and somewhat forgetful head "boffin" came in his immaculate evening dress (all the officers were in messkit of course) and in big brown boots; he didn't live it down for weeks!

So, do things never go wrong in the Conquer household? Well, yes, they do I regret to say – at least occasionally! My daughter was kept in bed with a sore throat – then the MO thought it was tonsillitis – then when her temperature rose to an impossible height she was taken in to Ely Hospital. It transpired that she had two cancerous growths in her neck (benign, thankfully) which had to be cut out. Twenty-four hours later I succumbed to the same thing (but one only) and after the op. found myself in the next ward to my daughter. The medics were never able to diagnose the precise cause of this peculiar affliction but we both still have the neck scars to prove it.

And then my beautiful English bull terrier (tricolour), the instigator and victor of several fights (he was jumped on by a terrier when he was a puppy and never forgave other canines – yet he loved cats and slept with them in his kennel) happened to pick the wrong one for once. He never recovered from the resulting liver damage.

There is really so much more to tell of what was really one of the highlights of my RAF career – Watton – but too many anecdotes spoil the message (or something!). So now we move on – I have been posted to Staff College, Bracknell to attend No. 46 Course in 1956. What is in store for us in the way of accommodation for the next year, we wonder.

CHAPTER EIGHTEEN

RAF Staff College, Bracknell – No. 46 Course

In my time there were two Colleges established for the advanced training of officers likely to be heading for promotion to the higher ranks of the Service: the Flying College at Manby, Lincolnshire and the Staff College at Bracknell, Berkshire. The former was solely for officers of the General Duties (Flying) Branch, most of them likely to remain in the senior appointments of the operational flying roles; the latter was for officers of all Branches plus some officers from the other Services and the Allied Air Forces.

The "raison d'etre" of the Royal Air Force is to fly operational aeroplanes – surely a statement of the obvious. Thus G.D., i.e. aircrew, officers will naturally be promoted to many more senior appointments than officers of the other branches – they will command all squadrons, most stations, thence to Groups and Commands, culminating in the most senior appointments in the Ministry. Yet there are many technical and administrative senior appointments which need a flow of officers from those other Branches to fill them, hence the Bracknell courses comprised members from all the branches and Services.

Thus, No. 46 Course at Bracknell comprised:

>   G.D. Branch   57
>   Technical Branch   9
>   (Engineers, Signals, Armament)
>   Equipment   3

Education	3
Secretarial	1
Medical	1
RAF Regiment	1
Army	4
Royal Navy	2
Royal Marine	1
Civil Service	3
Royal Canadian AF	2
Royal Australian AF	1
Royal New Zealand AF	2
Royal Rhodesian AF	2
USAF	4

Footnote: From the late 40s to the 60s there was also a second RAF Staff College at Andover but then the two were amalgamated. Even more recently, the Staff Colleges of all three Services have been amalgamated. See further reference to this in Chapter 20)

Naturally, this integration was common to all these annual courses, leading to many international friendships and clearing the way for future co-operation in joint activities – especially NATO. From my own subsequent experiences, (very limited compared to some of the other students on that course), I cannot emphasise enough how valuable were these courses in shaping our subsequent careers, in grooming us for responsibilities to come.

As at Shawbury ("So you thought you knew how to navigate" – remember?) so now – "So you thought you knew how to "think", "write", "compose", "reason", "argue", "persuade" eh? Well now you'll learn how it's really done". The first term was back to basics – and very wise too; it really is surprising how much of one's basic education had slipped away by the age of 35. I'm often now asked whether I went to University – yes, I did, this was IT.

Second term saw discussions, exercises and lectures on operational matters of all sorts, fighter and bomber phases, army and navy co-operation, joint operations; especially how to disseminate the bones of a problem, appreciate cause and effect, determine courses of action with likely effects, then learn from results – in short learn how to prosecute a war!

The third and last term was devoted to the study of real cases, future plans, the nuclear threat and counter-measures, all the most secret stuff. Frightening, by no means everyone's favourite subjects, but that's what the serious business is about.

Before recounting some of the more interesting and amusing of the travels and events of that year, how was I going to sort out family affairs when, once again, there was no chance whatsoever of accommodation at the College? A visit to Air Ministry (Personnel) led to the discovery of a possible hiring available in Addlestone, little more than 10 miles from Bracknell. A semi-d., shades of Bury St. Edmunds, or a detached house as in New Malden? No, this time a detached bungalow backing on to council playing fields, with private drive and large gardens – sounds the stuff of dreams, doesn't it? Until you see the house! I will not attempt a detailed description – let's just say that Joan and I dubbed it "Deep Depression Villa'!

As we had learned many times previously, beggars can't be choosers, and anyway it's only for a year. The bungalow was very dark, much in need of redecoration and the furniture was, shall I say, basic. We signed up for the inventory, to discover thereon a most unusual item – a cat! It was fat, lazy, named "Churdles", and it was unable to "miaow" – it grunted and barked – quite the most unlovable pet in all my experience.

So, the Addlestone house would not have been our ideal choice of home but then, as said already, where the Service made no housing provision for many of us, we counted our blessings – at least we had a comfortable and more-or-less modern temporary home within easy reach of the College, daughter's school and shops, I was now free to concentrate on "going back to my school'.

The course was divided into three Groups, each Group subdivided into Syndicates of six students. The staff comprised the Commandant (Air Vice-Marshal), Assistant Commandant (Air Commodore), three Group Captains directing the Groups and a Wing Commander directing each Syndicate – hence the term "Directing Staff"(DS). Daily work comprised lectures, by invited speakers, directing staff and students, written work from set exercises, syndicate discussion, study groups, play-acting, individual study (either in syndicate rooms or quarters). Study papers were criticised and assessed by DS and frequently offered for argument in syndicate discussion. Students were regularly asked for comment and criticism on all activities – could there possibly be a better way to apply maximum brain power to the benefit of Service development?

I have felt it important to lay special emphasis on the above because, in subsequent civilian life, I have often compared the efficiency of the RAF, in organisation and staff work, to the slackness, carelessness and inefficiency I have found in many other Government departments and civil firms, leading to absenteeism and the "couldn't care less" attitude of the workers. The fault lies with management – always!

I was very fortunate in my syndicate on 46 Course to have as DS the famous Neil Cameron – Marshal of the Royal Air Force Lord Cameron of Dalhousie, as he became later. Under the tutelage of such men who could possibly fail to reap maximum benefit from such training!

But was the course confined to study and work? By no means. Just about every sport facility was readily available, including free membership of that most prestigious Wentworth Golf Club. Several of us played there frequently but I have never really mastered the sport and my "rabbit" standard was most frustrating in the presence of so many "experts"!

However, by mid-year I discovered access to a sport even more to my liking – gliding! At RAF White Waltham, where I was first stationed as a sprog gunner on ground defence in 1940, we had a small gliding club with just four gliders, two side-by-side two-seaters and two single seaters (names escape me and records lost!). They were launched by cable, giving an initial takeoff height of about 6–800 feet and, in easy weather conditions, a circuit flight time of a couple of minutes, not very exciting one might think. Yet it was sometimes possible to achieve longer flights: although the geography of the area gave little chance of good lift and soaring conditions were never present in my limited experience (besides, those gliders were of too heavy construction for such luxury), I found that it was possible to gain extra height on takeoff by rougher treatment on the "stick". On one occasion I pulled almost vertical and attained 1200 feet which gave me a full five minutes on circuit. The instructor was not best pleased and gave me a rocket for putting undue strain on the winch! Despite that I succeeded in qualifying for my "C" certificate and thus regular solo flying when a machine was available.

Some of the course highlights were undoubtedly the several visits to military establishments at home and abroad. We visited the other Colleges at Cranwell, Andover, Camberley, Greenwich and Dartmouth, joining their students in discussions and exercises. Another visit to the Royal Navy at Weymouth gave us a chance to experience time at sea, some of us on a destroyer and some in a submarine; two of us, my mate Joe Saunders and I, even undertook a night recce of their port by canoe. How come? We had a great party that evening at the hotel on the front where we stayed the night and, strolling on to the beach at midnight, we found a row of pleasure boats chained up – that is all except one canoe, which had not been connected to the chain, with paddles therein. Temptation was too much – we launched and paddled off on calm seas all the way out to the RN docks, to the consternation of the officer of the watch on board the Destroyer in which we had sailed that day! Amazingly, no reporting action was taken! And we never did find the boat proprietor to pay for our "hire"!

The highlight of the course was undoubtedly the "Continental Tour" which took place at the end of the second term. The entire course travelled by coach to Dover, thence Channel crossing by ferry to Calais, coach to HQ AAFCE (Allied Air Forces Central Europe) at Fontainebleu, staying two nights in Paris, after which we divided into three parties visiting different Air Force bases: USAF at Bitburg, one of the RAF "Clutch" stations (at that time Laarbruch, Bruggen, Wildenrath and Geilenkirchen), and either the Belgian Air Force at Melsbroek or the Royal Netherlands Air Force at Eindhoven or Volkel. Much of our education at that time was taken up by the affairs of NATO, its organization, both operational and administrative, types and capabilities of aircraft, early warning and response times and much else concerning our readiness and operations during the so-called "cold war". In my case, this proved of vital importance in the light of my postings to come (see Chapters 19 and 21).

Two memories of that trip will remain with me for ever:

> a. An extremely rough crossing Dover–Calais. From the moment of boarding, the bar was full of thirsty officers, on

the loose for two hours. But within minutes of cast-off, several of my colleagues and I found our thirst had vanished and was being replaced by a distinctly nasty taste and "green in the gills". We dashed down to the bottom deck where there were long bunks of minimum comfort but also minimum "sway". There we spent the whole 90 minutes plus, until safe in harbour on t'other side. Amazingly, many of the gang remained upright in the bar throughout – strong stomachs maybe – but some were ill *after* the boat stopped rocking!

b. On the return journey we heard the news that we had invaded Egypt following the "nationalization" of the Suez Canal. I will not attempt to discuss here the merits or otherwise of the Suez venture – suffice it to say that the Americans didn't see eye to eye with Anthony Eden which led to our withdrawal and his resignation. One of my colleagues, Norman Hoad (with me at Watton, O.C. 192 Squadron, later Air Vice-Marshal Hoad), was almost puce with indignation over the invasion, whereas most of us were either neutral or, like me, in favour of forcing Nasser to re-open the Canal to international traffic. The long journey around the Cape was surely going to create havoc for east/west trade. Was Norman Hoad right? Certainly he was vindicated by the American stance and our withdrawal and eventually the Canal was re-opened – but who can say what would have been the outcome if the Suez invasion had continued?

Two final comments on the "Continental Tour". Journeying around Europe by coach is not, in my book, the ideal travel method, yet how else to convey 96 students plus half a dozen staff to hear and see so much of NATO in one week (with a day in Paris thrown in)? For reasons you will see in Chapter 20 this was the first of my SIX such tours from Bracknell!

Now we come to the end of No. 46 Course and 1956 and we await the dreaded news – where to now? I am one of the lucky ones – HQ No. 83 Group, Wahn, Cologne, as Group Navigation Officer – splendid, what's the catch? Only that your posting date is April '57 – so what do I do in the interval? Answer – remain at Bracknell – we'll find something to keep you occupied! Now I really didn't like the sound of that, I've had enough of "dogsbody" jobs in the past.

What do I do about our accommodation? You may stay in your Addlestone hiring until settled in Germany – well, thanks, that's one load off my mind. Now I have some suggestions:

> Let me go out to Wahn early; I could learn about the Group, its operational responsibilities and administration, visit all the Clutch stations, even sort out the problem of family accommodation. This would give me a "running start" into the new job. Negative.

> Send me on attachment to 201 Squadron, Pembroke Dock – I could get some more Sunderland navigation experience. Negative.

> Then attachment to my old Squadron – 527 at Watton? Negative.

Comes the final course interview with Group Director and Commandant – my course results are satisfactory and I am recommended as suitable for appointment to the D.S. in due course. Congratulations on appointment to 83 Group, sorry about the delay, but we have earmarked several jobs with which you could help us in the interim. Which leaves me short of breath and able to respond, merely, "Thank you, Sir". And so I am left to wonder over the Christmas period what might be in store for the next 3 months.

A week before the new course starts in January the Assistant Commandant sends for me to let me know he would hate to leave me unoccupied – he has a few essential jobs he needs attending to quite urgently. First, there are a couple of first term exercises which require revision following criticisms we made about them the previous year; clearly, I was just the chap to put them right! Two weeks of hard slog and the A.C. was delighted with them.

"Now, here is something right up your street Norman (on first name terms now!). You're a keen tennis player – the pavilion is in a pretty grotty state, as you rightly pointed out last season; perhaps you'd be good enough to arrange its renovation". A visit to the Station Commander (the College had its own station organisation with Squadron Leader CO, adjutant and staff, including "Works and Bricks") did not immediately raise a friendly welcome when I explained what I wanted. The civilian works staff were rather pushed at this time of year with the new arrivals, moves in and out of married quarters, etc. – couldn't it wait for three months? Well I thought so, but the A.C. did not. So, could W. & B. please supply tools and utilities, painting materials, and perhaps the Adj. could lend me the services of just one keen airman? A month later, allowing time out for bad weather, the pavilion was in much improved state and looking smart enough for the pending season's tournament.

Before departing from the Bracknell episode this time, I must just mention one of the most important and long-standing members of the College Staff – Head of the Drawing Office, Ben Irish. The production and reproduction of all the students' exercise papers, lecture notes, settings and stage requirements, plus a mass of photographic and presentation material, all these were on his plate with but two young assistants in the office/ studio. I still have on my study wall a framed pen and ink drawing of the College buildings which would be a credit to any modern artist. His work was always exemplary and he was a much admired senior member for many years. For several of the spare days during my extended stay I had the greatest pleasure in lending a hand in his daily commitments.

Apart from the work on revising the two first term exercises and then lending Ben Irish a hand with his essential artistry, the pavilion renovation work – a simple menial task out of keeping with staff work (in fact almost an insult to the course just completed) – proved that there had been no justification in refusing my alternative proposals for filling the gap between postings and so I felt it was down to me to rectify matters. I therefore took 21 days leave in February, and telephoned my successor on 527 Squadron who agreed to my visiting Watton and the Squadron. Flying Officer Vine, one of the Varsity pilots with whom I had flown previously on several occasions, managed to arrange a calibration task in Germany and booked me in as "second navigator".

We duly completed the calibration at Jever, then flew on to Wildenrath where, from the RAF Germany Communication Flight, I ascertained details of flights available to assist families in movement between Germany and the U.K. After a night stop there we flew on to Wahn; here I met Squadron Leader

Harry Coates, Officer Commanding HQ Unit, 83 Group, (soon to become a neighbour and close friend for many years), who informed me that my arrival on posting was expected in April, married quarters would be allocated but had to await the departure of my predecessor and his family, but that temporary accommodation would be available in a family hostel in Marienburg, Cologne. That night in the Mess, I met Squadron Leader Ray Hesselyn, my "predecessor to be" and learned that I was destined to be not only the Group Nav., but also the Group Planner. Time did not allow elaboration of that news and I was left to "ponder" at leisure as to what was entailed. No doubt, I should learn soon enough once I arrived "in post".

We returned to Watton the next morning, landing first at Marham to clear Customs with our "reasonable" load of booze. The last week of leave was devoted to the necessary preparations for departure from "Deep depression Villa".

CHAPTER NINETEEN

HQ No. 83 Group, Wahn, April 1957–May 1958

Arriving back at Wahn at the end of April, I reported to Group Captain Peter Powell (Group Captain Ops.) who, with Ray Hesselyn, explained the broad outline of my duties. It appeared that the Navigation job had limited scope but the tasks of Group Plans were more comprehensive. The main role of the Group was Early Warning and Defence against a possible attack from Russia with light bomber counter-attack if possible. The group controlled three of the "Clutch" stations – Bruggen, Wildenrath and Geilenkirchen – plus two stations of the Belgian Air Force. The Senior Air Staff Officer was a Belgian Colonel with several junior staff.

As a first step in familiarisation, Ray and I flew out to our three clutch stations where I was able to meet the three Wing Commanders Flying and some of the squadron commanders; it is always helpful to be able to put faces to voices when on the telephone. All seemed reasonably happy with their navigation and briefing facilities and with their allocated roles within the current plans. I was assured that if there were any complaints in future, I would be first to be told!

This is not the place to discuss operational plans, even though the secrecy factor is no longer applicable (30 years rule?). Suffice it to say that they were all fully formulated and in place (obviously!) but frequent test exercises were staged, particularly to check the "early warning" procedures. In fact, the first such practice was instigated from HQ 2nd ATAF (Allied Tactical Air

Force) in my first week on the job – my boss assured me it was not done for my personal trial or benefit!

There was always a "wash-up" after any such exercise. The AOC Air Vice-Marshal Harry Hogan and all concerned staff officers were present in the conference room and every aspect of the event was minutely examined so that necessary adjustments to the instructions could be made. On this, my first, such occasion the AOC was livid. The alert had been called at 4 a.m; he, the AOC, had awakened at his normal hour of 7 a.m. to discover the entire Group at "Readiness" – and he had not been called! The AOC was mad, so the SASO and the Group Captain Ops were mad, so what was the Squadron Leader Plans going to do about it? Just as well for Ray that he had already left the station. "I'm sorry, I really don't know Sir. I'll check our staff instructions forthwith Sir" quoth I. "It's alright Conquer, I realise you have only just taken over. Make sure it's put right for next time, will you." "Certainly Sir."

My memory as to the next moves in that saga have failed me, despite much head-banging and mind searching, but I am certain I made a firm note of that at the time. The rest of the meeting was largely "gobbledigook" to the brand new boy and I knew it was going to take me several weeks, nay months, to get familiar with all these planning aspects. Oh why could my appointment not have been just "Group Nav" as was at first intimated?! Anyway, just one month later came the next practice Alert – damn me, the AOC was not called yet again! This time there was no waiting for the "wash-up": I'm in the Ops Room at about 0700, a couple of hours after the alarm, when the Boss's ADC telephones: "AOC's office please Sir – immediately!". "Alright Conquer, explain yourself" "What Sir, you mean . . . ?" "That's exactly what I mean – why was I not called – again?!" Oh dear, oh dear, what had I done – or rather *not* done? Such a failure was inexcusable this time so I could but stutter an apology, hide my face in shame and wonder whether perhaps this was the end of my RAF career, I groped my way back into my office, grabbed all my notes, and discovered that the amendment I had typed for inclusion in the instructions was still in the file – and, of course, the op. order had not been amended. How could I have forgotten to process that amendment? That mystery remains until this day, but the orders were amended – with ASTERISKS – later that same day. I also added one further instruction to myself. "Group

Plans – immediately after receiving "alert" telephone AOC to ensure he is awake and active!"

I had always thought, following my brief attachment to 12 Group HQ in 1948, that a staff appointment at a Group HQ would virtually exclude flying – all liaison with units would be by telephone. Not so at 83 Group – here at Wahn we had a Communications Flight with several Meteors, a couple of Ansons, even a Chipmunk; pilots on the staff were always looking for chances to get airborne so I only had to ask to get lifts to any of our stations. And there is no better way to iron out problems than by personal contact, added to which the lads at squadron level always appreciated the chance to air their "moans" with someone "higher up the chain".

These frequent visits to stations, particularly those in the "clutch', paid many dividends. Friendships from past postings were rekindled and many new friendships resulted. Several of the Station Commanders and Squadron Commanders were past colleagues of mine or, as in one case, both a past and a future-to-be boss. Group Captain "Bobby" Burns, then commanding Wildenrath, was my CO at Charter Hall in 1945 (Part 1, page 000) and was destined within the year to be my CO again at Sundern – more news of that anon. Such visits were especially valuable when made during an active Command exercise: either the Wing Commander or Group Captain Operations would take me along so that we could both observe progress in the development of the exercise. Such experiences helped greatly when we were holding the post-exercise wash-up at HQ the next day.

This was the era of the "rapid reaction" requirement – when fighter pairs were held "at readiness" in special small hangars, with crews, fully rigged, on standby in the adjacent crew room, ready to go. The target reaction time, from that standby position to airborne, was two minutes!

So, whilst all this highly skilled military operations and planning was going on, what about my family – had I forgotten them? Well hardly – so, having presented some brief notes on "staff duties", let me return to the ever-present problem of accommodation. Within a couple of weeks of arriving, I had been able to arrange a flight back to UK to organize our move out of Addlestone and across the "ditch" to Cologne, where we were able to move into a pleasant small flat in the Marienburg guest house. This was really little more than two or three weeks in a hotel, because by that time I had been told that my predecessor and his family had returned to the UK and our married quarter in the Volkspark was ready for us. And what a super house it was; there was no doubt about it, the standard was much higher than any previous house in our experience at home. Here, in Germany, this house was rated as a Type IV, as befits the rank of Squadron Leader; yet it was easily the equivalent of a Station Commander's quarters in UK, listed as Type II.

Like most of those posted to Germany I imagine, one of my first thoughts on arrival was a car – a Mercedes, what else? In 1954 I had bought my first *new* car, a Morris Minor (only been on the waiting list for 8 years!). Anticipating the possibility of affording a somewhat better vehicle once in Cologne, I had sold the Minor just before leaving Addlestone. Now, I visited the Merc. dealers in Cologne to enquire about the new 190, a brand new model designed to supersede the 180. Yes, they could probably let me have one in about 6 months time – the enjoyment in test driving that machine was exceeded only by the knowledge that, as a member of RAF Germany, I could buy at 15% discount on the list price. The latter was approx. £850, so my Merc.190 would cost me £720. Makes you smile to think of it these days, doesn't it?

But what am I going to do about a car in the meantime? Well, Sir, how would you like this beautiful pre-war (1938) Mercedes 170 Coupe? All black leather upholstery, soft top, enormous bonnet, just like Goering used as a staff car? £150 – and we will buy it back from you when your new car arrives. Now I am really beginning to think my luck is in!

Until that 190 was 11 years old with 120,000 on the clock I only ever had one problem: that was when it was brand new, the day after it was delivered to my house in the Volkspark. The car was locked in my garage; one of the neighbours called and asked to see it; bursting with pride, I opened the garage door – but not the car. The door refused to respond to the key and remained resolutely shut. The rep. from the dealers arrived within the hour, asked me to turn my back, then used the classic car thief technique and drove it away. It was back an hour later – faulty door lock, easily replaced. Profuse apologies!

Looking back to those days, and despite my love of that 190, I have often thought about that 1938 Coupe with some nostalgia –

if it has been looked after it will be worth a fortune today! And talking of worth, the 190 was £720 new, I sold it after that 11 years for £1000!

This, my first experience in Germany (apart from that fleeting glimpse at Geilenkirchen during the Staff College Continental tour), left a number of impressions, some of which altered preconceived ideas. I had half expected hostile attitudes from their citizens – after all, it was only a dozen years since the war ended – and especially in Cologne, a city which suffered badly during the bomber offensive. Yes, there was the occasional cold stare but, by and large, we received a more friendly reception than I thought possible. I remember one particular evening when a party of half a dozen of us decided to try out a restaurant we had spotted on the way home. It was fairly late I suppose – around 10 p.m. – and they were just closing; rather half-heartedly, I thought, they agreed to stay open for us and, whilst waiting to place food orders, I requested a bottle of wine. It was brought to the table already opened and, whilst I had never before had the courage to do so in UK, told them to take it away and bring another, unopened. To the surprise of all (who had been a bit sceptical at my hasty action), the three waiters almost jumped to attention, dealt with the wine order correctly, and thereafter made us most welcome and served an excellent meal. When we left at about midnight, with much bowing and "auf wiedersehn", they begged us to come again. How strange!

Yet, even stranger: the annual Cologne celebration of "Rosen Montag", with its carnival atmosphere and parade of floats, bands and spectaculars, occurred shortly after that visit and many of us at Wahn were trying to arrange hire of upstairs rooms on the route to view the parade. The manager of said restaurant was only too pleased to offer twenty of us his flat above for the day, complete with waiter service as required. Yes, you're right – it was very good business sense on his part – many of us became regular customers thereafter.

One of the enduring memories of Cologne is the outstanding beauty of the Cathedral. We have all wondered at the miracle of the survival intact of our own St. Paul's through the London Blitz during the Battle of Britain; is it not even more of a miracle that Cologne Cathedral also survived without damage despite the massive bombardment inflicted on the city during the 1943/44 air offensive by the Allies? Having always been at one with the philosophy and tactics of squeezing the Nazi orange until the pips squeak, it was nevertheless a considerable relief to see that Cologne Cathedral escaped unhurt.

Another happy memory is our cruise up the Rhine from Cologne, with lunch at one of the numerous "castle" hotels abounding the river. Such a trip – one day, three days, a week – is a "must" for any visitor to the area.

My wife and I think with nostalgia of the rather splendid life we led in the Volkspark and what a contrast it was to the horrors of finding reasonable accommodation at most of my previous postings. There is no doubt that serving in RAF Germany, particularly for the family man, was luxury: the houses were spacious and well furnished, we had the services of a "daily", an excellent local school for the children run by the British Forces Education Service (BFES), and booze was ridiculously cheap – spirits at 7/- (35p!) a bottle.

And then holidays – leave was regularly granted when duties permitted (yet never once until my final year of service was I able to take my full annual entitlement!) and the whole of Western Europe was within easy reach by car, particularly via the Autobahn. These were the days before the arrival of Motorways in the UK and the German Autobahn system was a first experience of such fast motoring for us – the absence of any speed limit thereon was quite an eye-opener! The South of France, Switzerland, Austria, Italy – all were within a day's drive.

Also, in the Volkspark, it was good to be living in the midst of a group of colleagues and friends again, as we had enjoyed at Watton. Ronnie Noakes, our Padre, Group Captain "Robbie" Robinson (our SOA) and his wife Esmee, Harry Coates (OC Unit) and Gwen and many more with whom we formed lasting friendships.

This gives rise to thoughts of one of our best parties in the Mess at Wahn – the Summer Ball, Fancy Dress. Gwen Coates was a dab hand at the sewing machine and we spent many hilarious evenings designing our costumes. Gwen's was Latin American after the style of Carmen Miranda, complete with castanets; Harry was a Troubadour with guitar; I was a Chinaman, large circular hat, dangling moustache and most uncomfortable eye makeup; Joan wore a smock daubed with German road signs, UMLEITUNG (diversion) was prominently displayed across her buttocks!

It is early 1958 and rumours are beginning to circulate concerning a possible change of structure in our part of NATO so perhaps I should explain more about the then current setup. NATO Air Forces in Europe comprised the 2nd Allied Tactical Air Force and the 4th Allied Tactical Air Force. 2 ATAF controlled all British, Belgian and Dutch air forces, 4 ATAF controlled American, German (then in process of formation) and Italian air forces.

RAF Germany was the administrative HQ responsible for all the RAF stations; Belgian and Dutch stations were under national administration. 2 ATAF was the "controller" for all operations in the area and controlled all RAF, Belgian Air Force and Royal Netherlands Air Force squadrons. The RAF's No. 2 Group was responsible for RAF squadrons at Laarbruch, Gutersloh and Jever, plus the Dutch squadrons at Eindhoven and Volkel, with its HQ at Sundern; No. 83 Group controlled RAF squadrons at Geilenkirchen, Wildenrath and Bruggen, plus the Belgian squadrons at Melsbroek and Soosterberg.

It was now suggested that the establishment of two RAF Groups, with all their associated administration needs, was superfluous and that they be replaced by two much simpler control units directly under the ATAF. This would have the added saving of reducing the manning and logistic requirements of HQ RAF Germany, though the latter must remain, alongside HQ 2 ATAF at Rheindahlen Munchen Gladbach, to administer the RAF stations. The new "control units" were to be called No. 2 Tactical Operations Centre (2 TOC) at Sundern, a straight conversion from 2 Group, and No. 1 TOC at Goch in lieu of 83 Group. Hence one further saving – RAF Wahn would close and the station taken over, eventually, by the German Air Force. One further advantage of this reshaping would be that No. 1 TOC at Goch would be right alongside the main Type 80 radar early warning station at Uedem, north of Laarbruch, thus reducing the communication time, and thus the reaction time, between early warning and take-off!

It was not until March that we received confirmation of these changes and what it would mean for the personnel of the two Groups. Considering my luck in past postings I was dismayed at the probability of another move just after settling in at the Volkspark – perhaps to some far eastern post to which families were not invited? But no – whilst most of 83 Group chaps were off to form 1 TOC under Group Captain (now to be Air Commodore) Garvin, currently OC Laarbruch, Robbie Robinson and I were off to 2 TOC – Robbie as Group Captain Ops. and I (with acting promotion) as Wing Commander Plans, under Group Captain (now to be Air Commodore) Bobbie Burns, currently OC Wildenrath. (My promotion was a happy reassurance that Harry Hogan had not taken my alert "cock-up" too seriously after all).

A visit to Rheindahlen with Robbie soon confirmed the above and it was known that adequate married quarters were to be available for all involved. The effective date for the reorganisation was set for 1st May '58; I made a rapid flight to Northolt during April to arrange necessary uniform changes, flew to Gutersloh to visit Sundern (nearby) to arrange new quarters and we moved up, family complete, at the end of the month to a nice house at Sundern. When I think of how easily it all worked out on this occasion, it showed up all our previous moving problems in an even worse light.

No. 2 TOC, Sundern, April 1958–March 1960

The first few weeks were taken up by the transition – HQ 2 Group to become 2 TOC. Some Group personnel had already departed but key men were left to hand over, including Ops, Plans and Admin officers, some of whom were remaining on the TOC. As already mentioned, Bobbie Burns was the Commander, Robbie Robinson was Deputy Commander and Ops/Admin chief, Wg. Cdr. Ops of 2 Group, Lt. Col. Jan Flinterman, R. Neth. A.F. (of whom much more anon) was to remain with the TOC and I was Wg. Cdr. Plans. In addition Wg. Cdr. Ops had a staff of one Dutch major, two Dutch Lts. and (eventually) one German Lt. and Wg. Cdr. Plans had a staff of one Sqn. Ldr., one Flt. Lt. and two F/Os. This was a small staff, bearing in mind that our commitment was to be 24 hour watchkeeping, similar to the lines of the system we operated at Bicester some 26 years earlier.

The Unit was commanded by Sqn. Ldr. Harry Arden, ex-2 Gp, who was able to continue as before. He was responsible for all the accommodation, transport, supply and "works".

Daily "set-up" conferences in the early stages soon had the business operating smoothly. The centre of activity was the Ops.

Room, in which my first task was to set up the wall maps, covering the whole of northern Europe from UK and France in the west to Moscow and the Urals to the east, and from North Cape, Norway, to the Balkans. This was in fact just a repeat of my briefing room at Lakenheath and my 527 Squadron ops. room, although in the latter the main display was of radar stations, whereas in the others it was airfields and possible main targets, friend and potential foe. In addition, we had to instal a comprehensive communication system, linking the two TOCs, 2ATAF, 4ATAF, AFCENT plus the main radar early warning stations. We also needed to modify the existing station warning system, linking Duty Ops to all the officers on the station, both in their offices and married quarters.

Regularly we had to remind ourselves that we were in the forefront of any potential attack during the "Cold War", that our whole raison d'etre was to be the very first to initiate the alert and that all the preparations NATO had made for defence and counter attack depended totally on that alert. I think that then I felt a greater responsibility than at any other time in my service career.

Whilst at 83 Group, I had heard many stories about that ace Spitfire man who was W/C Ops at 2 Group, Jan Flinterman. When I arrived at Sundern, Jan was still in the final stage of the NATO Staff College course in Paris so the initial setup was begun in his absence, I confess that I was a little in awe of this man, or at least of the image of him that all the tales implied. How would we get on? Would he be so much more experienced and find me a bit of a novice in the serious business of this theatre? Also, how would he react to finding his 2 Group operations setup already in the course of revamping for 2 TOC?

He returned from Paris a couple of weeks later and I first saw him in one of the ops offices being greeted by his 2 Group chums, Major Harm Scheepstra spotted me and pulled me over to meet Jan. I can only tell you that I was profoundly impressed by him at that first meeting. I had heard and read of men with "presence", forceful character, an aura of power – this man had it, in abundance. I don't think I was ever quite so impressed in the presence of any other man, either in the services or anywhere else.

Perhaps the reader will not mind if I relate something of this man's career to date. Jan was just a year older than me; he was just 20 when the Germans invaded Holland, immediately started up a "fifth column", but when it got too hot realised that he could only get his revenge by escaping to fight. He got away on a fishing boat, went through France to Gib, reached UK early in '41 and immediately joined the RAF to train as a pilot. (He telephoned his mother who was now active in the resistance and told her he was learning to "ride a bike"!) In the final stages of his training at a Spitfire OTU in Scotland, he went to a local birthday party, danced with a girl twice and during the second dance stated firmly "I'm going to marry you!" She was already engaged to another but Marianne had fallen totally, followed Jan to Tangmere, where they were married in 1943.

Jan flew Spits on ops almost continuously for the rest of the war, at the end converted smartly on to Meteors, then returned to Holland, converted to the R.Neth. A.F and was immediately appointed to train his colleagues on Meteors and command their first jet squadron.

He was a natural sportsman, sailing from the cradle (like most Dutchmen), motor racing and rallying, twice winning the annual Tulip Rally, skiing – and still finding time to lead his fighter wing. This was my colleague at Sundern and a close personal friend until his death from cancer in 1995. I would like to enclose a copy of the speech I made at Jan's funeral service (see the Appendix) – I cannot think how better to express my regard for him.

Life on this tour was very different from any other. On permanent watch and instant readiness entailed a tight schedule of duties for us all. Either the Commander or his deputy was in immediate contact, day or night. The day was split into four watches: 0800-1300, 1300-1800, 1800-midnight, midnight-0800. One officer was on duty in the ops room permanently, with two others on immediate standby and three more at one hour's readiness. Three more were at three hours, one on leave. Immediate standby meant in the office or the Mess; at one hour meant in OMQ or perhaps on a short visit to nearby facilities; at three hours allowed for longer absences but in telephone contact.

On the face of it, this would appear to be very restricting – yet the Mess, where single officers lived, was only a few yards from the ops room and the OMQ for we marrieds was only a few hundred yards away. And being in the Mess or quarters was hardly an imposition.

Once the unit was set up and working smoothly, our duties

were not arduous. Maintaining routine contact with our masters, updating our intelligence data, sneeking some flying from our small comm. flight at nearby Gutersloh, writing reports, both operational and personal, all easily fitted in to our watch times. It was not long before Jan and I started to differ and I like to think we were both pleased to find that we could do so without rancour; our arguments were sometimes heated, yet we never "fell out" – in fact it always ended in laughter and actually deepened our friendship.

Barely a month after our arrival, Bobbie Burns sent for me and asked me if I would be prepared to take over as PMC. I could not fail to remind him of the Charter Hall incident and queried whether he thought he could trust someone who once didn't dress for dinner; he took it all in good part and said he thought I had grown up a bit since those days! The retiring PMC had been the W/C Plans in 2 Group so I suppose it was appropriate that I should be the one to take over. Bearing in mind the restricting nature of our job here, and that the initial planning work was in place, it was not a great hardship to take over the Mess. After all, the Committee members would do the work and I had but to supervise – and anyone who believes that lives in cuckooland! Still, I was pleased to take on again a job I enjoyed.

To the rear of the Mess, the grounds contained a small lake with, to one side, a peculiar iron construction which looked like a swimming pool slide but with two side rails rather than a centre board. My wondering as to its origin and purpose was soon to be answered. 2 Group staff had long since established an annual event known as "The Battle of the Murky Mere"! Jan was one of the prime movers of this circus so naturally it was to be continued. What a day it was! Several aircraft drop tanks declared u/s were kept in reserve and became canoes. Rival teams were formed – Ops, Plans and Unit all joined in. The competition was primarily to see who, launched in his "canoe" down the ramp (so that's what it was for!), could get the farthest distance across the lake. Sounds simple – until you know that the maximum depth of water was a foot to eighteen inches, beneath which was several feet of black mud.

The weight of one person in the canoe, plus frantic paddling on reaching the drink, sometimes attained ten yards. Put two in the canoe and you had two very filthy operators on ditching. Then of course, it was necessary for members of the other teams to try to prevent the one "in play" from getting very far; and so the end saw about a dozen extremely muddy men heading for the showers.

Jan was formally dressed as the Admiral of the Fleet, I dressed in an old made-up uniform as the PMC – Principal Marine Controller! All the ladies came to watch and rows of chairs were provided for the audience. All were warned once the "battle" had begun not to approach the banks of the lake. On that first occasion one of the wives ignored the warning in her excitement and before anyone could stop him, was promptly thrown in head first by one of the Dutch officers – and did that cause an uproar?! She had been freshly coiffed for the party which always followed in the evening and you can imagine her appearance as she emerged from the mud!

Several family events during our tour at Sundern are worth recording. British Forces Germany ran a fine hotel and skiing facility at Winterburg and so we were able to discover whether skiing was likely to be our "thing". Afraid not – we enjoyed a splendid week there, excellent food in great comfort, but neither Joan nor I had a "feel" for the sport. I did manage once to stay upright on the beginners slopes but even my expertise on roller skates (well, in my young days that is!) failed to translate into skill on skis. For daughter aged ten however it was a different story – she was a natural and I suspect that only the love of horses prevented her from following the sport later on.

It was here at Sundern that my daughter Gillian first got the riding "bug". A local riding school was possibly one of the best in Germany, with Herr Homrichhausen, a renowned horseman, as its leading instructor; he was, Gilly tells me, a harsh taskmaster. The facilities were also first class – large undercover arena, dressage training area, jump courses plus acres of practice grounds with access to miles of open country.

Early the following spring, I heard that one of my friends from our staff college course – Hans Neubroch – had been posted to the British High Commission in Berlin. I phoned to congratulate him on such an interesting appointment and he invited Joan and me to spend a long weekend with him there. That was an interesting car journey! Long queues at the famous "Checkpoint Charlie" took an hour to clear, then we were on our way up the autobahn to Berlin under the following warning: do not stop, divert or in any way cause suspicion – you will be under constant radar watch throughout by the Russians until you reach the Berlin entry point. So when a car rapidly overhauling us flashed lights, hooted and gestured for us to pull over, we did so with some trepidation. What had I done? I wasn't speeding, hadn't diverted or stopped to take photographs! It was one of the officers from the Charlie checkpoint – "Sir, you left your passport behind!" I shuddered, went puce with shame and probably said something like "Ta everso", or was it "Dankeschoen"?

We made it to Berlin without further ado and spent a most pleasant couple of days with the Neubrochs. Two particular memories remain of that weekend. We dined twice in the Commission mess, served by a very large woman of florid features who, it seemed, spoke no English or German, in fact she spoke not at all; she was Russian, as were all the staff – no doubt our members' rooms were bugged to boot. We went shopping, for a camera and film – AGFA, of course; whilst I was making my selection a Russian major stood alongside me, also examining some of the shop's wares, or so it seemed; actually, I think, he was examining me! Very disconcerting!

Some three months after our new organisation was established, we had the first full exercise of our war plans, beginning with a "no warning" alert – in the early hours, as always. This time I'm glad to say, there was no communications hang-up and all the required bodies were at their war positions within minutes. It was a full 48 hours exercise, involving fighter scrambles and subsequent recce and attack missions. It was a relief to know that our control machinery came up to scratch, as did the other Command components, and the exercise was declared a success, subject to some tightening up of a few procedures at the "sharp end".

It is worth saying at this stage, I think, that co-operation between the British, Dutch and Belgian forces was first class; we all worked as one Service and there was never any doubt in my mind that the whole NATO organisation was well devised and managed. Today, with the prospect of EU Forces, so called, working virtually in competition with NATO Forces, it is my view that disaster threatens – and many of my erstwhile colleagues of the early post-war years will agree, I'm sure.

Towards the end of '58, the "Boss" received a signal from Command HQ – "Why has Wg. Cdr. Conquer not yet attended the NATO Special Weapons Course? He is booked on No. 42

Course at Oberammergau on 14th October. Please confirm". I had not yet done so because it had never been mentioned when I was appointed to this job – yet as a planner/operator involved in possible nuclear strike operations I suppose one might have considered it part of the "job spec". I asked whether any of the other officers here had been on this course: well, Jan covered the subject at the NATO Staff College, of course, but none of the others had done so. I requested two more places on the course, therefore, one for my team and one for a member of Jan's team.

The course was for 10 days – Oberammergau is a beautiful spot – can we take our wives? Certainly – accommodation at the American camp there arranged. Splendid – so all three of us, with wives, motored down and enjoyed a holiday in that lovely corner of Germany/Austria/Switzerland. The Course content? Terribly hush-hush – six half-days of lectures plus a couple of exercise papers, leaving plenty of spare time to tour the area. Looking back on it, this was rather more of a "perk" than an operational necessity, a most welcome break from the daily watch grind at Sundern.

So, back to lighter topics. What about leave? After several months of confinement to the duty watch programme, the mind turns to thoughts of a holiday. There has been much talk of camping: now we're not thinking of the little ridge tent in which I spent many days with chums in our 'teens – we are introduced to the "joys" of the 12' x 10' mini-marquee, with sectioned bedroom, folding canvas beds and mattresses, kitchen cookers etc. etc., all folded for carriage on roof rack. Austria and Italy have well organised camping sites, we are told, with proper loos and shower facilities. So, we lash out on all the equipment and give it a go.

On our first night in Austria it rains; the tent is inundated. "Didn't you dig a soakaway round your tent before dark?" asks a neighbour. So next day I buy a spade – neither Joan nor Gilly thought much of that chore! So, on to Italy: three glorious days camped on the beach – on top of a ridge this time – near Pisa. Then it rained, and rained, and rained – a thunder cloud, a large CuNimb, circled the spot for three days. In the end we closed the tent up and moved into a B. and B. for a couple of days, then finally packed up a soaking wet tent and equipment to move across to Marina di Massa near Venice. Here we met up with Robbie and Esmee: they had parked too near the sea and were flooded; we camped unknowingly in the midst of a "musical" group, who played pop music fortissimo for 18 hours a day. On the third day the camp loos and showers were u/s.

On arrival back at Sundern "Anyone want to buy a beautiful tent and all this elaborate gear?"

Two events are now occupying much attention at the TOC. It is AOC's inspection time and, though that is largely a matter for the OC Unit and does not directly concern the other nationalities, it does require all sections to be on their toes, especially the PMC! Air Marshal Sid Ubee, RAF Germany Chief, is a most charming gentleman and finds no serious fault with our excellent facilities at Sundern. Meeting officers and their ladies at tea in the afternoon in the Mess, he is entranced by Jimmy Walton's gorgeous tiny daughter and picks her up; now Sid had lost an eye and kept the socket covered by a black patch – "Where yo' udder eye?" questions the child, much to the amusement of Sid and all the lookers-on.

The second, rather more important event, is the inauguration of the German Air Force's 21st Geschwader (squadron) at Ahlhorn, just to the north of Sundern-bei-Gutersloh. As mentioned earlier, the GAF is beginning to reform after the elimination of the Luftwaffe at the end of the war, and this is the first operational fighter squadron to appear. Naturally, this is a big event in the German (and the NATO) calendar, so there is to be full ceremonial with representation by all interested parties, from the German Premier, top brass from all NATO members, down to we minions at station level. Bobby Burns asks Jan and me to represent our Unit. The weather turns sour so the ceremony is held in a hangar: it begins with a march past by German troops, led by the traditional "oompa-oompa" band and a dozen or more standard bearers. I become aware suddenly that Jan is straining forward in his seat, rigid and red in the face – "Look at the bastards, they're at it again!" in a furious whisper. It is important to understand that this was only 13 years after the end of the war in which the Dutch had suffered most horrendously at the hands of the Germans. Some of Jan's family and many of his friends were captured, tortured and murdered by the Nazis and the sight of this resurgence was just too much for Jan to stomach, I took his arm and we promptly left the arena and motored slowly back to Sundern.

At about this time Exercise "Royal Flush" took place –

designed to test principally the Command's photographic reconnaissance skills. Several squadrons were involved, one at each of three stations under 2 TOC control – Wildenrath, Eindhoven and Jever. 2 ATAF wanted two of our officers to attend the latter two as observers (they would send an observer to Wildenrath), so Jan went to Eindhoven, I to Jever. It was a particular pleasure for me on this occasion to be at the "sharp end" with all the lads on Canberras – shades of 527 and Watton. The recce results achieved on this exercise were, as I remember it, excellent and considered the best ever; the other roles, fighter defence and strike, also participated, achieving intense effort by the whole 2 ATAF machine.

At Jever for the whole two-day exercise, I was not surprised that the Mess was "dead" that first evening – no-one was going to "indulge" during such intense activity. So I went to the camp cinema, a rare event for me! The film? "The Fly", never forgotten it – the most dramatic and astonishing film ending I've ever seen. I gather that a recent re-make is nowhere near as good but if you haven't seen the original and get the chance – just do not miss it!

I mentioned earlier that Jan was a born sailor. The British Forces Germany were keen on sailing as a sport and in the final stages of the war "sequestered" (to use a polite word) numerous boats from various sources for our use. Several of these – "Stars", sloops with 30 sq. mtrs. of sail – were established in a small lagoon on the Steinhudermeer, a large lake barely 50 miles from Sundern. I prevailed on Jan to teach me the art one weekend – and that was it, I was hooked! Subsequently, I spent a few hours on several weekends until, when I felt I really had the hang of it, Jan suggested that we do some real sailing. The Army ran a big sailing club at Kiel, with a dozen four-berth 50-sq.mtr. yachts, no engines, plus two 100 sq. 6-berth, powered, all-mod-cons. ketches, beautiful boats, all of them. Jan and I borrowed one of the sloops and spent a couple of days out of Kiel, in which he taught me enough to give me the confidence to "go solo".

They ran weekly courses for all the troops and airmen in Germany and so, at Jan's suggestion, I booked in for such a course a couple of months later. We spent one day on lectures and practical demonstrations and dry practices – sail hoisting and trimming, boat husbandry – then two days of local sailing, then three days on a mini-Baltic-cruise, each boat carrying three pupils with an instructor. Afterwards: "Now, what about these

100-squares, I ask". "They're for *real* sailors" I'm told, "You have to have a 'Baltic Mate's ticket' to sail those!" (Refer to subsequent events in Chapter 21).

All good things come to an end. Jan has been posted back to Holland to be Chief of Air Safety at their Ministry and, in early 1960, I am told to prepare for return to Bracknell on the D.S.

So, a final anecdote about Sundern: I am required to be "dined out", as is customary. A feature of such dinners is that the departee is required to "sing for his supper" and it has also become the habit for him to mount the table for his speech, prompted by shouts of "up, up, up!" But a recent visitor, an Air Commodore whom I shall not name, had lambasted that custom as "degrading, unbecoming in an Officers Mess, suitable only in pubs with sawdust on the floor!" So, when my turn came at the end of my outgoing dinner, and especially as the retiring PMC, I made arrangements to ensure that my colleagues were not disappointed. I had arranged an ample supply of sawdust, in buckets, so, to the anticipated cries of "up, up, up" I called "Mr. Vice, if you please" – whereupon Mr. Vice circled the room spreading sawdust; only *then* did I climb up onto the table for my short speech! And my cheerful boss Bobby Burns applauded with the rest.

CHAPTER TWENTY

RAF Staff College, Bracknell, April 1960–March 1963

In contrast to some of our previous appointments, family accommodation at both Wahn and Sundern had been superb. During the first part of the latter tour we had been allocated a small house designated Type 5 i.e. for junior officers. Nothing wrong with that, suited us just fine. But early in '59, some more junior officers had been posted in and a senior officer had been posted out so we were asked to move – into a Type 3 "palace". I should say NO? But now we are on our way again I'm wondering – is this going to spoil us for whatever might be available on our return to Bracknell?

I needn't have worried – no more "deep depression villa" this time! Not a *student* this time – I'm posted to the Directing Staff (DS) and so merit a married quarter on the station – and a very nice Type 4 it is too!

I believe I have covered adequately in Chapter 18 the organisation, the Course structure and content and the raison d'etre of the College. Nothing has changed in the meantime, of course, and I am very much looking forward to the challenge of being a syndicate DS. But first, a few words about our return from Germany.

I expect you can imagine the scene – car packed to the gills, barely space for wife and daughter despite the roomy Merc. 190, roof rack piled high, last minute purchases of booze and cigs., car still bearing RAF Germany number plates. Customs at Dover – "Anything to declare, Sir?" The only possible dutiable items are clearly displayed in the boot – nothing to declare other than those. "Would you mind emptying the boot, Sir?" "Thank you, now could you please unload the roof rack, Sir?" "And finally could the family move over there while we examine the contents of the car, Sir?" By this time the "Sir" strikes me as an insult not a politeness and I get stroppy. I stride off to find this man's boss and kick someone's a . . . ! Waste of time and temper – so now no-one is prepared to lend a hand and I have to repack everything myself. At least today I can say that that is the only time ever I was badly treated by a Customs officer. Frankly I think he was just jealous that I was able to import my car tax free!

A couple of weeks leave to see family and friends, arrange daughters transfer to a new school and we're ready to report to the College and move into our very nice, almost brand new, married quarters. My visit to Berkshire County Council Education Department to settle the school arrangements was almost on a par with our fracas at Dover Customs but this time I was *really* angry. At the BFES school in Germany, Gilly had successfully passed her 11+ exams, even though she was only 10 – surely that was a plus mark? But no, BCC would not accept that as a qualification, presumably because it did not happen in Berkshire; thus they would not accept our request to put her into a grammar school of our choice and insisted that she go to another elementary school in Bracknell, just for the summer term, to resit the 11+ there. Just how mind-bogglingly obtuse and infuriating can a council clerk be?! "So now that my daughter has officially passed the 11+ at a Government approved school, what happens if she now fails at this school – surely a possibility for a girl who is forced to re-sit after just a few weeks in a different environment among new friends?" My main concern was, of course, for the effect it could have on her confidence should that happen. "Well let's just hope she doesn't!" was the rejoinder. I was livid, but though I appealed through our local councillor, and to the Ministry, I got nowhere. Welcome home to the land of officialdom!

Having settled in to our new abode over a weekend, I report in to the College for duty on Monday morning – it is the start of the second term for No. 50 Course. "The Assistant Commandant would like to see you" says the Adj. Reporting to the "under-boss" I find he is Air Commodore Philip Warcup; we'd never met before, but we got on well and he and his wife Jean remained friends for many years (they were near neighbours of ours after we retired from the Service). "Welcome to the D.S. Conquer, I want you to take charge of No. 10 Syndicate in "B" Group. Your DG (Group Director) is Group Captain Jim Gale. I understand that after you finished the course in 1956 you stayed on for a few months and did a great job refurbishing the tennis pavilion, so I would like you to take over as officer i/c tennis – not too much of a chore – just organise a station team to compete in the Command annual championships and run our annual summer tournament", (is that all?) "Oh thank you Sir, you are too kind!" What an introduction – talk about the willing horse!

Next step was to meet the D.G. Jim Gale was of the Secretarial Branch, perhaps the most pleasant boss I worked for in my whole career, a real "gentleman of the old school"! He introduced me to the other Group D.S. I then met the six students in my syndicate and we were off for the start of their second term. I here confess that, although I found the course work none too arduous as a student, it proved much more difficult to see the various exercises through the eyes of six others. After all, they were all experienced officers, with fairly clear ideas of their own; the discussions were always lively and my main task was always to direct those discussions along the lines intended by the exercise author and within fairly determined parameters. It was too easy for speakers to wander into side issues and cross over the lines into irrelevant matters i.e. the art of "chairmanship" had to be developed and I found that it took a long time to achieve just that required level of control. Whatever my students thought of me I never did discover but I had some very bright lads, both in this syndicate and in my third term syndicate. Thus I was the tutor for twelve students during that first year of whom four later reached Air rank. The others, like me, plodded along in the middle ranks.

Perhaps I should explain further: it had always been a rigid rule that the syndicate D.S. was changed each term. This ensured that students assessments at the end of the course were a product of three D.S. opinions plus that of the D.G. who kept his eyes regularly on the work of all 30 (or in one case 36) of his students. Thus the risk of an assessment being unfairly biased did not exist.

As it was already April when I arrived, the tennis season was almost upon us and so the need to make haste with forming a College team was borne in on me almost before I got to know my students. But here I was lucky – one of the R.N. students on the course was Lt. Cdr. Bill Threlfall, a player of some renown;

anyone who watches Wimbledon will recognise that name – one of the best of the commentators at that tournament over many years. He was glad to captain the team and was also happy to help in sounding out the other students; we were then able to organise practice matches from which we could select a team. It was a foregone conclusion that Bill would win his singles matches and, with a suitable partner he found, almost certainly his doubles. As for the rest, we had several average amateurs but we were so short of talent at one stage of the summer that they even had to include me – a rabbit! Even so, we won about half our matches, thanks mainly to Bill and his partner.

One delightful piece of news came our way that summer – daughter passed her 11+ again, despite the tantrums when she was first told she had to re-sit (her mother had assured her when the result in Germany was known that she would never have to go through that again – and we both found it very difficult to persuade her that mother could not be held to blame!).

In July, at the end of that second term, the students and D.S. embarked on the annual Continental tour. How gracious of the system to insist that I must again spend two days in Paris, visit two Germany airfields and return laden with the usual perks of Gin and ciggies. This was my second such sortie – but very shortly you will read of more, several more!

That autumn I suffered my worst ever bout of sinusitis, one of my permanent weaknesses. The accompanying headaches were such that I could not face activity of any sort – so, to bed said the M.O., and take these for three days. "These" were sulphur tablets; for that three days I was rendered helpless and totally depressed – and have never taken a sulphur tablet since. At the end of that time I asked the M.O. whether smoking was the culprit – "Well it sure as hell doesn't help" he said. I have not smoked since – and I must say that the sinusitis has never been quite as bad again.

Though I was very much tied down by the tennis commitment, I was still able to fit in the occasional golf at Wentworth (the officers at Bracknell still had free honorary membership!), and also more frequent visits to the Gliding Club at White Waltham, where I managed to improve on previous performances and gain the "C" licence. During my year on the course, there had been a rumour that the Club would be getting a light aircraft so that we could progress from winch-launch to towed-launch, unhappily that had not come off and so we had still to make the best of two or three minutes flying at a time. Very frustrating!

Early in the third term, the station tennis tournament reached its conclusion with the "finals" day. Held at the weekend, we were able to run two matches at a time – women's singles and doubles (some WAAF, mainly wives), mixed doubles and finally the men's singles and doubles. The Commandant's wife kindly presented the prizes after each match. A couple of weeks afterward the Commandant, Air Vice-Marshal Maurice Heath, sent for me to tell me that his wife had found it rather arduous to have to wait around all day to present the prizes after each match. Next year would it be possible to arrange it so that all the prizes could be presented in one batch at the end of the day? I think my reply might have been a career-killer: "No, Sir, It would not. We cannot expect sweaty contestants to hang around until late in the day for their prizes. We will continue to do it as it is done at Wimbledon, if you don't mind". "Point taken" said the Cdt., "we will continue as usual".

The important "getting to know you" routine was regularly practiced at the College. During the year Commandant and Assistant C. invited students and their D.S. to cocktail parties at their quarters; D.S. also invited their students to a home function each term. On one such occasion, Joan and I were at Philip and Jean Warcup's for an evening and there met A.V.M. "Gus" Walker, he of the one arm, (We had Douglas Bader with no legs, Theodore McAvoy with his broken spine, Sid Ubee with only one eye, Sammy Hoare also with one eye, and Gus with one arm – all of them most remarkable "much-gonged" pilots!) I mention this occasion because I had never met the gentleman before and didn't see him again for a further five years – and yet, though we had spoken for only a couple of minutes together, he remembered my name instantly at that next meeting – a quite remarkable gift, one which I have never been able to emulate.

Towards the end of that first year Philip Warcup warned me that at the start of the New Year I was to take over the job of Plans 2. The organisation of the year's course was run by two members of the D.S: Plans 1 was responsible for syndication, planning the lecture and discussions programme, and the compilation and issue of the written exercises. Plans 2 was responsible for all the course visits, including transportation, bookings, accommodation and visit content for each event. My task was not an onerous one but, as you may well imagine, with 96 students and 24 D.S. to please, it did call for much attention to detail – especially for the week of the Continental tour. Work on the latter event had to start very early in the year and one of my clearest memories is of the massive volume of paper work and the number of files involved. Each year's planning filled a filing cabinet!

And so it became necessary for me physically to undertake that tour four more times; a planning trip early in the second term to test the route, the ferry, the headquarters and stations to be visited, the accommodation at each venue, particularly in Paris, the requirements of the hosts at each place and finally the transport needs for the division of the course into the several co-incident destinations. Naturally I had to make this planning trip in each of the two years, personally visiting every part of the tour. What a hardship! Then, to ensure that everything ran smoothly, I had to accompany the course on the tour itself. Thus, I ended up doing six such tours – one as a student, one as syndicate D.S. and four as Plans 2; it was certainly a record at that time and I imagine it stands to this day.

So started the next year – No. 51 Course, 1961. As Plans 2, I was not tied to syndicate times but was able to work reasonable "office hours". This gave me more time to deal with family matters. It also meant that we could once more plan for family holidays. Camping? – no, I don't think so, not again. Let's find a nice hotel in Devon. Here's an advert for a new small hotel between Hatherleigh and Holsworthy, let's try that for a couple of weeks. It was a disaster: the food was poor, there were no facilities nearby, and a pair of wretched peacocks woke us each day at dawn with their dreadful screeching cries. We had become friendly with another couple, Jill and Maurice, and after three days I confided that we were thinking of moving out and would tour the area to find an alternative. They were having exactly the same thoughts – "We have only stayed this long because we have enjoyed your company!" We all went searching by car and almost immediately spotted the Half Moon Inn in Sheepwash; and the licensee's name over the door? Wg. Cdr. "Sinbad" Inniss, recently retired from the RAF, where he was OC 111 Squadron and led the formation aerobatic team who later became the "Red Arrows"!

From this point on the holiday really took off. Excellent food, supervised daily by Sinbad's wife Ruth, fishing on the Torridge –

Sinbad owned six beats along half a mile of the river – and then sea fishing in Sinbad's boat which he kept at Appledore (guess how he acquired his nickname!). On many occasions recently, my family and I have enjoyed wonderful fish meals at the Beaver Inn in Appledore, the restaurant overlooking the estuary, the confluence of the rivers Tor and Torridge, remembering digging for worms in the beach opposite, followed by the briefly rough passage over the joining tidal waters before reaching the calm sea (sometimes) of the Bristol Channel.

Memorable as these fishing jaunts were, they were not the only highlight of that holiday. A few days after our moving into the Half Moon a strange, one-time-white, van arrived, covered in maps and place names from all over the world. The occupants – the Powers family, from Sydney, Australia. Stan, his wife Gwennie and daughter Wendy, had driven across Australia to Darwin, then by boat to Singapore, thence by land through India and the Middle East, Turkey, Greece, Italy, France, ferry to Dover, then sightseeing through Southern England. The van was also daubed with a multitude of signatures from people they had met en route. As I imagine they had done everywhere else, the Powers took the place "by storm"! They revelled in all our activities that week and this was, for us, the start of a friendship which was to last our lifetime.

As our holiday was ending, Stan mentioned that they proposed to motor to London in a few days time, stay for a while in Town, then sell the van and fly home. I asked if they had arranged hotel accommodation: they said they really hadn't thought that far so we invited them to stay with us at Bracknell – they could use our place as a base and do their visiting by train or van as they wished. They jumped at the idea and so a week later they arrived at Bracknell and stayed a fortnight.

Both Stan and Gwennie were lovely people, extremely strong characters yet gentle and charming souls. Stan was an identical twin: he and his brother were captains in the Australian Army, involved in the push to oust the Japanese from New Guinea; Stan was O.C. "C" Company, his brother was O.C. "A" Company, "A" and "B" Companies were the advance force in one battle, "C" was reserve. Shortly after the action began, Stan fell down – "Are you alright, Sir?" from his Lieutenant – "Yes – but my brother has just been shot". It was at that precise moment that his brother was killed. Absolute proof of that closest of ties between twins. Needless to say, Stan survived that battle, and several more, and only returned home when the last Japanese was ousted from the island.

During their stay with us we had a Guest Night in the Mess so I invited Stan to join me. What to wear he asked – I have no monkey suit! So we hired one. I introduced him to the Commandant and others before dinner and afterwards many of the lads flocked around him – with his broad Aussie accent and his very "presence" he had them eating out of his hand! The booze was flowing well in the bar when Stan suddenly spotted the piano – "May I?" he enquired – "Be our guest" in unison. I had no idea what to expect but it was immediately obvious that he was a talented pianist – especially for a sing-song. All the old numbers, both military and vaudeville, both clean and "suspect", it went on for hours. We returned home about 2 a.m. as the lads gave Stan a tremendous ovation; the event, and Stan, were much talked about for the rest of that course year.

One of the students and one of the D.S. had large families. Peter Latham, the student, had seven children, Ray Starnes had six. We celebrated Guy Fawkes day that November in the traditional manner, with large bonfire on the sports field, fireworks of course, and two vans – one with bangers and burgers, one as a bar. The affair was, of course, a great attraction for the children and when walking out there in the dark I ran into Peter Latham. "Whatho Pete. How many of the children are with you tonight?" Peter looked around and rather vaguely said "Oh, several!" On various occasions later he was not allowed to forget it. Ray Starnes, on saying farewell to Peter at the end of the course was heard to say "You'll be glad to know that our seventh is on the way!". (N.B. Peter Latham had recently been O.C. 111 Squadron and leader of the Red Arrows. He knew Sinbad Inniss of old!)

So then into 1962 and Course No. 52. Still Plans 2, so now I am setting up once again all those visits to the various establishments in the UK: the other Colleges, Army and Navy establishments and, starting immediately, all the preparations for another Continental tour. We don't have Bill Threlfall to lead our tennis programme this year but are once again lucky in having two students who have won tournaments as Command representatives.

All was fairly routine for the first part of the year until a call to attend a meeting in Philip Warcup's office: "We are taking a team to Australia in September for a presentation on military aviation matters to the R.A.A.F. Staff College in Canberra." Thereupon subjects to be covered were allocated to the half dozen D.S. present; my subject was to be the new V.T.O. (vertical take-off) aircraft then known as the Hawker P1127, since well established as the very versatile Harrier. The project was pretty hush-hush at that time but a visit to Air Ministry, Whitehall, Ops. Plans, followed by enquiries through the technical staffs, led to my being offered a visit to Hawkers airfield at Dunsfold to see some of the P1127 trials. Photographs were prohibited, of course, but I was allowed some of the confidential "bumph" which would enable me to swot up the subject in preparation for my talk to the Aussies.

This trip was very worth while, especially for me. A Britannia from Transport Command took the party from Lyneham to Singapore, from there by a BOAC Comet to Sydney, and finally a Fokker Friendship to Canberra. All the talks went down well at the RAAF College and the visiting party were treated to some notable Aussie hospitality! In return for a job well jobbed, Philip Warcup decreed we should enjoy five days "free time" in Sydney before embarking on the return journey. Stan and Gwennie, who had returned to Oz at the end of the previous year were thrilled to bits to hear from us and were quite delighted to welcome PW and yours truly to dinner. The following day, Stan insisted (as if I needed persuading!) on taking me sailing on the river estuary at Hornsby, just north of Sydney. He kept a very nice motor cruiser there and the waters were ideal – he and Gwennie spent many a long quiet day together on that boat. Many years later, he was out afloat one day alone; Gwennie and daughter Wendy were on shore, waving to him "time to come in no. 4!" when they realised he was not hearing, not seeing, not moving. The skiff was out tied to the boat so Gwennie threw off her top clothes, leapt in and swam out – Stan was dead, heart attack. A great shock for the girls, but what a peaceful end for Stan!

We flew back to Singapore by Qantas 707, where it seemed there was to be a delay in getting our return Britannia flight. Three days in Singapore – hardly a chore, what? But I had one cause to regret that delay: the Officers Mess at Changi boasted a delightful swimming pool, with ample loungers for the sun-worshipper; I should have known better, of course, having spent most of a year in the Med, but I forgot that the sun's rays reflect upward from tiled surfaces and, though I lounged under an umbrella, the sun got my back badly. That made 30 hours in a Britannia the most uncomfortable flight ever!

But some compensation – the Brit. pilot was an old chum from squadron days and he happily stowed two large cases in the cargo bay for me: I had acquired a 110-piece Noritake tea/dinner service – for £10 believe it or not! And it is still in use to this day.

There remains to tell of just one more task, possibly the most important and certainly the most time consuming, which I was required to undertake during this tour at Staff College. The Air Council had taken the decision to amalgamate the two RAF Staff Colleges, Bracknell and Andover; the latter was to close and the former expanded to compensate. This was considered by our Commandant to be unwise and there was little doubt that most of us on the College staffs would agree with him. To understand the pros and cons of the argument, it is necessary to explain the main reasons for setting up the two Colleges in the first place:

a. The classification of most of the studies at the Bracknell Staff College are unclassified, restricted or confidential. But towards the highlight of the course, in the third term, much of the information is Secret and some even Top Secret. All the British, Commonwealth, American and the few European (NATO) students were security vetted and therefore fully entitled to receive all the highly classified stuff. But we received many applications from other countries for student places for their officers e.g. Egypt, Nigeria, even China. It was therefore thought advisable to have a separate College, then at Andover, still mainly for British Forces but to include students of these other welcome nationalities. But for that college, the course would be split into six terms, the "foreigners" would leave at the end of the fifth term, allowing the full highly classified stuff to be dealt with for the British students alone in that sixth term.

b. It was found that some of these foreign nationals had limited grasp of English and minimal knowledge of the basics of military matters. It was therefore necessary to expand somewhat the early speech and writing exercises for their benefit; of course, syndicates were arranged to mix the foreign students with their British colleagues, so to give them added support with their exercise work.

So now the Commandant. "Conquer, I see from your student record on 46 Course that you wrote an excellent appreciation. Now I want you to write another for me." (Thinks I – after that flannel he's going to want something that stinks!) "As you've just heard, the Air Council have decided to abolish Andover and amalgamate the two colleges here at Bracknell. That is not to my liking. Now I want you to write a full appreciation on the subject but on this occasion the object of the exercise is not to find the 'best course of action', I want the conclusion to recommend that the situation stays 'as is'! I know you've been taught otherwise and perhaps it goes against the grain, but that's what I want you to do. There's no mad rush, but I want the final draft on my desk in one month's time". (If only this had happened in 2003/4, instead of 1962, I could have come back with: "So you want me to produce the same sort of paper with which Tony Blair justified the war on Iraq!")

Now a formal written appreciation is a lengthy document consisting of the following sections:

Review of the situation
The Aim to be attained
Factors affecting the attainment of the aim
Enemy courses of action that affect the attainment of the aim
Courses of action open to us to attain the aim
Selection of the best course to attain the aim
The plan of action

In this case the "Aim" had to be "To determine the most suitable and efficient organisation of our Staff College(s)". The many "factors" involved had to include those mentioned in a. and b. above. "Enemy courses" – this was not a wartime paper – meant factors which worked against the aim. The "possible courses" were what we already had or what the Air Council have now decreed. And my "selection" had to be the former. All I had to do (all?) was to visit all parties involved to get their ideas – Air Ministry (four departments), Andover, Joint Services Staff College at Latimer, NATO Staff College in Paris, Imperial Defence College in London and finally the Army Staff College at

Camberley and the Royal Navy Staff College at Greenwich. Remembering that this was supposed to be a "spare time" exercise, no-one was surprised that I wasn't around much for evening parties and the like for that month.

Maurice Heath approved the paper which, as instructed, recommended the "status quo" option. Much to my astonishment, and I suspect his also, when the paper was presented at the next Air Council meeting, their "Airships" changed their minds! Andover and Bracknell remained as they were for another ten years or more. But eventually the merger happened anyway – inevitable when you looked at the cash side of it. And now, recently, all the three services staff colleges have amalgamated into one – at Camberley!

We are now into the early months of '63, my tour at Bracknell is coming to an end, so what now I wonder. Why not another squadron? I have been off active flying for two tours, surely one last throw of the dice is not unreasonable? The "posters" laughed fit to bust. At your age? (42!) – not a chance. What about another spell in the Ministry, or how about staff plans in Flying Training Command? "Plans, plans, my life has been nothing but plans for a dozen years – give me a break!" "OK – how would you like to go back to Germany? Bruggen needs a Wg. Cdr. Admin. – right up your street." "Well, if that's how the cookie crumbles – it's likely to be the best I'll get – so Bruggen, here I come. By the way, who is the 'Boss' there now?" "Ivor Broom". After all those years – I first flew with Ivor back at Bicester in '41!

CHAPTER TWENTY-ONE

Bruggen, April 1963–September 1965

I had always subconsciously rather dreaded the possibility of playing the administrator on a station; it had seemed to be a "second best" job for the G.D. Branch, and yet most of the wing commanders I had known in that position had always seemed to be happy enough – or were they just resigned to their fate? We shall now find out, I mused.

I was certainly looking forward keenly to going back to Germany, knowing the high standard of living and fun prospects that that meant. But, of course, there was a snag: daughter Gilly would not be able to continue at her splendid school in Wokingham, where there were no boarders, and for the sake of her education it was essential in our view that she remain in UK. We therefore arranged for her to move to a C. of E. School, St. Helen and St. Katherine in Abingdon, where I regret to say she was not a "happy boarder". Such was at least one of the penalties of a Service life – yet, in retrospect, Gilly has always conceded that it was a good foundation for her subsequent career. (I understand that Nuns no longer run that school and it is now assessed as among the top twenty girls schools in the country).

I had decided to take our now ageing Merc. 190 back to Germany with us, perhaps to trade it in for a new one in due course. So now we would have the reverse of our return to UK three years before – car full, roof stacked high, but this time no officious Customs officer to get my back up. But events transformed this scenario more than somewhat. Having gone on ahead, to settle in to my new appointment, get to know the "Boss" and sort out accommodation, I was involved with a visiting Air Commodore from HQ RAF Germany who wished to address the station officers on future plans. Supervising preparations in the Ops. Room for his talk, I was checking sound and lighting equipment on the stage; unhappily someone had moved the whole stage forward a couple of feet and left a gap at the back, it was dark and I trod on a bit of boarding that wasn't there and fell into the gap, cracking my head open on a radiator. So, carted off to Wegberg Hospital in semi-conscious state, head encased in bandages, the day before we were due to move from our quarters in Bracknell!

Ivor was most helpful: he arranged for a "volunteer" to go over to UK to bring the family to Bruggen – George Faulkner, our Squadron Leader Engineer, did indeed volunteer his services and, I am glad to say, became a firm friend. But George turned out to be a stickler for "morals" and "appearances": when he arrived at Bracknell Joan naturally offered him a spare bedroom for the night – "Heavens no" says George "what would people think, my being with you in the house alone?" So he stayed in the Mess. I had booked the ferry from Dover to Calais and accommodation for the one night in a Calais hotel, before motoring on to Germany. "Good Lord no" again says George "we can't be seen to spend a night in the same hotel unchaperoned". So George cancelled those bookings and instead arranged the crossing from Harwich to Hook van Holland; that way they could spend the night in separate cabins, which he felt was acceptable. By this time, Joan felt that as George was the "conductor" she could but go along without complaint.

At the final stage of the journey, they stopped in Roermond to do some shopping. Shortly afterwards they were at the border crossing, only half a mile from the Bruggen main gates; the Dutch guard waved them through with much laughter at the heavily loaded car, but the German customs officer at the second crossing point was not amused. Certainly he did not demand a full check of the load but he was much mystified by the car numberplate: of course the car had been re-registered in England on our return three years before but in preparation for the second Germany tour I had refitted the previous RAF Germany registration plates; but in the interim that registration system had been changed, so the officer was flummoxed. Eventually he just shrugged and let them proceed. Seconds later George exclaimed "My wallet – I must have left it in Roermond". Joan, by now a very frustrated driver, turned the car to head back, dreading having to return through the border check-point, but almost immediately George exclaimed "I've found it". Great relief, and two hours later Joan was in Wegberg Hospital to see her trussed up husband.

I was released from Wegberg the next day and so was able to settle the family into our new quarters. As Wg. Cdr. "A" I was to be accorded a fabulous house, easily the equivalent of our second house at Sundern four years previously; but my predecessor's family was still in occupation awaiting transfer to UK and so we had been allocated temporarily a smaller house nearby. One often has to face this "double move" at the beginning of a tour, particularly where a house is ex-officio for one of the senior appointments.

Just a week later, we received an informal visit from the AOC which was planned to coincide with the CO's monthly parade and inspection. Still wearing my ghastly turban of bandages (the scar is even now a deep furrow across my scalp) and no cap, I nevertheless insisted on commanding my wing on that parade, despite Ivor's offer to excuse me. Both Ivor and the AOC made an informal inspection of the parade – Flying Wing, consisting of the two squadrons Nos. 80 and 213, Admin Wing and Tech Wing. As they came across to my wing they stopped bang in front of me and the AOC saluted; grinning he said "That's got you Conquer – you don't know whether to salute or not, do you?" "No problem Sir" says I, whipping up a smart *left* arm! Much hilarity in the Mess at lunchtime.

Whilst I had a fairly clear idea of the numerous responsibilities of the job, I soon discovered that there were many more angles to it in Germany than in the UK. The number of people on the station for a start: counting the numerous families with many children, station personnel, plus a Command Maintenance Unit, a German "works" unit, a strong American Air Force unit and the Command Police Dog School, we numbered in excess of 2500 souls. There were four Messes, two schools (for children, not dogs), and about 200 houses (married quarters) and umpteen barrack blocks for single personnel. The amount of real estate was something to see – a very large airfield with four hangars for the squadrons and Tech Wing, a veritable town of buildings, both office and domestic, and – oh yes – an 18-hole golf course! It was quite a station, was Bruggen.

At that time, our operational task consisted of photo reconnaissance (80 Squadron) and strike (213 Squadron), both squadrons equipped with Canberras. Apart from routine flying exercises and simulated operational flights, Bruggen was tasked with an instant reaction strike role, two aircraft permanently on immediate standby in special small hangars. If I remember aright, the record reaction time upon receiving the alarm was under three minutes – crew into aircraft, engines started, take-off direct from hangar. Needless to say, this demanded that the "ready" aircraft be fully armed whilst on standby: that raised quite a few problems in itself, problems which I shall not discuss here – fortunately those matters were not on *my* plate

Security was probably the most onerous responsibility at that time. Because of the vastness of the "estate" really tight security was almost impossible. The main "at risk" area was, of course, the weapons bunker and fortunately the responsibility for that rested squarely on the shoulders of the American detachment. They also dealt with the arming and disarming of the aircraft. The next priority was the perimeter and all the dispersed aircraft; here, unlike the situation at Lakenheath 12 years earlier, I had a large RAF Police section and the RAF Police Dog School and so, by continuous patrols and exercises training those dogs, we were able to keep a fairly close watch on the outskirts, day and night. Double main gates at the station entrance, with sentries on the outer gate and a fully manned guardroom at the inner, proved adequate protection there. I do not recall any major breaches of security during my tour, in fact the overall threat seemed much less there than we had believed the IRA presented at Lakenheath.

I was very fortunate to have a most competent bunch of lads on my wing. Mike Culhane, my chief policeman, was well versed in all the angles and I was content to leave the policing and security matters entirely in his hands. My senior Secretarial officer, Tom Reading, was an able assistant and I could leave all accounting and admin. problems to him. Flt. Lt. John Murphy, a friend there and for many years since, coped easily with the housing and "works and bricks" problems, which were never-ending. Catering, Education, Medical and Physical Fitness officers all ran almost faultless sections, leaving me with very few concerns in the day-to-day running of the show. The other wing commanders were a good bunch: Frank Bowen-Easley, OC Flying Wing, the two squadron commanders Bob Simpson, 80 and Stan Slater, 213, Norman Searle, OC Tech. Wing, John Prentice, commanding the MU. and finally David Wilkinson (I think it was), the senior Doc, I could not have wished for better colleagues.

Then of course there was the "Boss", Ivor Broom, bless his cotton socks. Ivor was one of your really keen operational types: his war record was inspirational – a tour on Blenheims in '40/'41, when the "chop rate" was probably one of the worst of all time, briefly training new crews at Bicester in '41/'42 (myself included), back to a Blenheim squadron for a short time, then transferred to Mosquitos, which he flew almost continuously for the rest of the war. Two DSOs and two DFCs spoke volumes. Bruggen was good for Ivor – he displayed great talent for command. Though he did not suffer fools gladly, his personal confidence and his consideration for others amplified his natural air of authority, I, like many others, enjoyed working for and with him. He later rose to Air Marshal with a K, then retired from the RAF to become the head of National Air Traffic Control. We remained friends until his death just a couple of years ago.

Little more than a month after our arrival our appointed married quarters became available – next door to Ivor and opposite Bob and Stan – and we moved in with little fuss. A large house, with an even larger garden, the latter ideal for our young boxer bitch Candy; we had been so glad to be able to bring her with us, yet barely six months later she developed a kidney complaint necessitating a visit to a local vet. I was not entirely happy with his diagnosis but he was convinced it was necessary to operate – she did not recover. We felt gutted and, yes, guilty – but what else we could have done I know not.

I was assigned a permanent housekeeper, one Frau Ramnetz, an absolute treasure. On our previous tour we had had some part time help with the chores but this was different; Frau Ramnetz was ours full time, had run the house for my predecessor, and was so efficient that it seemed almost churlish to give her instructions. And yet she was never averse to adding any extra little jobs to her day that either Joan or I might suggest; she spoke some English and we always considered her as part of the family.

Early on, and not long after a reasonable settling-in period, Ivor had briefed me about a forthcoming Royal Visit. Both 80 and 213 Squadrons were to be presented with new Standards and Princess

Margaret had apparently eagerly accepted the RAF's request to make the presentation. It had been hoped to programme the event for mid-1963 – but then they found out that Conquer would not be there in time to plan it so it was postponed – no, sorry, only kidding!

"Her Royal Highness The Princess Margaret would be most pleased to present the new Standards to No. 80 and No. 213 Squadrons at Bruggen but I regret to tell you that her public engagements schedule is already full for the year 1963. However, if it would be convenient, she would be delighted to do so on a similar date in 1964". That, or words to that effect from the Palace, was the real message, and so I found myself under instructions from Ivor to set up a working party to arrange the programme and the event.

The most important feature in any programme for such a Royal event was that it should cover every single minute in detail. Now that is fairly simple when the visit is to last for, say, an hour; but Princess Margaret had let it be known that should would like to be shown the workings of the station and, especially, the domestic side: school(s), children's play facilities, clubs/messes and, during the afternoon, perhaps tea with the officers' ladies. Thus, if the parade for the presentation of the standards were to be held in the morning, say at 1100 hours, then it would mean the Princess arriving at about 1030. To end the day with tea in the Officers' Mess would mean departure at about 1630; thus the entire visit would last for six hours – 360 minutes of minute (pun intended!) detail.

By agreement with all the senior station officers the "working party" was set up in the SHQ conference room to include one representative from all affected parties – virtually every section on the station – a specimen programme for the day being presented to the Boss and the squadron commanders in December 1963. It broadly included:

       1030   Arrival by helicopter
       1100   Parade and presentation of standards
       1150   Meeting with Squadron Officers in Briefing Room
       1230   Luncheon in Officers' Mess
       1400   Visits to Station and Domestic areas
       1600   Tea with the Ladies
       1630   Depart

Put like that it all seems fairly simple but, as I am sure any reader who has ever had experience of such an occasion realises, from such little acorns big oak trees grow – and consume many many working hours to achieve success.

"Who is to command the parade – will you be doing that yourself, Sir?" seemed a logical question in the early stages. "Lord no" says the Boss "I have to accompany HRH throughout – including on the parade rostrum. No, you're the senior Wing Commander, my deputy, that's your job" says he. Ah well, it's not as though I'm a stranger to the role but I had to admit it was quite a few years since I last did sword drill! Also, when I checked up on the drill format I discovered that it involved over 80 words of command – it was, in fact, the very first "double" standards presentation in RAF Squadron history.

That on-the-spot decision by the Boss did not go unchallenged. A recent change in the Wing Commander Flying appointment (Frank Bowen-Easley had been promoted and posted) had introduced a certain Charles Crichton to the scene, himself just promoted to that appointment. He strongly expressed the view that as the presentation was to the two squadrons, and as he was O.C. Flying Wing, then *he* should command the parade. I might have been prepared to stand aside but felt compelled to oppose that view – both squadron commanders were senior wing commanders, normally the Group Captain would therefore command the parade, but in this case it should be his deputy, the only wing commander on the station senior to the two squadron commanders – that is, if seniority is to have any meaning at all. The Boss agreed and the issue was settled. (The Crichton–Conquer relationship thereafter was not entirely harmonious – he even suggested that at times when the Group Captain was away from the station he, as OC Flying Wing, should be acting Station Commander. The Boss squashed that one also!)

In the ensuing few months, Ivor frequently carried out informal inspections of the sections to be visited by HRH and often then attended our "workshop" meetings with suggestions for improvement. Very early on, he and his wife Jesse took a special interest in the various Mess facilities and wished to see renovation and improvements in the Ladies Cloakroom: Joan was asked if she would take on that task and I was pleased that she did so readily. All were surprised at the very low budget which she submitted for the task but she had accepted the responsibility and Ivor and I let her get on with it. After the visit we were highly chuffed when the Princess commented how nice it had been to visit such a pleasant room in pastel shades – for once none of that awful "gold and red glitter"!

I could write many pages solely on the following months leading up to that Royal visit but so many other matters need reporting more. But one more personal anecdote I cannot omit: I must obviously have a new uniform for this parade so a few days leave in UK whilst taking daughter back to school after the Easter hols., with a visit to Moss Bros for measuring and initial fitting. One unfortunate result of my Blenheim prang has been that my right leg is substantially shorter than the left – some 2 inches to be precise. Delivery of the new uniform took much longer than expected – it arrived barely a week before the Royal visit – so imagine the panic when I discovered the tailor must have been cross-eyed – he'd made the left leg the shorter! Moss Bros. were so concerned they made a new pair of trousers immediately and the senior Moss flew out in person to deliver and fit them!

The parade that day followed the standard format of all such presentation parades – except that for the first time, as already mentioned, two Squadrons were to receive their Standards, thus doubling the main part of the ceremony and the inspection time by the Princess. To perfect such a parade required many practices and rehearsals, classroom briefings with diagrams for all officers and NCOs, "spacing" meetings on the ground, wet weather practices in a hangar and finally full squadron rehearsals both "wet" and "dry". The Squadron Commanders and I also had to practice our sword drill together several times – we were all a bit rusty in that department!

Some of these rehearsals were the cause of much merriment – particularly on the part of the troops. To see Joan, Anne and Jean, our three wives, and for the final rehearsal Jesse Broom, strutting their stuff as "Princess stand-ins" occasioned mirth in the ranks – and much gossip and laughter at parties during that time.

I suffered one moment of panic on the day itself: I was momentarily stumped when the 80 Squadron standard bearer returned after receiving the new Standard to "take post" and almost began to utter the commands for the next move following the presentation(s), thus almost forgetting the presentation to 213 Squadron. Fortunately, in an almost unbearable 5 seconds of silence, my brain found the right page in the book and the ceremony continued in order. Once again, it was brought home to me how close one can come to disaster when in the public eye!

To conclude the Royal visit story, it remains only to say that the event was a success, no-one put up any major "blacks", and the only disruption to the schedule was created by the Princess herself at teatime in the Officers Mess – she was so enjoying her chats with "the Ladies" that she refused to leave on time despite frequent "nudging" by her aides. The delay of almost 40 minutes created some alarm at her evening appointment – with the A.O.C.-in C. and staff at Command HQ!

Mention of parties brings to mind "Noddy's trio". Early in my tour at Bruggen I had discovered a pianist and a guitarist among the mess members – both of 213 Squadron. We began quite simply by strumming away one evening to find that we were not at all bad – leading to pleas for Saturday evening entertainment. Well, any excuse for a party, One of my habits whilst on the drums was to nod my head to the rhythm; hence I soon acquired the nickname "Noddy". All that remained was for me to take on the part fully at the next Fancy Dress Ball complete with red top and nose, tail hat and blue boots. Don't know about Noddy – I felt a right "Charlie"!

Staying with the subject of the Summer Ball, it is always difficult to think up something new as a theme – but our PMC certainly came up with a winner during my second year there – 1964. The title was simply "Down on the Farm"; but it was the originality of the different units – notably 213 Squadron – which gave the event such distinction. All of us dressed the part: I managed to "acquire" a Norfolk jacket, plus fours, cap and 12-bore; Joan, Jesse, Jean and Anne were suitably garbed as milk-maids; but the "pieces de resistance" were all the lads of 213 who came as a flock of sheep! They all arrived, suitably late, on hands and knees, covered in sheep-skins, in a flock – a dozen of them – shepherded by their CO., the "farmer". They even attempted some of the dances on all fours. I have to say that, in my 30 years experience, that was one of the most memorable of all mess functions, second only perhaps to "The Battle of the Murky Mere"!

During the summer hols that year, Gilly my daughter, now 16, asked if she could get a part-time job on the station. She was, and always has been, very fond of animals, particularly horses and dogs, so I asked Mike Culhane if he could use her services in the Police Dog School. Certainly, she could help the handlers by cleaning kennels and grooming the dogs. What about pay? I suggested that Mike should pay her a fair wage privately and I would recompense him – ". . . and that's just between we two!" This, of course, started her lifelong love affair with German Shepherds (or Alsatians if you prefer). On one occasion I was conducting the CO on a routine inspection of the School when Mike took me to one side and said "Watch this". Gilly was just about to enter the cage of "Satan', one of the really nasty aggressive dogs: he growled as she opened his gate (and only Mike's restraining hand stopped me from going to her), to which Gilly rasped "Get down, how dare you growl at me". At which the dog cowered down, wagging his tail, and whimpering as she stooped to caress him. "And that's a dog even his handler is scared of" says Mike, "Gilly has him eating out of her hand!"

Reader will recall from my time at Sundern my enthusiasm for the Kiel Yacht Club and sailing the Baltic. Needless to say, my second Germany tour gave me the opportunity to resume those facilities on several occasions. It was during one of those visits that I managed to qualify for the Baltic Mate's ticket. This in turn led to my being asked to deputise for one of the instructors on the school who was indisposed. With Ivor's approval, that gave me the opportunity for a whole week at Kiel, including conducting four boats in their qualifying tour around the Danish islands. For a comparative "sprog" at the game, that was honour indeed.

I mentioned earlier on that Bruggen boasted an excellent 18-hole golf course, a prize feature not only of the Station but also of the Command. I confess that I rarely took advantage of it myself, preferring to devote what little spare time I had in that job to other things. However, on one visit I met one of the USAF officers who had just been told he was posted home – would I like to buy his golf clubs? An almost new matched set, two woods and eight irons, putter and bag – £10! Now who is going to refuse an offer like that? Those clubs saw me through the rest of my playing days until failing legs finally led me to quit the game a couple of years ago. The local professional declined to buy them – too old – but offered me £40 for the bag! I gave the lot to our local branch of the Aircrew Association for sale at their Summer Fete.

Towards the end of my second year at Bruggen, Ivor Broom returned to the UK on promotion to be replaced by, of all people.

Ted Sismore, What is this, I asked, a Bicester reunion? Ivor's departure was, to coin a phrase, truly memorable – on two counts. First, he was "dined out" in style according to custom, but with one very unusual feature – Ted, his replacement, was also at that dinner. As expected, the responsibility for the "thank you and farewell" speech fell to me and, of course, I made mention of our former meetings and history, at the same time welcoming the newcomer and commenting on our rival performances in the race for the Cape Town record 18 years before. In his reply Ivor, tongue in cheek, pointed out that he, the retiring CO and Ted, the incoming CO, were both pilots, ". . . whereas Norman, the 'Administrator', is a navigator. What does that say about the Ministry's "equal careers' policy?" What indeed – that hurt! And it was barely a month later that I was to be informed that I would not be promoted further and would therefore be retired on my 47th birthday. You will see, as it turned out, that their "Airships" did me a very good turn by that decision!

The second memorable event was the actual departure of Ivor and Jesse from Bruggen. The station possessed a very nice small sailing boat, with trailer, which was used by club members on river or nearby lake. Said members decided that a splendid gesture of farewell would be to tow the boat all round the station, fully masted, with Ivor and Jesse aboard, taking farewell bows to all the men and families who would line the route. Ivor thought it a splendid idea and it certainly created a memorable spectacle, both for the Brooms and for us all. One snag: those who planned the route around the airfield forgot about an overhead power cable at one point; the second half pictures were much spoiled by the mast, snapped in two at head height – and I think Ivor himself only ducked just in time!

We are now well past the half-way mark in my Bruggen tour, Ted Sismore is well settled in the chair and, like Ivor, he enjoys the occasional trip in one of the squadron Canberras, usually with one of their navigators as crew. Then one day he calls me into his office and "I'm off flying for an hour or so. Like to come with me Norman?" Thinking "to hell with that job I'd just started" – "Rather", says I "where are we going?" "Oh, only local," says he, "no navigation needed"

I suppose that should have warned me – yet I was still taken aback when without warning, at about 20,000', he started throwing her about all over the sky. Now aerobatics is fine when you know what to expect but, taken by surprise, it ain't clever! I leave to the readers imagination what prompted him to do that. Needless to say, we did not fly together again,

It always comes as a pleasant surprise to hear from old colleagues, especially those who have already left the Service. One day in '64 I received a telephone call from Johnny Battle, an old navigator friend from the Shawbury days. Calling from Brighton he explained that he was now working for a Canadian insurance company, Manufacturers Life, could he come out to see me at Bruggen? "Certainly, delighted. Come and stay with me here – spare beds, no problem." His primary purpose was, of course, to sell. Yet I was pleased about that because I had been assessing my own situation and was no longer sure that "don't worry about the family – the Service will provide" was good enough protection; my total life insurance at that time was £1000!

We made John welcome and he soon explained his business and how he operated and could he demonstrate his "programming technique" on me? I was quite astonished at the logic of his approach and could not gainsay his deductions and the need to attack the problem. "Do you want to do something about it? Then how much can you afford to devote to a solution?" I learned later that he (and his colleagues at the crunch point of the interview) were always happy to hear the reply "£5 or 10 a month", absolutely chuffed to hear occasionally "£15 or 20"! When I said "Would £100 a month do?" John simply fell of the chair! And this is where I would pay him a great compliment – he applied about £17 a month to suitable life insurance and put the rest into a Building Society ". . . to guarantee a mortgage when you retire from the Service – funds in short supply means priority given to members". For that advice I have always been grateful – it turned out to be prophetic.

Needless to say, I arranged for him to see several other officers on the station who were equally glad to have such advice. I was to discover that, like me, very few officers had made suitable financial provision for their families in the event of their death – and yet we were all flying for our living i.e. at more risk than your average citizen.

A few weeks later I had another call from John. "Would it be possible for me to visit again and bring a colleague with me – I believe you remember George Masters who used to be a Controller at Goch during your time at Sundern?" John had

had several recommendations from me and others he had "programmed" during his first visit but had not had time to see them all. So, "Yes, of course, and I should be delighted to see George again." The following day "Norman, John again. Our Branch Manager would like to come with us to meet you. Could we add him to the team?" Well why not – plenty of room.

And so Kerry Fone, that Branch Manager, entered the lives of the Conquer family. On his first night at Bruggen, after a very pleasant evening meal with the "team", Kerry asked Joan and me out to dinner the next evening at a splendid castle restaurant beside the Rhine; there he extended the totally unexpected invitation to join him at the Brighton Branch should I decide to retire from the Service. I don't think he, or the others, had any inkling of their Airships recent decision about my future, so I could only think that Lady Luck was looking over my shoulder. And yet my first reaction was "Me – sell life insurance for a living – you must be crazy!" Was he? I think not. I gave the obvious reply "Thanks for the offer – I'll think it over" but I'm sure that the grey matter did not work overtime for me to reach the foregone conclusion. More on this subject very soon!

I have failed to mention so far one of the least pleasant features in the life of a Wg. Cdr. "A" – crime/misdemeanours/offences and punishment. Whilst rarely involved as "judge" (except perhaps when one of his NCOs/airmen has disobeyed the rules or if appointed as an officer in a Court Martial i.e. as President or Member of the Court) he has nevertheless to ensure that all the necessary procedures are followed, advise the CO on steps to be taken and also advise those accused of their rights and responsibilities. I was fortunate during my tour at Bruggen not to have many incidents of this sort, but a couple of "comic cuts" capers were quite amusing at the time – for some of us, anyway.

A sergeant engine mechanic in the MT Section had a near-miss on the autobahn one day: a truck pulled out into the outer lane without warning and, though he braked hard, the truck badly damaged his offside front wing – didn't stop, naturally. Our boy was mad, so mad that he plotted revenge against all German trucks. He welded a massive "sword", three feet long, to his rear axle, protruding outward from his offside rear wheel. Then he rode the outside lane of the autobahn, cutting up the tyres of moving trucks. I can't remember how many trucks littered the road with slashed rubber that day – but enough to get the Polizei really, really mad in their turn. The result? Great diplomatic effort to calm the pending international crisis, whilst the lad was smartly dispatched back to UK on "jankers".

On another occasion my friend George Faulkner, recently promoted to Wing Commander Tech., was posted home to Air Ministry. In RAF Germany we were all issued with special petrol coupons to run our cars and, of course, they were for our personal use only. George had already left the station and his wife Martha had stayed behind to clear their married quarters, conduct the "march-out" as it was known. Of course, she still needed the car so George had unwittingly left her with the remainder of his coupons. Someone "sneaked" and the message was passed to me with the request that I "do something about it".

I persuaded the CO that he should leave it to me – well he wanted a quiet life so I said I'd deal with it quietly without fuss. I checked on Martha's fuel supply, accompanied her to a nearby garage, filled her car with my own coupons and suggested she come to me if she needed more before departure. George came to collect her a fortnight later, I took him out to the local and over a pint and a laugh told him this was an official warning. Case closed.

Mention of legal and disciplinary matters leads me, unhappily, to end the Bruggen saga with a sad event. All RAF operators and administrators, of all ranks, dread the aircraft prang. Ivor Broom enjoyed a completely air-accident free two and a half years but even he would concede that, on a full time operational flying station, that was a matter of great good fortune. Sadly, Ted Sismore was not to enjoy the same luck.

Not long before I was due to leave the station, a crew of 213 Squadron lost an engine during a practice bombing sortie. Not in itself a serious problem on a Canberra – always as happy and as manoeuvrable on one engine as on two – but, tanks being almost full, they needed to burn off fuel to reduce weight to the safe limit for landing; so, back at base, the pilot did so by practising landings and overshoots – not a good idea with a dead engine and contrary to the rules of airmanship. Regrettably, the pilot 'lost it' on the third run and the crew were filled in the crash.

The loss of a splendid crew (and a fine aeroplane) was a tragedy for the squadron and the station – a rare event thankfully, but perhaps felt even more during peacetime then were the more frequent losses during the war. The task of arranging the Court of

Inquiry which inevitably followed, with its mass of paperwork, interviews with all concerned and finally allocation and acceptance of blame, was not a pleasant one and this event cast a cloud over what had been one of my most memorable and happy tours in the Service.

As previously mentioned, my tour is nearly over and it is "report to Adjutant" time – but in this job he is one of my staff officers, so he reported to me instead! Knowing my official date of departure from the Service – 16th February, 1968 – and having made up my mind already to take up Kerry Fone's offer, I requested a posting in south east England to be near Brighton – how about Biggin Hill? And get this – unlike all those requests and promises for a pilot's course, this request was granted! So, I am off to the Officers and Aircrew Selection Centre, Biggin Hill – September 1965.

Needless to say, I am not entirely happy to be leaving Germany. Some aspects of the Wg. Cdr. "A"s job I'm pleased to leave behind; in particular being second-in-command and deputy Station Commander is not the best job in the world. Yet I look back on it as a rewarding period of my life, many lessons learned, many friendships made, and it certainly lent another splash of colour to the overall Service experience. One regret was that I did not update my car – the Merc.190 was now 8 years old and clocking almost 100,000 miles – what a fool not to take advantage yet again of those special purchase terms available to those serving in Germany.

So, once again, after being "dined out", comes the task of packing up, marching out of our superb married quarters and saying farewell to our wonderful housekeeper, Frau Ramnetz, and finally au revoir to our many friends, new and old, on the conclusion of what I considered a most memorable tour. Having made enquiries, we learned that we had already been allocated ex-officio married quarters at Biggin Hill so we would not have to face the trauma of temporary ad hoc arrangements like those we had suffered in so many earlier postings.

CHAPTER TWENTY-TWO

O.A.S.C., Biggin Hill, October 1965–February 1968

Our journey home was easy, with only one minor hiccup – yet another confrontation with a (plainly) stupid Customs officer. This gentleman insisted that as our car had been bought in Germany, we would have to pay import duty, despite the age of the car and its mileage and that it had already been imported to England nearly six years before! Fortunately, as had happened before, his Chief, summoned by me in defence, soon put the lad straight and I was barely able to mask a chuckle at his discomfiture.

After a suitable period of leave a phone call confirmed that our new married quarters awaited us: certainly not comparable to the plush property we had just left at Bruggen, but a pleasant enough Type 4 in a patch of similar properties, all fairly new, There were, in fact, two sites of OMQs at Biggin – one occupied mainly by the BH staff officers, the other largely devoted to officers working in Air Ministry appointments in London. Such facilities were certainly not available 15 years earlier when I was at Adastral House.

Over the many years since I retired from the Service, I have found that one of the aspects of the RAF which interests many people, often even more than tales of operational matters, is the selection of officers and aircrew. Why are some favoured more than others? What special abilities does a lad need to be accepted? How important is medical condition, education, practical knowledge, manual dexterity? What are the main characteristics you look for? When all considered, how often are your decisions right/wrong? And shouldn't paper qualifications suffice to prove the worthiness of the candidate? (This public interest has led me to give talks on the subject to popular clubs such as Probus and Forum).

At my first interview with the Wing Commander "Org." I was told that I would start my tour there with a 2-weeks course on "Selection Technique". Well, really, I thought – I've been commanding and reporting on my junior officers for some 20 years now, surely such a "course" must be superfluous. (Rather along the lines of that "3 days of lectures on how to navigate to Gibraltar" at Lyneham in 1943 – Chapter 6!) Do I really need yet more training when I'm due to retire from the Service in a couple of years time? But in that fortnight I learned a great deal – "my eyes were opened wide", as they say. In fact, it was a sobering experience to realise that that couple of weeks training would have been invaluable to me many years before and would have helped greatly, especially with that dreaded task of writing officers' annual reports.

I hope to answer all those questions in the preceding paragraph by describing the OASC organisation and procedures, preceded by a brief history of the selection process, and culminating in justification of the methods which have been adapted and updated over the years. Before arrival at BH, I had really thought that this posting would just be something of a "rest cure", perhaps uninteresting, but an easy way to lead me into retirement: far from it – I found it one of the most enjoyable and rewarding of all my Service appointments.

During the war years there were, of course, several advances in selection technique: the adoption of short objective tests – General Intelligence, Elementary Maths, Basic English – and eventually a Pilot Co-ordination Test. Even so, boarding officers were free to disregard the results of these tests and rely solely on subjective assessment should they wish. Yet still there was no training for Boarding Officers – there were some who believed that the ability to ride a horse was as good an indicator of flying aptitude as any other!

It was soon realised that the cost of failure at advanced stages of training was so great – particularly for those sent to flying training schools in Canada and South Africa – that by 1942 pilots were being "graded" at Elementary Flying Training School in UK; this "grading" was based primarily on the time taken to first solo. Those pupil pilots rejected at this initial stage were offered transfer to other aircrew categories – Observer (combination of navigator/bomb aimer/air gunner), Wireless Operator or Air Gunner – or, if preferred, transfer to a Ground Branch. As far as those other aircrew roles were concerned, only towards the end of the war was a selection system designed, pre-flight, to judge potential solely for those roles. The main point here was, of course, the tremendous urgency to get as many aircrew of all categories trained and into operational service to prosecute the crescendo of the Air War.

By 1944 Air Receiving Centres had been established all over the country employing objective testing methods measuring performance against fixed standards. Constant monitoring of results followed by continual checks of actual performance in training allowed fine tuning of the system; continuity thereafter in the post-war years resulted in our modern high-tech system (once described by an American Colonel of my acquaintance as "the most sophisticated and effective personnel selection system in the world").

Commissioning of Pilots and other Aircrew during the war resulted partly from recommendation at first interview, then approved or modified, or sometimes even originated, by instructors during the training period. Those graduating as Senior NCOs were kept under constant review by Squadron and Station Commanders and many were eventually commissioned from those NCO ranks; in fact many who first served on squadrons as NCOs eventually rose to high rank.

After the war, much greater emphasis was placed on the commissioning potential of candidates during initial assessments, until eventually the "All Commissioning" policy was adopted for all new Pilot/Navigator recruits. Between 1946 and 1962 Selection Boards were re-named and re-located several times, with only one constant – the full-career, permanent commission, intake for cadets to the Royal Air Force College, Cranwell. The College was, and is, of course, the prime route to the highest ranks of the Service. In those early post-war years we had the Aircrew Selection Centre at Hornchurch, the RAF Technical College at Henlow and the Ground Officer Selection Centre at Uxbridge. Finally, in 1962, all were combined at the Officer and Aircrew Selection Centre, Biggin Hill.

(Although this is the final chapter of my book, readers may be interested to know that the organisation rested there, progressed, modified and modernised, especially in the light of the major technical advances in modern aircraft, until 1992. OASC was then moved to its present location at the RAF College, Cranwell).

Thus, the history of RAF Selection; now what of the organisation of the Centre. In concert with the development of the selection system, it became necessary to train people to administer the tests. The Women's Auxiliary Air Force (WAAF) supplied the first trainees for this task; then, post-war, men took on some of those tasks and so there is still to this day a mixed staff of airmen and airwomen at the OASC.

Boarding Officers were experienced Wing Commanders and Squadron Leaders, mainly from the General Duties (i.e. Flying) Branch; they also formed the nucleus of the Training School which, as already mentioned, became the essential initiation for every future Boarding Officer. Boards are set to cover selection of pilot/navigator, other aircrew, ground officers; Board Presidents, their Deputies and Review Officers are appointed from those experienced in the boarding process. The whole is programmed and controlled by a Wing Commander "Org", plus a small staff to deal with arrivals/departures and reports.

The size of the task at OASC is, of course, measured by the numbers of candidates who arrive for assessment – this in turn is measured by the number of graduates needed to meet the requirements of the Service, Two variable factors contribute to these calculations: the percentage of candidates who can be expected to qualify at selection, the percentage of those selected who will qualify in training. To take the latter first, training wastage has varied enormously over the years; during the war it peaked at over 60%; for many peacetime years it averaged 45-50%, as it was in my time at BH; towards the end of the century, with the steady run-down of the Service, with fewer more sophisticated, more expensive aeroplanes, it is about 30-35%. Conversely, wastage during the selection process gradually increases, primarily due to the much higher standards demanded to enter training in the first place. At this time at BH we were processing 100+ applicants a week, from which barely 10–15% were accepted; it is perhaps unfair to average such figures because the standard of applicant varied so much over a year – much higher in summer following the end of the school year.

Applications come to OASC from several sources: Careers

information Offices, University Air Squadrons, Careers Liaison Officers, or from Station Commanders for those already serving. The whole boarding process is followed by the majority of candidates, assuming success at each stage.

Obviously an aircrew candidate who failed either medical or aptitude testing would not continue, unless he/she had expressed a willingness to consider alternatives.

So may I now describe the whole selection procedure in some detail. Part 1 consists of the Aptitude test, a Medical examination and a First Interview.

    a. The *Aptitude Test* consists of a battery of tests which are known predictors for Pilot, Navigator, Air Traffic Control or Fighter Control. Different tests are applied for other Aircrew (NCOs).

    b. The *Medical* is a rigorous basic examination by specialists. Those applicants subsequently selected are required to return to OASC for extended aircrew medical testing.

    c. The *First interview* is conducted by a Wing Commander Board Chairman with a Squadron Leader Member. Neither knowing nor heeding aptitude or medical results, the Board's aim is to assess the applicant's personality, character, motivation and suitability, both for the role requested and, in most cases, for a commission in the Royal Air Force. The interview lasts for about 45 minutes, Chairman and Member share the questioning and each records notes as the other questions. The candidate is assessed on a 1–9 scale under the following headings:

    Appearance and Bearing
    Manner
    Speech and Powers of Expression
    Activities and Interests
    Academic Level/Potential
    Physical Level/Potential
    Awareness
    Motivation
    Overall impact

After the interview the Board discuss and agree a Board Grade (0–7) with comments on strengths and weaknesses. Candidates awarded BG 0 go no further; those with BG1 and BG2 may or may not go on, depending on the Board's qualifying remarks; all with BG3 and above go through.

This might be a good point to mention a couple of the most amusing incidents from my Boarding Interviews. A sharp and handsome young man of 20 entered the interview room in style! He gave a brisk "Good morning, Sir" and sat in the obvious candidate's chair before I had the chance to invite him to do so.

I recited to him the Board's aim, ". . . personality, character, motivation, etc . . ." and then asked if he had any question for us before we began, "Yes, I hope you won't think me rude, Sir, but isn't most of what you have just said a load of bullshit?"

I confess, I laughed; and although my next reaction was almost to dispatch him hence, I caught the gleam in my colleague's eye. "Well now, Hamilton-Brown (a pseudonym)" said I, "if you succeed in completing this selection board, I will make sure that I am the Review Officer who sees you at the final interview – and then I will give you the opportunity to answer your own question." We did just that. He sailed through all the tests with high assessments and his first comment at that final interview was "I have learned a great deal, Sir, and I apologise for my stupid remark earlier". That was nearly 40 years ago – and, although that gentleman is not Chief of the Air Staff, he is an Air Marshal.

In a totally different situation, I was interviewing a young Cockney airman who wanted to be an Air Loadmaster. Being a near-Cockney myself (I was if a south wind blew the sound of Bow bells in my direction) I could understand him perfectly, but my Squadron Leader from Yorkshire was totally "at sea". I liked the boy a lot – but just could not pass him at that stage. After the interview I took him to one side and said "Look lad, I think you could be a very good loadmaster, but with your extreme Cockney accent, you could be a danger to your crew – your Captain might not be able to understand you on the intercom. Go back to your station, see the Education Officer, and ask him to try and soften that accent." He did so; six months later I had the great pleasure of interviewing him again, he sailed through the Board and was selected. But I could barely restrain the hilarity at his now polished tones – with a difference – "Oh most frightfully yes, Gaw blimey"?

After Chairman and Member of the interview Board have collated their reports and awarded the appropriate Board Grades, selected candidates, grouped into syndicates of 5 or 6, go forward to the Part 2 procedure, divided into the "Exploratory phase", consisting of a Discussion Exercise, a Leaderless Exercise (a physical, "over the sticks" type task in the hangar) and a Group Planning Exercise, and then the "Confirmatory phase", comprising an Individual Problem and the Command Situation Exercise (again in the hangar).

Let me now expand on these various exercises, their format, purpose and place in the overall assessment process:

a. *Discussion Exercise.* Syndicates are given three of four general topics to discuss among themselves. The Board plays no part in the discussion, merely introducing the subjects. Notes are taken to assess tolerance, maturity, originality, powers of expression, sincerity, intellect.

b. *Leaderless Exercise.* An active exercise in the hangar. The syndicate are set the task as a team – for 30 minutes they use equipment (planks, ropes, a chair) to manoeuvre the team from start line to finish while the Board members take notes and Board President observes on closed circuit TV. Purpose two-fold: firstly, to test group compatibility, co-operation, physical ability, perception, resourcefulness; secondly, introducing candidates to the concept of working as a team and acquaint them with basic rules for subsequent exercises. To conclude, the Board Chairman highlights the rules, offers hints on practical bridging with planks etc., and reinforces the need for a leader in these exercises. More Board notes and points awarded.

c. *Group Planning Exercise.* The syndicate re-assembles in class, seated at tables as directed by the Board to ensure involvement by even the quietest members. Each is given a copy of the exercise setting, consisting of map and brief for an imaginary situation. There can be two or more possible solutions and the aim is for the syndicate to reach an agreed group plan. Three phases:

Private Study for 15 minutes – read, make notes and do calculations.

Discussion for 20 minutes – options, compare calculations, arrive at team solution. No chairman – free-for-all. Board assess influence, perception, judgment and involvement of each member. Board Chairman notes the developing plan.

Question Period. Half an hour in which Chairman questions each candidate on setting, problem, calculations, rejected plans and agreed solution. Throughout, the Board Member notes responses, mental agility, flexibility and, especially, reaction to pressure. Finally, Chairman conducts a "wash-up", issues written notes on time, speed and distance calculations (more tomorrow!).

The last task of the day for the candidates is a Physical Fitness test in the Gymnasium conducted by P.T.I.s.

The Board Chairmen and members conclude their day by discussion of findings todate, agreeing percentage marks for the Group Planning Exercise, discussing all the candidates' performances during the Exploratory Phase, awarding overnight scores and individual assessments. The Board President has been keeping an overall watch on all the syndicates and forming his own assessments. Finally, each pair of Board Members briefs the President on their findings and discuss any significant differences of opinion.

The final day sees the confirmatory phase of Part 2:

The Individual Problem. Similar to the Group Planning Exercise, but now each candidate is issued with a different problem setting taken from a wide selection. He is allowed 25 minutes to assimilate the detail, make necessary calculations and determine his "best course of action". He is then debriefed by the Board Member for 10 minutes, questioned on his solution and made to justify it against several alternatives. The Board Chairman makes notes throughout and both officers record their assessment. All the other 4 or 5 candidates follow in turn.

Finally, the Command Situation Exercise. Back in the hangar on the physical tasks, but now each candidate is appointed in turn to LEAD the team "over the sticks" on different exercises, 15 minutes each, from the available 20 sets. Each again involves moving the team and equipment over a course, usually by "bridging", but now the one appointed candidate is in charge. Here the Boarding Officers are looking for comprehension, influence, confidence, judgment, drive, decisiveness, flexibility.

In all cases during these exercises, the Board member has been directing the conduct of the work whilst the Chairman has kept notes; both discuss results as they go along. The Board president has been keeping a watching brief by CCTV, but bear in mind that he has perhaps 6 syndicates of 5 or 6 candidates each to survey.

In conclusion, to end the selection process, the Board Chairman conducts a review of general administration and organisation of the candidates' stay at OASC, giving them the opportunity for comment on their treatment and to confirm their Branch choices. When they have left, The Board discuss their findings, agree assessments on a 1–9 scale, commenting on observed qualities; a Part 2 Board Grade is then awarded. Adding "credits" from the Part 1 Interview, taking account of Physical Fitness results, they arrive at an overall Board Grade and a recommendation of acceptance or otherwise. Where rejection is recommended, they suggest advice or encouragement, if merited, in case of future re-application. Finally the Board brief the President on findings and recommendations and, subject to his agreement, or modified by his objections, a Final Board Grade is approved for the detailed reports now to be written for the Director of Recruiting and Selection.

So now, after all those "selecting" duties as a Board Chairman the reader is already wondering what on earth I did with all my spare time. It took a few months to settle into that routine, with new batches of up to 50 candidates arriving every Sunday, allocated separate rooms in a reserved barrack block, ready to begin the process at crack of dawn on the Monday. When the last departed on the Thursday, we could settle down to a couple of days writing reports – and perhaps even find time for a drink in the Mess – or begin to consider what we were going to do about housing in a couple of year's time!

Eventually, needless to say, the dreaded "secondary duties" reared their heads. The Government of the day was getting increasingly nervous about the global situation. The Russian Bear was roaring, the Cold War was upon us, the Cuban incident and all that: so what about Home Defence? This was a subject of concern which had steadily declined since *The* War and now, suddenly, the Commandant was instructed to liase with certain other stations, Councils and Civil Authorities, with a view to setting up a Civil Defence Committee. Guess where I came in – right on – Station Defence Officer, again! And also a member of that Committee. My memory is hazy about details but I seem to recall that we did not achieve very much during my stay there. But, my word, couldn't we really do with such an organisation in this 3rd Millennium?

Then, as many will recall, Biggin Hill has for many years held an annual Air Show – very appropriate for the most famous Battle of Britain Station. That, of course, required a special Organisation Committee, which sat regularly throughout the year, its really hectic period beginning in January through to the Show in August/September. So, who was well suited to be a member of that Committee – who else but yours truly? And then, of course, the Show was usually attended by several VIPs, who had to be formally welcomed in the time-honoured fashion – by a Guard of Honour. And who had the experience to command such a guard? Who else?

About half way through my time there, the Commandant was looking for a new Wing Commander "Org" and it seemed likely that my name was in the frame. However, I made the point that my Service career was approaching its end, wouldn't it be more appropriate for the job to go to one of the Wing Commanders who was destined to serve to age 55? He could provide much better continuity. And so my dear friend "Koz" Cosby was elected – very appropriately, he was one of the best known Battle of Britain aces and stayed on to run the show for several years thereafter.

I have not so far touched on the domestic scene but, as already mentioned, the main issue facing us now was the problem of housing. Within a year or two my RAF service would be drawing to a close, I should be leaving Biggin Hill as a civilian, and Joan, Gilly and I would need a home of our own. Incidentally, daughter Gilly, now 17, was leaving school and she had opted for a one year's residential course at Brighton Secretarial College. We had long discussed the possibility of University but she was quite firm in her ambition to get a good job "in the City", of which we heartily approved.

So – where shall we live? What sort of house can we afford? But first, are we sure about a new job in the insurance business? One can easily imagine the hours of soul-searching in that situation, bearing in mind that I would be 47 at the start – not the ideal age to begin a new career, yet how much better than staying on in the Service until age 55 which would make that new start far more difficult. Many specialist aircrew i.e. flying full time in the rank of flight lieutenant, carrying on to age 55, retired then on very comfortable pension terms and had no need of further employment. But career officers in the middle ranks, such as myself, often found it most difficult to find further reasonable employment and rued their decision to carry on in the Service to that age.

Needless to say, I re-established contact with the lads in the Brighton Branch of the Company not long after arriving at BH and by the time I had spent several days, on and off, seeing them in action at the office I became convinced that this was for me. That decision made, and being assured by Kerry that a warm welcome awaited me there, I felt free to set about the establishment of our next home.

At first, I thought the Company might prefer me to live locally in Brighton but my "Boss" to be felt that I would be better placed for business in the London, Kent, Surrey, Berkshire areas. So we started looking to buy around East Grinstead, Crawley, Redhill – all giving short range access to likely business but also not too far from the office. Needless to say, I was working on the premise that I would operate from home, only visiting the office when necessary – probably weekly (all of which proved to be exactly right).

What could we afford? Well, bearing in mind that I had been unable to save a single penny during my 28 years service, we would need to rely on a terminal grant of three years' pension (expected to be about £3500) and cover the rest on mortgage. If I could start by earning about £2000 a year (Kerry thought that a reasonable figure) then, as things were in the mortgage business at that time, I could expect to borrow up to £5000 (most Building Societies then operated on about two and a half times income). We would need to buy all our furniture, utensils, etc. Thus I was seeking a house for around £6-7000. Not very much to our taste was available at that figure, needless to say.

But now, Lady Luck emerged on our side. In 1962, just before our second posting to Germany, we had visited the annual Ideal Homes Exhibition at Olympia and had fallen in love with the "House of the Year", a most beautifully designed semi-bungalow – so much so that I had written to the architects in Norwich for a copy of the plans. Eventually, we had written off the possibility of ever being able to afford such a house. Yet now, having watched the development of a new house in Biggin Hill main road, we suddenly realised that it was our "House of the Year"! I approached the foreman and asked him whether this was the first of several he would be building. "No", says he, "and in any event I am leaving this firm and setting up on my own". So, could I be his first customer and would he build that house for me? "Do you have a site?" he asks. Good Lord, no – I'd never even considered it before. "Right, leave it to me, I'll see what I can find".

Within a week: "I know where there is a super plot going, in a private park, near East Grinstead, interested?" The owner had a seven-acre garden, the bottom three acres of which were an orchard, and this area he had decided to sell in three one-acre plots, building a short drive linking those plots to the road. This was a site, a garden, in a private park, a setting beyond our wildest dreams; surely we could never afford it. How much is the site? £4200. How much would you charge to build that house here? £7000. How were we going to afford £11,200 for that house?

By now, Joan and I were so besotted with the prospect of owning such a house in such a setting, I was determined that, come what may, we would do it! A last minute increase in my anticipated pension from £1240 to £1320 meant a terminal grant of £3960. Next, I decided, against advice, to commute almost half my pension: I was offered the amazingly generous rate of 13:1 which, applied to my agreed commutation of £600 of the pension, produced £7800. I then further decided to request the maximum possible mortgage and was offered 2.5 times my expected £2720 income (£720 pension plus £2000 business income) rounded up to another £7000. I would thus depart the Service with nearly £19,000 available, money beyond imagining during my life to date. This would enable us to buy the house, furnish it, set Gilly up for her secretarial course, and give us a cushion against a possible slow start in the business.

Plans were converted into action late in 1966, the middle plot was purchased (friends in the Mess: How on earth can you afford £4200 just for an acre of land? You're mad! And so often I wondered if they weren't right!), and the first sod was dug just 3 days before the introduction of a new tax on land purchased, not yet developed! I managed to keep a close eye on the development throughout, our builder was absolutely first class, the work went without a hitch, we marched out of our BH married quarters and moved into our first home on August Bank Holiday Monday 1967.

Throughout most of my time at BH I had been able to make infrequent visits to the Brighton office, mainly to cement old friendships with John Battle, George Masters and Kerry Fone, also to get to know other members of the "firm" and to learn some of the basics of the business. Now that time is drawing to its close, I manage to take some of the leave which I had saved up from the past – yes, it was always considered reasonable in the Service to forego some of one's leave entitlement during busy spells, which we had at BH most of the time, thus "saving" for the future. More time at Brighton enabled me to study theory and practice in the profession, so providing a "head start" when it came to the real thing the following year.

There was one further advantage in these attempts to get ahead of the game, so to speak. In frequent discussions with my colleagues at OASC, I became more than ever convinced that, as became apparent at Bruggen, few of them had made adequate provision for their families in the event of disaster, and very few had made any effort to get into the housing market in preparation for their retirement from the Service. So many, like me (until John and George came to Bruggen!), had left their planning very late but now said they would be more than ready to "catch up" and could I advise and make provision for them. Naturally, I could not do so personally whilst still in the RAF, but they would either see one of my future colleagues or be happy to await my move to civilian status. This gave me numerous invaluable contacts for the future.

An amusing off-shoot from the above personal discussions was the reception I frequently got when I walked into the Mess bar of an evening: "Watch out chaps, here comes the Money Man!" All said in good humour, thank goodness.

In final discussions with the Adjutant, now that my departure was imminent, I discovered that I was entitled to 28 days Terminal Leave and, in addition, I had a further 21 days of unused leave. My retirement date would be 16th February 1968, my 47th birthday, thus my active service would terminate on 29th December – ". . . with Christmas coming up let's call it 20th December." So now I would have virtually 2 months in which to get my feet firmly under the table at the Brighton Branch – who could ask for a more easy and profitable transition?

The final traditional farewell was to be invited by Commandant, Mess Committee and colleagues to be "Dined Out" just before Christmas. At that dinner, the PMC and Commandant spoke to briefly review my career, wish me well and present me with a splendid silver tea service, which graces our sideboard to this day.

It would be quite impossible to summarise 28 years, so how to finish? The Royal Air Force was not my first choice of a career, the war was the instigator. But as a lucky survivor from those war years, I found the life exhilarating and a strong challenge. We had many a laugh – it was "Service With a Smile".

APPENDIX

AT THE CREMATION OF JAN FLINTERMAN

A Eulogy

JAN FLINTERMAN – by Wing Cdr. Norman Conquer OBE RAF (Rtd)

Jan Flinterman – Jan Flinterman – I shall remember Jan Flinterman for so many reasons. As a wartime Pilot in the Royal Air Force his deeds are well documented and recognised by his Honours from Britain, France and his native Holland. I am sure that his post-war service as a principal figure in the development of the Jet-age Royal Netherlands Air Force has already been commented upon by Jan van Arkel.

I first met Jan in 1958 when, with Officers from the British, Dutch, Belgian and German Air Forces, we transformed R.A.F. 2 Group, with whom Jan was serving as Wing Commander Operations, into the N.A.T.O. 2nd Tactical Operations Centre at Sundern bei Gutersloh. Jan had just graduated from the NATO War College in Paris, I from the RAF Staff College at Bracknell. Having heard already the Flinterman Legend, I approached our first meeting with some trepidation and not a little awe – but I need not have worried – he was very much "one of the lads"; never once did I see any sign of hauteur or pomposity in his make-up – but common sense, wisdom and a superiority in so many ways which I believe set him as a giant among men.

His leadership was unquestioned, even by those senior in rank, he was one of that rare breed – those who lead from the front by example. Jan's record as a sportsman is well known too: as a life-long sailor – if not of the 7 Seas, then of 4 of them to my certain knowledge; and let us not forget his successes as Admiral of the Fleet in the Battles of the Murky Mere. And then, too, he was renowned as a Motor Sport enthusiast, on Motorcycle and in Rally Car. As with all other aspects of his life, he took these activities seriously and displayed the highest capability in them all.

He was the only man I ever knew with whom I could argue constantly at work or at play and yet remain always the closest of friends. As he excelled in so many things, so too in argument: in fact, I fondly imagine that, at some time in the past few days, confronted at the Pearly Gates by the man after whom he named his son, he spent a couple of hours putting him right on a number of events which haven't gone too well during this century on Earth. It was not long after we met that Jan retired prematurely from The Air Force to take over the running of his Family Motor business following the death of his Father. But before very long, he was head-hunted by Martin Schroeder back into the flying business as Operations Director of Martinair at Schipol. And then, for his final career stage, several years later he was again head-hunted, this time by General Bertie Wolff, back into Government service with the Netherlands Space Administration team: had he not by that time reached a rather advanced age, I am sure he would have been first in the queue for active service in Space Travel.

Of all the many activities he enjoyed one must make special mention of his devoted service to the Royal Air Force Association in Holland. I believe all members of the RAFA have good cause to be grateful for his guidance and active contribution in making yours the most successful of all RAFA branches and for his many years as your President.

Yet, asked what he regarded as his greatest success in life, the one single achievement which meant most of all to him, I think he would have said, without hesitation, winning his lovely wife Marianne away from the Scottish Clans that day half a century ago.

Marianne, his son Peter, daughter-in-law Norah, his grandchildren Natalie and Jamie, will all miss Jan so much. His many, many friends, among whom I am most privileged to be counted, will hold life the poorer without him.